Trinitarian Soundings
in Systematic Theology

In memory of Professor Colin E. Gunton,
and to his beloved wife, Jenny

Trinitarian Soundings in Systematic Theology

Edited by

PAUL LOUIS METZGER

t&t clark

Published by T&T Clark International
A Continuum imprint

The Tower Building, 11 York Road, London SE1 7NX
80 Maiden Lane, Suite 704, New York, NY 10038

www.continuumbooks.com

First published 2005
Reprinted 2006

British Library Cataloguing-in-Publication Data
A catalogue record for this book is available from the British Library

Typeset by Free Range Book Design & Production Ltd
Printed on acid-free paper in Great Britain by Biddles Ltd., King's Lynn, Norfolk.

ISBN   0567084000 (hardback)
         0567084108 (paperback)

Contents

Contributors

BRUCE L. MCCORMACK is Frederick and Margaret L. Weyerhaeuser Professor of Systematic Theology at Princeton Theological Seminary. His publications include *Karl Barth's Critically Realistic Dialectical Theology: Its Genesis and Development, 1909–1936* (Clarendon Press, 1995) and 'Beyond Nonfoundational and Postmodern Readings of Barth: Critically Realistic Dialectical Theology', *Zeitschrift für dialektische Theologie* 13 (1997): pp. 67–95, pp. 170–94. Professor McCormack was awarded the Karl Barth Prize in 1998.

PAUL LOUIS METZGER is Associate Professor of Christian Theology and Theology of Culture, Multnomah Biblical Seminary. His publications include *The Word of Christ and the World of Culture: Sacred and Secular through the Theology of Karl Barth* (Eerdmans, 2003) and a forthcoming work with Eerdmans titled *Eating (Jim) Crow: Confronting Race and Class Divisions in the Consumer Church*.

MURRAY RAE is Senior Lecturer in the Department of Theology and Religious Studies at the University of Otago, Dunedin, New Zealand. His publications include 'Kierkegaard, Barth and Bonhoeffer: Conceptions of the Relation between Grace and Works', in *International Kierkegaard Commentary: For Self-Examination and Judge for Yourself!*, ed. Robert Perkins (Mercer University Press, 2002), and *Kierkegaard's Vision of the Incarnation: By Faith Transformed* (Clarendon Press, 1997).

PAUL BLACKHAM is Associate Minister (Theology), All Souls Church, London. Dr Blackham's activities include providing theological leadership for the Evangelical Anglican movement.

PETER M. B. ROBINSON is the Incumbent of Emmanuel Church, Richvale, Toronto and Adjunct Professor of Theology at Wycliffe College, University of Toronto. He is editor of *InCourage*, an Evangelical Anglican theological journal in Canada. His publications include 'Cappadocian Distinctions on the Being of God', in *Alive to the Love of God*, ed. Kenneth Pearson (Regent College Publishing, 1998).

COLIN E. GUNTON was Professor of Systematic Theology at King's College London and co-editor of the *International Journal of Systematic Theology* until his death in 2003. His publications include *The Christian Faith* (Blackwell Publishers, 2002) and *The Promise of Trinitarian Theology* (T&T Clark, 2nd edn, 1997). Professor Gunton held honorary doctorates from the University of London, the University of Aberdeen, and the University of Oxford. He was also a Fellow of King's College London.

STEPHEN R. HOLMES is Lecturer in Theology at St Mary's College, St Andrews University, Scotland. His publications include *Listening to the Past: The Place of Tradition in Theology* (Paternoster, 2002) and *God of Grace and God of Glory* (Eerdmans, 2001).

STANLEY J. GRENZ was Pioneer McDonald Professor of Theology at Carey Theological College and Professor of Theological Studies at Mars Hill Graduate School, Bothell, Washington until his death in 2005. His publications include *The Social God and the Relational Self: A Trinitarian Theology of the Imago Dei* (Westminster John Knox Press, 2001) and *Theology for the Community of God* (Eerdmans, 2000).

R. N. FROST is Associate Professor of Historical Theology at Multnomah Biblical Seminary. His publications include '*The Bruised Reed* by Richard Sibbes', in *The Devoted Life: An Invitation to the Puritan Classics*, ed. Kelly M. Kapic and Randall C. Gleason (InterVarsity Press, 2004), and 'Puritanism', in *The Dictionary of Historical Theology*, ed. Trevor Hart (Eerdmans, 2000).

DEMETRIOS BATHRELLOS is a Greek Orthodox priest who teaches at the Institute of Orthodox Theological Studies, Cambridge, the Theological Seminary of the Archdiocese of Thyateira and Great Britain, London, and at King's College London, where he is a visiting research fellow. His publications include *The Byzantine Christ: Person, Nature, and Will in St Maximus the Confessor* (Oxford University Press, 2004).

GEORG PFLEIDERER is Professor (Ordinarius) for Systematic Theology/Ethics at the University of Basel. His publications include *Karl Barths praktische Theologie* (J. C. B. Mohr (Paul Siebeck), 2000) and *Theologie als Wirklichkeitswissenschaft* (J. C. B. Mohr (Paul Siebeck), 1992). He is also the co-editor of the first four volumes of *Christentum und Kultur: Basler Studien zu Theologie und Kulturwissenschaft des Christentums* (Theologischer Verlag Zürich, 2002–2004).

JAMES M. HOUSTON is Emeritus Professor of Spiritual Theology and Founding Principal of Regent College, Vancouver, British Columbia, and formerly a fellow of Hertford College, Oxford. His publications include *The Mentored Life: From Individualism to Personhood* (Navpress Publishing Group, 2002) and *I Believe in the Creator* (Eerdmans, 1980/Regent College Publishing, 1995).

MIROSLAV VOLF is Henry B. Wright Professor of Systematic Theology and Director of the Yale Center for Faith and Culture at Yale Divinity School. His publications include *After Our Likeness: The Church as the Image of the Trinity* (Eerdmans, 1998) and *Exclusion and Embrace: A Theological Exploration of Identity, Otherness, and Reconciliation* (Abingdon Press, 1996), a winner of the Grawemeyer Award in Religion for 2002.

PAUL D. MOLNAR is Professor of Systematic Theology at St John's University, Queens, New York. His publications include *Divine Freedom and the Doctrine of the Immanent Trinity* (T&T Clark, 2002) and *Karl Barth and the Theology of the Lord's Supper: A Systematic Investigation* (Peter Lang Publishing, 1996). He also served as a consulting editor for *The Dictionary of Historical Theology*, ed. Trevor Hart (Eerdmans, 2000).

KELLY M. KAPIC is Associate Professor of Theology at Covenant College, Lookout Mountain, Georgia. His publications include *The Devoted Life: An Invitation to the Puritan Classics*, which he co-edited with Randall Gleason (InterVarsity Press, 2004), articles in *Foundations* and the *International Journal of Systematic Theology*, and a forthcoming book on the theology of John Owen with Baker Academic.

ESTHER D. REED is Senior Lecturer in Theology and Ethics at the University of St Andrews. Her publications include *The Genesis of Ethics: On the Authority of God as the Origin of Christian Ethics* (Darton, Longman & Todd, 2000/Pilgrim Press, 2002) and *A Theological Reading of Hegel's Phenomenology of Spirit* (Edwin Mellen, 1996).

ROBERT W. JENSON is a co-founder of the Center for Catholic and Evangelical Theology, a co-founder of *Pro Ecclesia,* and has served as Senior Scholar for Research at the Center of Theological Inquiry, Princeton, New Jersey. His publications include *On Thinking the Human: Resolutions of Difficult Notions* (Eerdmans, 2003), and a two-volume *Systematic Theology* (Oxford University Press, 1997, 1999).

Foreword

Bruce L. McCormack

Eberhard Jüngel once said of Karl Barth that he 'lived intensively'.[1] The same was true of Colin Gunton. One always knew when Colin Gunton was in the room. His presence was palpable. In the question-and-answer sessions that inevitably followed the presentation of academic papers at conferences, he seemed always poised to come off his seat, to lend support to one speaker, to reject vehemently the position of another, or simply to add a pertinent observation. He was full of nervous energy because, for him, wherever theology was being done, there was a great deal at stake. In late night discussions in a pub, one would find him at the centre of a large coterie of graduate students. Most were his own but there were always outsiders who wanted to join in the fun. And so he would hold court, dispensing wisdom, addressing challenges, answering questions, offering opinions – and listening, too. What students loved about Colin was that he took their ideas with great seriousness. He understood them as junior colleagues, men and women whose thinking was a great source of stimulation to his own. And so they would buzz around him or sit enthralled, hanging on his every word. Theology was exciting when Colin was around because it excited him so and his excitement was contagious.

Colin Ewart Gunton was born on 19 January 1941. He grew up in Nottingham, where he attended the same church as the girl who would one day become his wife. Colin and Jenny began dating in their mid-teens and were married as soon as he finished his first degree at Hertford College Oxford in 'Greats' (i.e. classics). In 1966, he began his study of theology at Mansfield College Oxford. Being married while studying theology was frowned upon at Mansfield in those days. The fact that Colin chose not to submit to the powers that be in this regard tells us a great deal about the way he thought theology

1

should be integrated with everyday life – a point I will return to in a moment.

Upon completion of his B.A. in theology in 1966 and an M.A. a year later, Colin began work on his doctoral degree under the direction of a young Lutheran theologian from America (by way of Heidelberg) by the name of Robert Jenson. The degree would take six years to complete – with good reason. His teaching career was launched only two years into his research when he became a Lecturer in Philosophy of Religion at King's College London in 1969. And, of course, Colin had to become an ordained minister in the United Reformed Church before completing the degree – which again said a lot about how he understood the nature of theology, its purpose, its public. In spite of these activities, the dissertation turned out to be a first-rate study of the doctrine of God in Charles Hartshorne and Karl Barth, one which reflected not only refined skills in doctrinal theology but also considerable philosophical acumen.[2] The capacity demonstrated in these years for turning out important work even while juggling the responsibilities of a home life and local church involvements was a harbinger of things to come. He was installed as Associate Minister of the Brentwood United Reformed Church in 1975, a post whose obligations he gladly fulfilled until his untimely passing.

The rest of the story is better known and may be told quickly. Colin became Lecturer in Systematic Theology at King's in 1980 and Professor of Christian Doctrine four years later. He served as Dean of the Faculty from 1988 to 1990 and later, after reorganization of the fields at the University of London, as Head of the Department of Theology and Religious Studies from 1994 to 1997. Under his leadership, King's became one of the most vibrant and exciting centres of theology to be found anywhere. Colin founded and directed a Research Institute in Systematic Theology, which drew distinguished scholars from all over the world to give papers and join in the spirited theological conversation that was a customary feature of life there. In 1998 he helped to found the *International Journal of Systematic Theology*, which he would co-edit until his death. The decade of the nineties saw him appointed to a number of distinguished lectureships, which took him to Oxford, Princeton, Ottawa, Montreal, and Brisbane. He also served as Visiting Professor at the Universities of Kiel and Copenhagen (in 1996 and 1997 respectively). He was awarded honorary doctorates by the University of London (1993), the University of Aberdeen (1999), and shortly before his death, by his Alma Mater, the University of Oxford. He was also made a Fellow of King's College – again just prior to his passing.

And yes, he also managed to find time to write or edit twenty books and dozens of articles. At his death on 6 May 2003, Colin Gunton was widely regarded as the most significant English theologian of his generation, a man who helped to restore dignity to the study of dogmatic theology at a time when its fortunes were in decline.

But this is not the whole story. We do not even understand Colin Gunton, the theologian, if we do not have an appreciation of who and what he was when at home, away from the demands of his academic life. Everything one needs to know about Colin Gunton one finds in a statement recently made by his beloved wife, Jenny: 'The family and church family had no idea of the work he was doing and the sphere of his influence—he was frequently in the church kitchen washing up!'[3] That was Colin. He loved his local church. He preached regularly—at least once a month.[4] He once said to me that a church should never have more than around eighty members. He wanted to know not only each person's name but what was happening in the lives of each of them and one could not do that in a large church. And he loved his family. He and Jenny had four children, all fully grown now (Carolyn, Christopher, Jonathan and Sarah). When they were young, he kept his travel to a minimum so that he could eat with them and read to them. As voluble and excited as he could become in his public life, Colin was calm and peaceful at home. He was an avid gardener; he collected as many different plants as he could find and made a point of learning all their Latin names. He loved to cycle, something which he and Jenny did in Holland quite frequently. And he loved holidays in the Lake District.

Each of the contributors to this volume will have their favourite recollections and memories, but these are some of mine: suddenly catching sight of Colin riding a folding bicycle through the streets of Princeton while cars whizzed about him, when I didn't even know he was in town; trotting breathlessly beside Colin as we walked from Rutherford House to the bottom of Leith Walk (in Edinburgh) in search of an open pub, and wondering how it could be that a man half my size could walk my legs off; sitting with him in The Greenhouse in Princeton, arguing about Karl Barth; seeing Colin and Jenny worshipping together at Westerly Road Church in Princeton, Sunday by Sunday (the church at which my wife ministers); attending an amateur performance of a selection of Shakespeare's sonnets with Colin and Jenny in Brentwood; listening to Mozart in their home; and the sheer pleasure of listening to Colin field questions after delivering a paper of his own.

The faces of those I have loved most in life all seem to fade to a blur the further removed I am from them in time and space. Without photographs, I fear that I might forget how they looked—all save one. Every detail of Colin Gunton's face remains firmly etched in my memory. I can call his face to mind and hear his voice as clearly today as on the day after I last saw him. He was to me a mentor, a theological comrade-in-arms, a friend. His passing has left a gaping hole in my life—as it has in the lives of so many others. The essays in this volume are proof, however, that his legacy lives on. King's College as Colin knew it may be no more, but what happened at King's in those magical years is now happening in numerous other places around the world. Thanks be to God for the great gift Colin was to all of us.

Notes

1   Eberhard Jüngel, 'Karl Barth', in *Barth-Studien* (Zurich-Köln: Benziger Verlag/Gütersloh: Gütersloher Verlaghaus Gerd Mohn, 1982), p. 15.
2   Colin E. Gunton, *Becoming and Being: The Doctrine of God in Charles Hartshorne and Karl Barth* (Oxford: Oxford University Press, 1978).
3   Letter from Jenny Gunton to Paul L. Metzger, 6 October, 2004.
4   See Colin E. Gunton, *Theology through Preaching: Sermons for Brentwood* (Edinburgh: T&T Clark, 2001).

Introduction:
What Difference Does
the Trinity Make?

Paul Louis Metzger

'The Trinity is the greatest mystery of the Christian faith. Therefore, leave it well enough alone.' So argued one seasoned scholar in his critique of the renaissance of Trinitarian theology. Of course, it is true that the Trinity is the greatest mystery of the Christian faith. On this point, no doubt, all of the contributors to this volume would agree. However, as will be shown, they would disagree with the follow-up exhortation to leave the Trinity 'well enough alone' when it comes to sounding the implications of this greatest mystery for other Christian doctrines, practices and cultural engagements.

One reason for this is that, according to the biblical witness, the divine mysteries are revealed. In this light, we are not talking about a God hidden *behind* divine revelation. Rather, 'God is for us fully revealed and fully concealed *in* His self-disclosure', as Karl Barth maintained in his treatment of the divine attributes.[1] Ultimately, much of the renaissance in Trinitarian theology involves reflecting on the revelation of the Triune God, and seeking to think outward from it.

A second reason why the contributors would not share this scholar's view of Trinitarian theology is that they embrace Karl Barth's and Robert Jenson's conviction that the doctrine of the Trinity is central to the theologian's overarching task. Jenson writes, 'It is from Barth that twentieth-century theology has relearned that this doctrine has and must have explanatory and regulatory use in the whole of theology, that it is not a separate puzzle to be solved but the framework within which all theology's puzzles are to be solved.'[2] How can it be otherwise if the Triune God is the one with whom we must deal, the one on whom all things depend, and the one to whom all doctrines and practices of Christ's church must be directed?

Building on this twofold rationale, the aim of the volume is to show how the doctrine of the Trinity is a deep well from which to draw fresh insights when analysing other key doctrines—from prolegomena to eschatology and theological ethics. *Trinitarian Soundings in Systematic Theology* explores interfaces between Trinitarian thought and major themes of systematic theology. Given the scarcity of systematic theologies done in a Trinitarian fashion, this multi-author exploration of systematic theology from a Trinitarian perspective suggests a path to follow in the formulation of each particular doctrine represented in the volume. The common thread that links the chapters is the conviction that a Trinitarian perspective illumines each of systematic theology's traditional loci.

Trinitarian Soundings promises to become an important work given its unique presentation of major themes of systematic theology in their classical order, yet from a Trinitarian point of view. Its contributors include veteran theologians as well as younger scholars who are energetically employing this Trinitarian focus. The contributors represent various theological traditions and geographical locations, which surely brings richness to the theological enquiry. Dedicated to the memory of a pioneer in the resurgence of Trinitarian theology, the late Professor Colin E. Gunton, this collection represents a distinctive treatment of systematics, intent on showing the vitality of approaching all aspects of the faith from a self-consciously Trinitarian perspective.

More selective treatments are offered in *The Trinity in a Pluralistic Age*, edited by Kevin Vanhoozer (Eerdmans, 1997) and *Persons, Divine and Human*, edited by Christoph Schwöbel and Colin Gunton (T&T Clark, 1991), demonstrating that the renaissance in Trinitarian theology has a bearing on the subjects of religious and cultural pluralism and personhood respectively. While Robert Jenson's two-volume *Systematic Theology* (Oxford University Press, 1997, 1999) and Colin Gunton's *The Christian Faith* (Blackwell, 2002) offer fruitful examples of Trinitarian theologies, an edited volume such as this suggests that there is no one way of doing Trinitarian theology, but rather, a variety of ways.

Trinitarian theology is not another theological fad—here today, gone tomorrow. Those theological movements that have displaced or discredited the doctrine of the Trinity over the course of church history are themselves ever-recurring digressions, having a negative bearing on systematics, the Christian life, and cultural engagement. According to Gunton, Friedrich Schleiermacher, the father of theological liberalism, espoused a Sabellian notion of God, thereby rejecting 'the traditional teaching of the church that God is triune both in his action and in his eternal divine or "inner" being'. To Gunton, this move undermines our confidence in the gospel of Jesus Christ, the structures of creation, and 'the course of history'.[3] While espousing a Trinitarian concept of God, Christian thinkers in the early modern period did not fare much better. Michael Buckley has gone so far as to argue that early modern Christian apologists themselves gave rise in part to the origins of modern atheism by failing to employ the doctrine of the Trinity (specifically Jesus) in their defence of the Christian faith against its critics.[4]

No doubt, some conservative theologians who are blind to their own particular digression will say that Trinitarian theology is simply a restatement of the doctrine of the Trinity. To the contrary, Trinitarian theology is not a restatement, but a revisiting of systematic theology in view of the Trinity. Moreover, over against a classical theistic–non-relational–substantialist metaphysic and foundationalist framework, Trinitarian theology frames consideration of divine and human being in interpersonal, communal terms, and views this interpersonal God as first in the order of being and knowing, with all that this shift implies for human concepts, language and culture. What follows then is not a conservative, foundationalist theological project, but rather a constructive theological enterprise that recovers and extends the Trinitarian tradition in order to reshape classic systematic loci in particular ways.

One way or another, the contributors have been influenced and shaped by Colin Gunton's life and teaching. Two of the themes that will appear in the book are relation and mediation, which influence and shape the practice of theology. Theology is best done in community, a community in which there is space for otherness and difference given God's personal space for otherness in the divine life and in the world. These themes marked the life and teaching of Professor Gunton, and it is in part due to his legacy that they have taken on renewed signifi-cance in the present day. Colin did theology in community, and for all his zeal and conviction, he gave space to others to develop their own particular approaches to Trinitarian thought.

I wish to express thanks to each of the contributors for their partici-pation in this theological enterprise and for developing Trinitarian insights in distinctive ways. Special thanks go to those who have served as dialogue partners through the stages of this book's development: my wife, Mariko (and our children, Christopher and Julianne—partners at play!), and fellow contributors Ron Frost (with whom I initially discussed the idea of an edited volume along these lines), Kelly Kapic, Demetrios Bathrellos and Peter Robinson. Heartfelt thanks also go to Robert and

Blanche Jenson and Bruce McCormack for conversations about Colin's life and theological legacy during my time of residence at the Center of Theological Inquiry in Princeton, New Jersey. Their shared affection for Colin ministered deeply to me. I wish to express appreciation to my colleague Nathan Baxter for proofreading the manuscript, to my assistants, Matthew and Kristin Farlow, Halden Doerge, Joshua Butler and Winky Chin, for their work on the project and for their passionate pursuit of Trinitarian theology, and to Doug Goebel for his support in the early stages of the volume. I am indebted to Jenny and Sarah Gunton for the biographical information on Colin and his family, and to Eerdmans, SCM Press, and Professor Christoph Schwöbel (who serves as the executor of Colin's literary estate) for their permission to include a slightly revised version of an essay by Colin from *Act and Being*. I am also grateful to Eerdmans for allowing me to use an abridged edition of Professor Miroslav Volf's essay, 'Trinity and Church', from *After our Likeness*, and to Westminster John Knox Press, *Horizons in Biblical Theology* and the Association of Theological Schools for permission to publish the late Professor Stanley Grenz's essay in this volume. Lastly, I want to thank the people at T&T Clark International, especially Philip Law, Slav Todorov, Sarah Douglas, Becca Vaughan-Williams, Fiona Murphy, Geoffrey Green, Timothy Bartel and Father David White for their editorial expertise and encouragement in bringing this book to print.

What difference does the Trinity make? The Trinitarian God certainly made a profound difference in Colin Gunton's life and teaching, and through him in the lives and teaching of others. It is our hope that the reader will get a sense of this God's profundity in the pages that follow. If so, it will serve as a fitting tribute to Colin's memory, and to his wife, Jenny, with whom he shared his life's journey in pursuit of this God.

Notes

[1] See Karl Barth, *Church Dogmatics*, II/1, *The Doctrine of God*, ed. G. W. Bromiley and T. F. Torrance (Edinburgh: T&T Clark, 1957), p. 341 (italics added).

[2] Robert W. Jenson, 'Karl Barth', in *The Modern Theologians: An Introduction to Christian Theology in the Twentieth Century*, ed. David F. Ford, 2nd edn (Oxford: Blackwell, 1997), p. 31.

[3] Colin E. Gunton, *The Christian Faith: An Introduction to Christian Doctrine* (Oxford: Blackwell Publishers, 2002), pp. 176, 179.

[4] Michael J. Buckley, SJ, *At the Origins of Modern Atheism* (New Haven and London: Yale University Press, 1987), p. 33.

1

Prolegomena

Murray Rae

A prolegomenon or foreword to theological enquiry is traditionally thought to be required in order to describe the means by which God is rendered accessible to human thought. It is commonly assumed in such an exercise that the processes of human enquiry specified therein are responsible for such rendering, and that these processes are determined by historical context and prevailing credulities. As early as the second century, the Apologists sought a 'point of contact' with the cultured unbelievers of their time and a common method of enquiry that could lead through the portals of faith. Justin Martyr, for example, was content to speak of Christianity as the 'true philosophy' and to appeal to the 'moral conscience' and the 'light of divine Reason' in accounting for the genuine theological insight of philosophers like Socrates and Plato. Such insight provided a means of access to what is more fully revealed in Christianity. Confidence in human reason was also characteristic of theology in the late Middle Ages and continued through both Roman Catholic and Protestant Scholasticism. The task of theological prolegomena, accordingly, was to set out by what rational means human thinking could gain access to theological truth. Subsequent movements of thought claim to have found a basis for theology in the 'feeling of absolute dependence' (Schleiermacher), in the religious intuitions of humankind (Troeltsch), in humanity's capacity for self-transcendence (Rahner), in the shared questions of human existence (Tillich), and so on. The task of prolegomena in these approaches is to describe the pre-theological scaffold that makes the construction of theology possible.

A prolegomenon to Trinitarian theology on these terms is, however, mistaken, and for two reasons: first, because no prolegomenon to theology can avoid substantive theological content, if not explicit, then certainly implicit, and second, because if God is the Triune God, revealed in Jesus Christ through the power of the Spirit, and testified

9

to in Scripture, then theology is not predicated upon any human capacity or mode of thinking, but upon the initiative of God in making himself known to us and reconciling the world to himself.

A prolegomenon to Trinitarian theology, therefore, will not strictly be *pro*legomenon, a word in advance of God's speaking, but a *post*legomenon, a word in response to revelation that is enabled by God himself.[1] Such is true, for instance, of Peter's confession: 'You are the Messiah, the Son of the living God.' Jesus responds, 'Blessed are you, Simon son of Jonah! For flesh and blood has not revealed this to you, but my Father in heaven' (Matt. 16.16–17). The ground of Peter's confession is not his own capacity to formulate theological truth, but the revelatory act of God himself. This is the triune condition of all theological speech, which is only to be undertaken, therefore, in the broad context of worship and prayer. A maxim usually attributed to Pope Celestine I (d. 432) has it that *lex orandi est lex credendi*, the rule of prayer is the rule of believing. Sometimes this is explicitly rendered in theological discourse, as for example in the *Confessions* of Augustine, or the *Proslogion* of Anselm, in which can be found the dictum *Credo ut intelligam*, I believe in order to understand, but the principle holds good for all theology. Theology is closely bound up with doxology[2] and with the life of faith; it is an activity of the church, of that community gathered by Christ and empowered by the Spirit to serve God in worship and in mission. Theology's warrant, therefore, is not found through appeal to reason, religious inwardness, or popular spirituality, nor in a demonstration of public relevance, as has frequently been attempted, but solely in the fact of God's presence in the church.

The foregoing paragraphs set out a conception of the theological task that is widely contested. In what follows we shall offer, through a series of theses, some defence of this conception, not however by appeal to reason or experience, but rather by expanding upon the logic of this account. This will be a derivative logic, founded upon and having the character of witness to the one Logos of God made flesh in Jesus Christ. It is true, as Colin Gunton cautions, that 'if we turn away from God's actual historical self-identification in Jesus, we simply manufacture an idol'.[3]

There can be no prolegomenon to theology that does not itself contain substantive theological claims

By describing the theological enterprise as a participation in and response to the revealing and reconciling action of Father, Son and Spirit, we are already claiming that God is to be understood as the Triune God and not otherwise. Not only is this description offered in response to the initiative of God, it is dependent also upon apostolic witness as preserved in Scripture, and upon the tradition of reception and reflection by the church. This 'advance description'[4] of the theological task is therefore not prior to any substantive theological content but is merely a description, set at the beginning of our own theological speech, of all that has been said and done in advance of our speaking, and which makes our speaking possible—as reception, reflection and handing on.

Other things are called 'theology' that presume to begin elsewhere, but the prolegomena to these activities too will also involve theological, or atheological, claims. If, for example, a theology is proposed 'within the limits of reason alone', that is, without attending to revelation, then it is presumed that God is not sovereign over the epistemic relation between humanity and himself. Or if it is contended that talk about God is a possibility grounded in the human, then it is likewise supposed that God is an object at our disposal rather than the Lord. In both cases, it is implied that God is known otherwise and has a different character than is revealed through the life death, and resurrection of Jesus. These other enterprises called theology, therefore, are something other than Christian. None of these remarks serves to decide the truth or falsity of competing theological claims. They merely demonstrate that no prolegomenon to theology is anything but theology itself.

Theology is response to the Word

Confession of the Triune God is both preceded and enabled by the triune action of God in which the Father gives his Word to humanity, and sees to it through the Spirit that humanity is able to hear and under-stand, and thus to be reconciled with himself. Theology therefore—and this must be true also of the description of theology attempted in prole-gomena—is an activity that follows the utterance of God's own Word. That it *follows* the Word means both that it *comes after* the Word—it is *a posteriori*—and that it *attends to* the Word given in Jesus Christ. 'Following' has also a third sense, that of discipleship. Theology is the thinking done by those engaged in that calling and task.

Responsible theological speech, on this account, is judged to be so only by the standard of the Gospel as it is preserved in Scripture. Here we find the sole criterion of the correctness of theological speech. Clearly enough, theologians themselves do not speak infallibly; the task of explicating and restating the gospel in ways appropriate to each new age is a venture of faith that depends for its success on God's faithfulness to the church. Theologians have no capacity in and of themselves to speak the truth. Indeed, they are capable, by virtue of the freedom granted to humanity by God, of allowing their own interests to obscure and distort what has been given. In that case, their formulations will fail in their responsibility to proclaim the gospel, and are thus to be reckoned as heresy. Theologians have no guarantee against this possibility, but can only pray that through the course of time and by his faithfulness to the church as a whole God will preserve the Gospel among his people. Trusting in that faithfulness, and in glad recognition of the immutability of God, theologians must seek repeatedly to follow and let their thinking be shaped by the word once delivered to the saints.

Theological speech is not predicated upon any human capacity or mode of thinking

In the light of God's self-disclosure in Christ as Father, Son and Holy Spirit, it is necessary to say that speech about God is made possible by virtue of God's own speech and not otherwise. We do not decide in advance that flesh and blood cannot reveal the truth of God. There are no *a priori* grounds for such an assertion, or indeed for the converse claim that humanity does have the capacity to render God accessible. Only in the light of the fact that God has spoken, and reveals himself as the Lord, do we learn that he is sovereign over the relation between humanity and himself. He freely gives himself to be known. He is not seized by human effort or ingenuity. It is no accident that the theologian most responsible for the resurgence of Trinitarian theology in the twentieth century was also the most adamant about the incapacities of human thought. Karl Barth writes,

> God's revelation in its objective reality is the incarnation of his Word... It becomes the object of our knowledge; it finds a way of becoming the content of our experience and our thought; it gives itself to be apprehended by our contemplation and our categories. But it does that beyond the range of what we regard as possible for our contemplation and perception, beyond the confines of our experience and thought... It becomes the object of our knowledge by its own power and not by ours.[5]

The ground of Barth's assertions here is that God has identified himself. Human thought seeks God on its own terms, but God gives himself to us on his own terms. Lest this be thought of as an act of violence against humanity, and a violation of our freedom, let it be recognized that God exercises his sovereignty as servanthood and love. That is the content of what is disclosed in Christ. God does not compel our assent, but waits upon it, even enduring crucifixion for the sake of our freedom to disbelieve.

Truthful theological speech is itself an action of the Triune God

The claim of the apostle Paul that 'no one can say "Jesus is Lord" except by the Holy Spirit' (1 Cor. 12.3) is a principle that holds good also for the explication of that confession. Such explication is theology's task. This does not have the trivial sense that the words of the confession themselves cannot be uttered without the Spirit, but rather that whoever knows what they are really saying knows it only because of the Spirit's enabling (cf. John 14.13). Truthful theological utterance[6] on this account depends on the agency of the Spirit and, notably, has both Christological reference and a Christological ground: the Spirit 'will glorify me, because he will take what is mine and declare it to you. All that the Father has is mine. For this reason I said that he will take what is mine and declare it to you' (John 16.14). Under the guidance of God's Spirit, our speech about God is tied to Jesus in and through whom the Father himself is made known.

Reinhard Hütter has recently described the theological task as a form of suffering, by which is meant that theology is not constituted by what its practitioners do and say on their own account, but rather by what they 'suffer', by what they undergo as members of the community that is formed by and drawn into the Spirit's witness to Christ.[7] Pathos and not *poiesis*, Hütter argues, is the defining characteristic of the church's life and of that particular responsibility of ecclesial life that is theology. Only on this understanding do the theological formulations and utterances of the community of Christ have any binding and authoritative status, precisely because, when understood this way, they are part of God's testimony to himself. Theology cannot have any independent existence, therefore, but is to be understood as a particular mode of participation in the Spirit's work of mediating Christ himself.

God is known in a reconciling act

It is the goal of divine revelation to overcome the distance between God and humanity, a distance caused by sin. Sin refers not first of all to the moral disorder of the world, though that is one of the dimensions of sin, but primarily to the alienation of humanity from God. Sin is the effort of humanity to go its way in defiance of God, and thus apart from him. This has its effect also at the level of our knowing and thinking. Our thinking and reasoning is estranged from God and is no longer oriented to the one Word of God by which the world is upheld.

This one Word of God, given to the world in Christ, 'should have been fully sufficient', says John Calvin, 'for the production of faith, if it were not obstructed by our blindness and perverseness. But such is our propensity to error that our mind can never adhere to Divine truth; such is our dullness, that we can never discern the light of it.'[8] The Bible likewise makes it plain that humanity is at a loss to heal the rift opened up between itself and God; indeed its effort to do so through ritual or reason is yet one more assertion of human hubris and opens the rift still further.

For revelation to achieve its goal of reconciled relation to God, therefore, the alienation of our minds must be overcome. Paul says, 'Do not be conformed to this world, but be transformed by the renewing of your minds' (Rom. 12.2). Does Paul expect this to happen by human contrivance? No! He does not urge that we should transform ourselves, but that we should be transformed, and this according to the logic he has already made clear to the Romans earlier in the epistle: 'Do you not know that all of us who have been baptized into Christ Jesus were baptized into his death? Therefore we have been buried with him by baptism into death, so that just as Christ was raised from the dead by the glory of the Father, so we too might walk in newness of life' (Rom. 6.3–4). The epistemic dimension of this new life is the reorientation of our minds and of all our thinking to Christ. Not apart from, but in and through Christ, humanity is enabled to know and to speak of God. Again, we must recognize that this does not render us incapable of error. The struggle against sin, and against epistemic alienation, continues, but those who have been baptized into Christ know now that only when, by the power of the Spirit, our words accord with God's own Word will theological speech attain its goal of faithful interpretation of that Word.

Theology is set within the context of worship and prayer

In beginning his series of lectures on Christology, Dietrich Bonhoeffer proclaimed that thinking about Christ begins in silence before the Word. 'We must study christology', Bonhoeffer says, 'in the humble

Furthermore, theology is not to be construed as a merely human endeavour. It is a mode of participation, enabled by the Spirit, in the Triune God's identification of himself. Whoever speaks of God does so only as God himself makes eloquent the stuttering and hesitant speech of those who bear witness to the gospel of Jesus Christ. Precisely through such enabling, God identifies himself further as servant and Lord. Witness to the gospel is the task and calling of a particular community, the ecclesia, gathered by Christ and constituted by the Spirit as his body. Theology belongs within this community as part of its response-ability to make the gospel known. Making it known involves receiving it, wrestling with it, interpreting and understanding it, all in service of the commission to tell this news to a world in need. Søren Kierkegaard is again worth quoting here: 'From the Christian point of view', he says, 'everything ought to serve for upbuilding'. And further,

Everything essentially Christian must have in its presentation a resemblance to the way a physician speaks at the sickbed; even if only medical experts understand it, it must never be forgotten that the situation is the bedside of a sick person. It is precisely Christianity's relation to life (in contrast to a scholarly distance from life) . . . that is upbuilding, and the mode of presentation, however rigorous it may be otherwise, is completely different, qualitatively different, from the kind of scienticity and scholar-liness that is 'indifferent', whose lofty heroism is so far, Christianly, from being heroism that, Christianly, it is a kind of inhuman curiosity.[21]

Far from being mere curiosity, Christian theology ought properly to be the joyful acknowledgement and interpretation of the fact that God in Christ, by the power of the Spirit, has made himself known as Saviour and Lord.

Notes

[1] See discussion of this point in Alan J. Torrance, *Persons in Communion: Trinitarian Description and Human Participation* (Edinburgh: T&T Clark, 1996), pp. 15–16.

[2] Again, see Torrance, *Persons in Communion*, ch. 5.

[3] Colin E. Gunton, *Father, Son and Holy Spirit: Essays Toward a Fully Trinitarian Theology* (Edinburgh: T&T Clark, 2003), p. 26.

[4] I take the phrase from Robert Jenson, whose account of 'What Systematic Theology is About' makes many of the points that I will also make here (albeit much less adequately). See Robert W. Jenson, *Systematic Theology*, I, *The Triune God* (Oxford: Oxford University Press, 1997), ch. 1.

[5] Karl Barth, *Church Dogmatics*, I/2, *The Doctrine of the Word of God*, ed. G. W. Bromiley and T. F. Torrance (Edinburgh: T&T Clark, 1956), pp. 172–3.

[6] By 'truthful theological utterance', we do not refer primarily to propositions about God that may be deemed to be true, but rather to those forms of speech that emerge

from and are constitutive of reconciled relation to God.

[7] See Reinhard Hütter, *Suffering Divine Things: Theology as Church Practice* (Grand Rapids: Eerdmans, 2000).

[8] John Calvin, *Institutes of the Christian Religion*, tr. John Allen (Philadelphia: Presbyterian Board of Christian Education, 1936), 3. 2.33.

[9] Dietrich Bonhoeffer, *Christology*, tr. John Bowden (London: Collins, 1966), p. 27.

[10] Hütter, *Suffering Divine Things*, p. 114.

[11] Søren Kierkegaard, *Philosophical Fragments*, ed. and tr. Howard V. Hong and Edna H. Hong (Princeton: Princeton University Press, 1985).

[12] For further explication of the contrasting epistemologies outlined here and of Kierkegaard's discussion of them, see Merold Westphal, *Kierkegaard's Critique of Reason and Society* (University Park, Penn.: Pennsylvania State University Press, 1987), pp. 1–18.

[13] Søren Kierkegaard, *Concluding Unscientific Postscript to Philosophical Fragments*, ed. and tr. Howard V. Hong and Edna H. Hong, 2 vols (Princeton: Princeton University Press, 1992).

[14] Martin Luther, 'The Place of Reason in Christian Life', in *Luther's Works*, lxiv, *Table Talk* (Philadelphia: Fortress Press, 1967), p. 183 (WA, TR 3, 2398).

[15] Martin Luther, 'The Right and Wrong Use of Reason', ibid., p. 71 (WA, TR 1, 439). I am grateful to Iain Taylor for drawing my attention to these comments of Luther's.

[16] Jenson, *Systematic Theology*, I, p. 4.

[17] This incidentally is another reason why prolegomena along traditional lines are mistaken. Theologians are not responsible for inaugurating a theological discourse. Rather, they are called to join in a long-running discourse that has already been established—by God.

[18] Jenson, *Systematic Theology*, I, p. 25.

[19] Ronald Thiemann, *Revelation and Theology: The Gospel as Narrated Promise* (Notre Dame: University of Notre Dame Press, 1985), p. 153 (italics original).

[20] Yet, one might also argue, as Colin Gunton has done, that the doctrine of revelation, the account of God's identifiability, belongs within the doctrine of salvation. With this, too, we can agree, as it has also been noted above that God is known in a reconciling act. These various possibilities draw attention to the integrated nature of theology. See Colin E. Gunton, *A Brief Theology of Revelation: The 1993 Warfield Lectures* (Edinburgh: T&T Clark, 1995), p. 111.

[21] Søren Kierkegaard, *The Sickness Unto Death: A Christian Psychological Exposition for Upbuilding and Awakening*, ed. and tr. Howard V. Hong and Edna H. Hong (Princeton: Princeton University Press, 1980), p. 5.

2

The Relational Dynamic of Revelation: A Trinitarian Perspective

Paul Louis Metzger

Revelation is relational. Christ, canon and church—the three forms of the word of God—constitute the relational dynamic of revelation. Whenever this dynamic is lost, radical objectivism, or its opposite, subjectivism, is just around the corner. The Spirit preserves this dynamic in two ways. First, the Spirit shapes Scripture to reveal Christ. Second, the Spirit enacts new encounters with the living Word through the interface of the church's proclamation with the witness of Scripture. Thus, Christian Scripture and church proclamation participate in the revelation of Christ. This essay will seek to unpack from various angles the significance of this twofold claim.

The Perichoretic Pattern of Revelation[1]

Christian Scripture is the Word of God because it bears witness to the living Word through the Holy Spirit in the life of the church. However, Scripture becomes a collection of lifeless words when we divorce it from its relation to Christ and the proclamation of Christ. The key is to safeguard this relational dynamic. In so doing, we will safeguard our own participation in the revelatory event. The Spirit not only shapes Scripture to reveal Christ, but also enacts revelation anew in the life of the community as it is centred on the text, which is centred on Christ. Our words become the Word of God to the extent that they bear witness to the written Word, which bears witness to the living Word. The same Spirit through whom Christ was conceived and who discloses Christ as the revelation of the Father formed Scripture to reveal Christ

21

and enacts new encounters with the living Word through the witness of Scripture in church proclamation.[2] Such Christological and pneumatological concentration safeguards the relational dynamic of revelation.

In the opening volume of the *Church Dogmatics*, Karl Barth presents us with a version of this dynamic.[3] Christ, the living Word, is revelation. Scripture, the written Word, is revelation's primary witness. And the proclaimed word of the church is revelation's secondary witness. The beauty and value of Barth's model of revelation is that he positions the written Word in close proximity to the living Word and proclaimed Word. Donald Bloesch goes so far as to state of Barth's view that 'there is something like a perichoresis in these three forms of the Word in that the revealed Word never comes to us apart from the written Word and the proclaimed Word, and the latter two are never the living Word unless they are united with the revealed Word'.[4] For Barth, *sola scriptura* does not signify the solitary confinement of the Bible, but rather, that the Bible is the sole conduit between Christ and church proclamation. The other side of this claim is equally important: Scripture only has significance within this relationship. Only within this perichoretic or interpenetrative framework do Scripture and church proclamation participate in the revelation event.

The Classic Hermeneutic and the Hermeneutic of the Gospel

Perhaps the real question before us is 'Why the Bible?' What makes it so central to Christian faith? From what does it derive its authority? Without seeking to demean theories of inspiration, truthfulness and the like, it is important to set the matter in a larger context. In keeping with what has been said so far, we turn to two quotations, one from George Lindbeck and the other from Stanley Hauerwas. The statement from Lindbeck concerns the relation of Scripture to Christ. The statement from Hauerwas concerns the relation of Scripture to the community.

The Trinitarian Consensus of the Classic Hermeneutic

The quotation from Lindbeck is taken from his discussion of 'The Classic Hermeneutic: Premodern Bible Reading' in 'Scripture, Consensus and Community':

> a certain way of reading Scripture (viz. as a Christ-centered narrationally and typologically unified whole in conformity to the Trinitarian rule of faith) was constitutive of the Christian canon and has, it would seem, an authority inseparable from that of the

Bible itself. To read the Bible otherwise is not to read it as Scripture but as some other book, just as to read Homer's *Odyssey* for philological or historical purposes, for example, is to turn it into something other than an epic poem.[5]

Lindbeck here draws our attention to the absolutely fundamental fact that Scripture's truth claims are bound up with bearing witness to the living Word and salvation in him. John 20.30–1 illustrates well the point we are making. The purpose of John's Gospel, according to this text, is to present Jesus as God's Christ, and to show that eternal life is found through faith in him. John's Gospel is not written as history or biography or theology, though it includes elements of each, but as a Gospel—a proclamation of the glad tidings of Christ and salvation through his name.[6] In a very real sense, this could be extended to Scripture as a whole. As John 5.39–40 makes clear, Jesus' audience searched the Scriptures because they believed them to bring life. These very Scriptures bear witness to Christ, yet they refused to come to him to find life. Against the backdrop of the classic hermeneutic noted above, which, as Lindbeck claims, involved approaching Scripture 'as a Christ-centered narrationally and typologically unified whole in conformity to the Trinitarian rule of faith', we do indeed turn the Scriptures into something they are not when we read them with non-Trinitarian lenses; in fact, instead of serving to inspire life, a faulty reading of the Bible can take away life—even unto death (see John 5.44–7).

Further to the discussion of the classic hermeneutic, Martin Luther went so far as to claim that 'What does not teach Christ is not apostolic, even though Peter or Paul teach it; again, what preaches Christ is apostolic even though Judas, Annas, Pilate, and Herod do it.'[7] For his own part, Jonathan Edwards' conception of the Son as 'the communication of divine Wisdom' served as the foundation stone for his constant employment of typology. As Amy Plantinga Pauw argues, 'Since Christ is the full revelation of God to the world, the ultimate antitype, all other manifestations of God in Scripture and in the created order are types of this perfect and eternal wisdom, "images and shadows of divine things."'[8]

Such a classic hermeneutical frame of reference must be retrieved in the present theological, hermeneutical context, where the doctrine of biblical revelation is often viewed with suspicion. There is no such thing as a non-dogmatic or non-theological engagement of the biblical text, or of any text or language for that matter.[9] Moreover, anti-Trinitarian frames of reference lead to fundamental problems for approaching the Bible and revelation. To illustrate by way of a historical parallel, the early Socinians, whose orientation was supposedly non-dogmatic, advocated an inspired and trustworthy Scripture, yet were closed to a Trinitarian perspective. They sought to divorce Scripture from its Trinitarian frame of reference. Their Unitarian view of God had repercussions for Scripture's authority and inspiration.[10] Perhaps it is the case that the seed of liberalism is sown on orthodoxy's soil. That is to say, an over-objectified view of the Bible leads ultimately to radical objections to the Bible. A Trinitarian frame of reference is important for developing a doctrine of revelation, including Scripture's status in the revelational framework, for God reveals God by God through Scripture in the life of the church. Scripture's content, even the means through which Scripture is mediated, is ultimately Trinitarian. Once this view is lost, the radical objectification process is bound to begin.

Objectification in the form of detached speculation is not ultimately objectivity, but disguised subjectivity. Søren Kierkegaard contends against radical objectification and detached speculation. As he sees it, the human knower is fully involved in the knowing process, and so, detached speculation is inhuman:

> The law for the development of the self with respect to knowing, insofar as it is the case that the self becomes itself, is that the increase of knowledge corresponds to the increase of self-knowledge, that the more the self knows, the more it knows itself. If this does not happen, the more knowledge increases, the more it becomes a kind of inhuman knowledge, in the obtaining of which a person's self is squandered, much the way men were squandered on building pyramids, or the way men in Russian brass bands are squandered on playing just one note, no more, no less.[11]

It is an impersonal, sub-human form of knowing that seeks after autonomy. A truly human approach to the matter, on the other hand, involves participation, or what Colin Gunton refers to as 'mutual indwelling'. Gunton draws attention to John's Gospel's distinctive emphasis on such 'mutual indwelling'. According to Gunton, 'The knowledge of which he speaks is first of all the knowledge by acquaintance that is a function of the interrelatedness of persons',[12] a point John drives home in chapter 17 of his Gospel.

The Gospel Community Context of the Classic Hermeneutic

Such a conception has a bearing on the relation of canon to Christ and community: one should not—in fact cannot—separate the text from the interpretive community or the Christ to whom it bears witness. One must view the propositions of Scripture and church proclamation, too, in an 'intrinsic' relation to Christ over against an 'extrinsic' frame of reference.[13] Jesus Christ is the Truth who is mediated to us through the person of the Spirit through the writings of those historical personages closest to Christ—his apostles—and those witnesses who follow after them in the course of history. Indeed, there is mutual indwelling, albeit in a unilateral manner, from Christ to canon to community. This leads us to the quotation from Hauerwas, who claims in his discussion of the moral authority of the Bible that

> The authority of scripture derives its intelligibility from the existence of a community that knows its life depends on faithful remembering of God's care of his creation through the calling of Israel and the life of Jesus.
>
> To construe the authority of scripture in this way, moreover, is most nearly faithful to the nature of biblical literature as well as the best insights we have learned from the historical study of the Bible. The formation of texts as well as the canon required the courage of a community to constantly remember and reinterpret its past.[14]

The point to be made in relation to Hauerwas's claim is that the authority of the Bible is made intelligible by the community's dependence on *remembering*, and what we would term *re-enacting*, the history of salvation wrought in Christ. The remembrance of the Passover (Exod. 12.14, 26–7), its fulfilment in the Last Supper (Luke 22.7–38) and Eucharistic celebration (1 Cor. 11.23–6) bear witness to this truth. By extension, Lesslie Newbigin claims that the community is the 'hermeneutic of the gospel',[15] and, I would add, of Scripture. The Christ-centred and Spirit-gathered community—not just any community—makes Scripture intelligible (or unintelligible, as the case may be), demonstrating its meaningfulness and authority through embodiment of Scripture's narration of Christ's kingdom and his kingly ambitions.

The Spirit, the Classic Hermeneutic and the Gospel Community

In view of the preceding discussion centred on Lindbeck and Hauerwas, we find that questions of the Bible's meaning, truth and authority must be set forth in a larger context—one that accounts for the relational dynamic of revelation involving Christ, canon and community. However, missing from Lindbeck's and Hauerwas's statements is an explicit account of the Spirit (which brings us back to inspiration), who according to the classic model of typological reading formed Scripture along the lines of prophecy and fulfilment centred around Christ, and who shaped the community and Scriptures. The Spirit constituted the Scriptures first through the apostolic community and the ensuing community through the Scriptures by way of that community's re-enactment and retelling of God's story in Christ.

By saying this, am I not failing to place Scripture in a larger context, harking back as I am to a theory of inspiration? To be sure, it is too often the case that Scripture's authority and power are viewed atomistically rather than 'perichoretically', so to speak. No doubt, as inspired it has inherent authority. But in keeping with what was said above, its inherent authority is the result of the Spirit's ongoing activity of constituting Scripture *in relation to* Christ and His community, both of whom the Spirit also constitutes dynamically and continually. If proper consideration is not given to the Spirit's constitutive work in shaping Scripture in relation to Christ and re-enacting Christ's story through Scripture in the community of faith, the danger exists of 'locking up' Scripture in solitary confinement, as fundamentalist Christianity so often does. Yet on the other hand, if one fails to give consideration to the Spirit's inspiring *of the text* in this dynamic relation involving Christ and the community, then one may be in danger of viewing Scripture simply as a book filled with useful information about ancient artefacts and customs as well as of perceiving the community of faith's retelling of the story as nothing more than its best religious sentiments projected onto Christ and God—a form of communal relativism or subjectivism.[16]

The Scriptures participate in revelation as the primary witness to Christ through the Spirit. Once again, John's Gospel makes clear the argument we have been developing. The Spirit of Truth, as he is called (John 14.17), the Counselor (John 14.26), will come and teach the disciples all things, and will remind them of everything that Jesus had said to them (v. 26). The Spirit reveals the Son, and as Paul says in 1 Corinthians, the deep things of God (2.10). In so doing, the Spirit constitutes the relational dynamic involving Christ, canon and community. The Spirit continues to uphold and constitute the Scriptures as the apostolic witness to Christ, just as the Spirit continues to uphold and constitute the humanity of Christ. For its own part, the present community of faith enters into this relational dynamic if and when through the Spirit it stands in dependence on the apostolic witness of Scripture to Christ.

The Revealing Spirit

In view of the preceding discussion, how then does the Bible continue to speak today? What is to be made of the claim noted at the outset of the essay that the Spirit enacts revelation anew through the interface of Christ, canon and community? Have we lost sight of this Trinitarian dynamic? The answer is 'no', and for three reasons.

The Spirit and the Present Word: the Vision of Christ

First, the Spirit enacts revelation anew by bearing witness to the identity of Christ through Scripture in the life of the community. This pertains to the vision of Christ. Here we are speaking of Christ's presence to the community in and through the Scriptures by the Spirit. Scripture and church proclamation bear witness to Christ's reality, mediating his presence in the present age through their identity descriptions. However, they could not do so if Jesus were a remote figure in the historical past. A particular of history can only serve as the universal of faith if that universal has in fact become a particular within history, which is exactly what has happened. The eternal Word who is God, and through whom the world was created, became flesh in history (John 1.1, 3, 14), died, rose again, ascended into heaven (Heb. 1.3b–4), and will come again to judge the living and the dead (Rev. 19.11–16), as the creed proclaims. As Gunton remarks,

> According to the past witness of scripture, Jesus is not a person marooned in the past but one who lives forever to make intercession for us and will return at the end of the age as judge. Past revelation reveals a figure who is past, present and to come: yesterday, today, and forever.[17]

We are called upon to remain in Christ, and for his words to remain in us (John 15.7). We are to inhabit the world of the text, which discloses reality to us. Christ's story is that reality to which the text itself bears witness, for he is the living Word who became flesh to redeem flesh from its fall to decay. The text bears witness to the fact that both it and we inhabit Christ's recapitulating work in the Spirit through whom God is redeeming and perfecting world history. All of Adamic history, including that of Israel, finds itself taken up and transformed by Christ's thirty-three years of life on earth in the Spirit.[18]

How is it then that the Bible speaks today? By bearing witness to our place in Christ's story—the story of his ongoing, ascended presence as first-born and first fruits between Golgotha and glory. It is within this dynamic history that our own story finds its shape and meaning. As we abide in the text, which identifies Christ's story, the Spirit enacts revelation anew, incorporating us into the meta-narrative of salvation history.

The Spirit and the Personal Word: Vital Affections for Christ

Moreover, the Spirit enacts revelation anew by shedding light on our experiences again and again in new ways as we come before the Bible in search of guidance and comfort. This pertains to the heart's vital affections for Christ. Here we are speaking of personalization. While the meaning disclosed in the text is not new, the experiences we bring to the text, and on which the text sheds light, are. The former point regarding meaning pertains to 'inspiration', whereas the latter point regarding experiences pertains to 'illumination'. The Spirit who searches the deep things of God, disclosing them in Scripture, also searches our own hearts through the Word of God, as it is proclaimed. As Scripture says, 'The Word of God is living and active, sharper than any double-edged sword. It penetrates to dividing soul and spirit, joints and marrow. It judges the thoughts and attitudes of the heart' (Heb. 4.12). The Spirit personalizes the written Word to us, addressing our heart's affections in relation to Christ as manifest in our experiences that we bring before the text.

The focus here is on personalization—not 'principalization'. The Christian faith is not a set of propositions to which one assents, but a personal relationship mediated in large part through propositions. Nor is it a matter ultimately of behavioural modification. Although one cannot know Christ apart from obedience to his Word (see John 14.21), it is not simply a matter of putting on certain Christian virtues. Apart from proper affections, virtue formation simply becomes a form of Pharisaism. As Paul, the former Pharisee, writes in 1 Cor. 13.3: 'If I give all I possess to the poor, and surrender my body to the flames, but have not love, it profits me nothing.' It all comes down to whether or not we have the love of God in our hearts. In commenting on this text, Jonathan Edwards claims that none of these virtuous acts would 'make up for the want of sincere love to God in the heart'.[19]

John's Gospel places much emphasis on the affections of the human heart. In John 5.39–40, Jesus rebukes the leaders, telling them that they do not search the Scriptures to find him because they do not have the love of God in their hearts. They do not accept Jesus, although he has come in his Father's name. Their desire for the praise and glory of man had displaced their affection for God (John 5.44).

Christ-centred affections will manifest themselves in certain virtues. However, the converse is not equally true: one can have virtues without godly affections. Bloesch makes note of this distinction between graces (what I call 'affections'[20]) and virtues in his discussion of 'Evangelical contextualism', which he associates with such names as Karl Barth, Dietrich Bonhoeffer and Helmut Thielicke. Bloesch writes,

> Evangelicals in this tradition speak more of graces than of virtues. Virtues indicate the unfolding of human potentialities, whereas graces are manifestations of the work of the Holy Spirit within us. It is not the fulfillment of human powers but the transformation of the human heart that is the emphasis in an authentically evangelical ethics.[21]

The foregoing should not be taken as dismissing the importance of Christian virtues. It is simply a matter of the proper ordering of vital affections and virtues. For Luther, 'We do not become righteous by doing righteous deeds but, having been made righteous, we do righteous deeds.'[22] Or as Barth said in his discussion of St Benedict's rule: it is not by performing godly deeds that the kingdom of God enters into our midst, but by the kingdom of God entering into our midst that we will perform godly deeds.[23] With this proper ordering of affections and virtues in mind, we now come to the third way in which the Spirit enacts revelation anew in the life of the community.

The Spirit and Participation in the Word: the Virtues of Christ

Lastly, the Spirit enacts revelation anew through the community's participation in the life of Christ. This pertains to the virtues of Christ. Here we are speaking of personalization involving participation. Person-to-person encounter through the mediation of Scripture involves application to life: 'As the Father has loved me, so have I loved you. Now remain in my love. If you obey my commands, you will remain in my love, just as I have obeyed my Father's commands and remain in his love' (John 15.9–10). Just as the Son bears witness to the Father by remaining in his love through obedience to his commands, so, too, we bear witness to Christ by remaining in his love through obedience to his commands. The same chapter indicates that Christ's command is that Christ's disciples then and now love one another just as he loved us, laying down his life for us, thereby obeying his Father's command (John 15.12–13, 17).

Apart from obedience, one cannot know Christ in his Word, nor participate in the ongoing dynamic of revelation. John 14.21 makes clear that Christ continues to reveal himself to the person who continues to obey him in love. Hauerwas's work is important in this regard. Although Kevin Vanhoozer argues that Hauerwas goes too far in claiming that the community gives Scripture its sense through practice in Christian virtues, he applauds Hauerwas for arguing for the significance of obedience in interpretation. As Vanhoozer claims, spiritual training 'helps us to discern the meaning that is already there'.[24] *Sola scriptura* would indeed be heresy if it were to signify solitary confinement, whereby one divorces the Bible from obedience to it.[25] According to Hauerwas, literalist fundamentalists and liberals are 'two sides of the same coin', approaching the text as if it were accessible apart from the church and training in Christian virtues.[26] Fortunately, we are not left alone with these two extremes, as the next section shows.

A Kernel of Wheat: Crucifixion and Contextualization

As Scripture's meaning and intent are bound up with obedience in the context of the community, so, too, are its significance and relevance for the present. Dietrich Bonhoeffer illustrates well the point we are making. Scripture speaks to us in the present tense as we present ourselves before it—reading the Bible over against ourselves, as Bonhoeffer himself did.[27] For Bonhoeffer, 'The present age must justify itself before the biblical message and in that way the message must become present.'[28] In this sense, the community of faith participates anew in revelation.

Bonhoeffer's life and those like his in the community of faith provide us with an illustration of what Newbigin calls the hermeneutic of the Gospel. Bonhoeffer placed himself under Scripture in the context of the community at Finkenwalde, and thus Scripture bore witness to Christ in and through Bonhoeffer's life of radical obedience. Bonhoeffer understood well the relationship between Christ, the canon and the community. According to Bonhoeffer, the whole of Scripture is Christ's book,[29] and Christian community is crucial to reading Scripture 'wisely and to live as Christians in the world'.[30] To this, we would add consideration of the Spirit. Without a relational model of revelation, one that involves personalization and participation in the life story of the crucified and risen Christ through Scripture in the community by the Spirit, there is no basis for contextualization—no word of God for today.

Newbigin makes the connection between the cross and contextualization,[31] a connection Bonhoeffer experienced all too well: a kernel of wheat must fall to the ground and die if it is to bear fruit (John 12.24). That was the case for Jesus. It is the case for us today as well. In the

Christian life, life comes through death. It is only through participation in Christ's resurrected life through sharing in his sufferings
(Phil. 3.10) in his community that we come to know God, and for God
to continue to make God's self known. As Luther said, 'true theology
and recognition of God are in the crucified Christ', and again, 'God can
be found only in suffering and the cross.'[32] The Spirit enacts revelation
anew in the community of faith through prophetic witnesses and
martyrs to the crucified and risen Christ revealed in Scripture. To
commandeer a claim made by John Howard Yoder, 'People who bear
crosses are working with the grain of the universe',[33] a universe
disclosed by the Spirit in Christian Scripture and the community of faith
as the ongoing story of the crucified and risen Christ.

Notes

[1] 'Perichoretic' refers to the mutual indwelling of the Father, Son and Spirit in the divine
life. I am using perichoretic imagery in this paper, not to indicate a form of being that
humans possess, but to speak of God's being toward us, which the canon and the
church participate in through Christ and the Spirit.

[2] This chapter will focus on the second and third persons of the Trinity in revelation.
This is not to ignore the Father, for the Father reveals himself through the Son and
Spirit. To appropriate Irenaeus' famous line in the current context, God reveals
himself through his two hands—the Son and Spirit. Jesus is the revelation of the
Father. As John puts it, 'No one has ever seen God, but God the one and only, who
is at the Father's side, has made him known' (John 1.18). And again, 'If you have seen
me [Jesus], you have seen the Father' (John 14.9). Now to know Jesus as the revelation
of the Father is the work of the Holy Spirit (See 1 John 4.2–3). Colin Gunton says it
well: 'Although we cannot know God's naked – unmediated – self-presentation, we
can know him by knowing the Son, as the Fourth Gospel repeatedly insists. And we
know the Son because the Father sends the Spirit in order that we should be able to
do so. And those who know the Son know the Father': *Act and Being: Towards a
Theology of the Divine Attributes* (London: SCM Press, 2002), p. 38. In the end, to
talk of the Son and Spirit in revelation is to talk about the Father, for they are the
personal agents through whom God reveals himself to the world.

[3] Karl Barth, *Church Dogmatics*, I/1, *The Doctrine of the Word of God*, ed. G. W.
Bromiley and T. F. Torrance (Edinburgh: T&T Clark, 1975), pp. 111–12.

[4] Donald G. Bloesch, *Christian Foundations*, i, *A Theology of Word and Spirit:
Authority and Method in Theology* (Downers Grove, Ill.: InterVarsity Press, 1992),
p. 190. Bloesch uses the terms 'revealed' and 'living' interchangeably for speaking
about Christ. Later on, Bloesch draws attention to Barth's connecting of this threefold
model of the Word of God with the unity of the divine persons within the Trinity (p.
314, n. 10). See *Church Dogmatics*, I/1, pp. 120–4.

[5] George A. Lindbeck, 'Scripture, Consensus and Community', in *The Church in a
Postliberal Age*, ed. James J. Buckley (Grand Rapids: Eerdmans, 2002), p. 204.

[6] See D. A. Carson, *The Expositor's Bible Commentary*, VIII, *Matthew* (Grand Rapids:
Zondervan, 1984), pp. 38–9.

7 Martin Luther quoted in Schubert M. Ogden, *On Theology* (Dallas: Southern Methodist University Press, 1992), p. 54.

8 Amy Plantinga Pauw, *The Supreme Harmony of All: The Trinitarian Theology of Jonathan Edwards* (Grand Rapids: Eerdmans, 2002), p. 13. Pauw refers the reader to Wallace E. Anderson, Mason I. Lowance and David H. Watters (eds), *The Works of Jonathan Edwards: Typological Writings*, XI (New Haven: Yale University Press, 1993) for Edwards' notebook entitled 'Images and Shadows of Divine Things'.

9 In his work on Barth and Derrida, Graham Ward claims that 'Language is always and ineradicably theological': *Barth, Derrida and the Language of Theology* (Cambridge: Cambridge University Press, 1995), p. 9.

10 See Klaus Scholder, 'The Relationship between Reason, Scripture and Dogma among the Socinians', in *idem, The Birth of Modern Critical Theology: Origins and Problems of Biblical Criticism in the Seventeenth Century* (Philadelphia: Trinity Press International, 1990), pp. 26–45.

11 Søren Kierkegaard, *The Sickness Unto Death*, ed. and tr. Howard V. Hong and Edna H. Hong (Princeton: Princeton University Press, 1980), p. 31.

12 Colin E. Gunton, *A Brief Theology of Revelation: The 1993 Warfield Lectures* (Edinburgh: T&T Clark, 1995), p. 118.

13 See Gunton, *A Brief Theology of Revelation*, p. 99.

14 Stanley Hauerwas, *A Community of Character: Toward a Constructive Christian Social Ethic* (Notre Dame: University of Notre Dame Press, 1981), p. 53.

15 Lesslie Newbigin, *The Gospel in a Pluralist Society* (Grand Rapids: Eerdmans, 1989), p. 222.

16 For his own part, Hauerwas does not deny the Spirit's work. Rather, he emphasizes the Spirit's work in relation to the community. Kevin Vanhoozer draws attention to the fact that for literary critic Stanley Fish, to whom Hauerwas looks for insight, the 'interpretive' community's reading practice 'produces the meaning', not the biblical text. In similar fashion, Hauerwas argues that the 'meaning that interests the church is not "the meaning of the text" but rather "how the Spirit that is found in the Eucharist is also to be seen in Scripture"': Kevin J. Vanhoozer, *First Theology: God, Scripture and Hermeneutics* (Downers Grove, Ill.: InterVarsity Press, 2002), p. 211. Vanhoozer's quotation from Hauerwas is taken from Stanley Hauerwas, *Unleashing the Scripture: Freeing the Bible from Captivity to America* (Nashville: Abingdon Press, 1993), p. 23. Later, Vanhoozer argues that Hauerwas's claim that 'Scripture does not make sense apart from a church that gives it sense . . . imperils the very distinction between textual meaning and community interpretation' (p. 278). This calls to mind Vanhoozer's mention of Francis Watson's claim: locating authority in reading communities and their practices 'owes more to postmodernity than to patristic theology'. According to Vanhoozer's restatement of Watson's argument, the 'ruled reading approach' replaces 'the communicative agency of God' with 'the being of the community' (p. 290). The problematic feature in Hauerwas's view is that the meaning of Scripture is too closely tied to the community, and so does not provide sufficient space for the text's otherness. For all practical purposes, this rules out Scripture's prophetic critique of the community by the Spirit.

17 Gunton, *A Brief Theology of Revelation*, p. 81.

18 Along these lines, see the genealogy of Luke (3.23–38) and Matthew (1.1–17). In the former, Christ is of the line of Adam, and in the latter, he is of the line of David and Abraham. While Paul tells us that Christ is the last Adam, who is a life-giving spirit (1 Cor. 15.45), Matthew discloses Christ as the one who takes up and recapitulates

Israel's history, as illustrated in Christ being led by the Spirit into the wilderness to be tempted by the Devil, emerging triumphant in obedience to God (Matt. 4.1–11).

[19] Jonathan Edwards, *Charity and its Fruits: Christian Love as Manifested in the Heart and Life* (Carlisle: Banner of Truth Trust, 1969; repr., 2000), p. 55. See also Edwards' discussion of the Pharisee on p. 53.

[20] I have employed the term 'affection' (English for *Affectus*) as it is used in Philipp Melanchthon's 1521 edition (in contrast to the 1543 edition) of the *Loci Communes Theologici*, in *Melanchthon and Bucer*, ed. Wilhelm Pauck, Library of Christian Classics (Philadelphia: Westminster Press, 1969); see for example p. 27.

[21] Donald G. Bloesch, *Freedom for Obedience: Evangelical Ethics in Contemporary Times* (San Francisco: Harper & Row, 1987), p. 191. Grace according to Luther is Christ's love by the Spirit creating new desires or affections, a point we develop below. God's Spirit is the grace of God, who transforms our hearts' desires and with them our deeds, making them righteous. Luther himself maintains that every act of fallen nature is 'an act of concupiscence against God' whereas every righteous act is due to the love of God being poured out into our hearts through the Spirit: Martin Luther, 'Disputation against Scholastic Theology', in *Martin Luther's Basic Theological Writings*, ed. Timothy F. Lull (Minneapolis: Fortress Press, 1989), pp. 14, 19. These points are made in theses 21 and 84 respectively. The solution to the problem that 'every act of concupiscence against God is evil and a fornication of the spirit' is the divine love that the Holy Spirit pours out into our hearts (Rom. 5.5). As Luther states, 'the good law and that in which one lives is the love of God, spread abroad in our hearts by the Holy Spirit': 'Disputation against Scholastic Theology', p. 14, thesis 22, and p. 19, thesis 84.

[22] Luther, 'Disputation against Scholastic Theology', p. 16. Luther's comrade Melanchthon speaks of the same matter in the following way: 'internal affections are not in our power, for by experience and habit we find that the will (*voluntas*) cannot in itself control love, hate, or similar affections, but affection is overcome by affection': Melanchthon, *Loci Communes Theologici*, p. 27.

[23] Karl Barth, *Church Dogmatics*, IV/2, *The Doctrine of Reconciliation*, ed. G. W. Bromiley and T. F. Torrance (Edinburgh: T&T Clark, 1958), p. 18.

[24] Kevin J. Vanhoozer, *Is there a Meaning in this Text? The Bible, the Reader, and the Morality of Literary Knowledge* (Grand Rapids: Zondervan, 1998), p. 379.

[25] See Hauerwas's discussion of heresy and *sola scriptura* in *Unleashing the Scripture*, p. 27.

[26] See Hauerwas, *Unleashing the Scripture*, pp. 9 and 17.

[27] Stephen E. Fowl and L. Gregory Jones argue that Bonhoeffer claimed that we must 'read Scripture *over-against* ourselves, allowing Scripture to question our lives': Stephen E. Fowl and L. Gregory Jones, *Reading in Communion: Scripture and Ethics in Christian Life* (Grand Rapids: Eerdmans, 1991), p. 145, italics in original.

[28] Dietrich Bonhoeffer, quoted in *Dietrich Bonhoeffer: Witness to Jesus Christ*, ed. John de Gruchy (London: Collins, 1988), p. 188.

[29] See Fowl and Jones, *Reading in Communion*, p. 145.

[30] Fowl and Jones, *Reading in Communion*, p. 144.

[31] Newbigin, *The Gospel in a Pluralist Society*, p. 145.

[32] Martin Luther, 'Heidelberg Disputation', in *Martin Luther's Basic Theological Writings*, p. 44.

[33] John Howard Yoder, 'Armaments and Eschatology', quoted in Stanley Hauerwas, *With the Grain of the Universe: The Church's Witness and Natural Theology* (Grand Rapids: Brazos Press, 2001), p. 6.

3

The Trinity in
the Hebrew Scriptures

Paul Blackham

Trinitarian theology is the subject of renewed interest. The solutions to
the problems of third-millennium life are being rediscovered in the
divine life of the Three who are One. In the past, such Trinitarian
thinking was deeply nurtured by an appreciation of the profoundly
Trinitarian theology of the Hebrew Scriptures, but today this renaissance has been slow to arrive. In this chapter, I want to think about the
theological assumptions that have prevented the depth of exegesis that
we so desperately need at this time.

Assumptions about the Living God have profound exegetical implications. This vital fact must be appreciated from the outset as we think
about grasping the Trinitarian faith of the Hebrew Scriptures. This
chapter will focus less on examining the many Hebrew Scriptures that
display the Trinitarian faith and more on examining the theological
assumptions that may hide or reveal this Hebrew doctrine of God. The
details and theological distinctions in the Hebrew Scriptures are tragi-
cally missed or 'flattened out' when viewed from a doctrine of God that
excludes such possibilities in advance.

As Moltmann[1] and many others have shown, a classic approach to
the doctrine of God produced in the Greek philosophical tradition
begins with a definition of a single divine essence before later (and
usually much more briefly) dealing with the three divine persons.[2]
Thomas Watson's *Body of Divinity*, a classic work which I deeply
appreciate, offers a basic definition of God that illustrates the problem:

> God is a Spirit, infinite, eternal, and unchangeable, in his being, wisdom, power,
> holiness, justice, goodness and truth . . . By a spirit I mean God is an immaterial
> substance, of a pure, subtle, unmixed essence, not compounded of body and soul,
> without all extension of parts.[3]

If the most important and foundational claims about the Living God can be made before the actual divine Persons are even mentioned, to what extent can such a doctrine of God claim to be genuinely Trinitarian? If the so-called *essence* of God is defined *a priori*, in advance of a careful investigation of the Three Persons who actually *are* the Living God, then we must expect that our thinking about God will tend to default to a kind of monotheism.

The tension between monotheism and Trinitarianism is something of which we are all aware. The contemporary assumption that Islam, Judaism and Christianity all worship the same God is nourished by the tradition of classical theism. It is not at all clear why someone would want to make the claim that these three religions all worship the same God, but the fact that this assumption is made so easily indicates the extent to which the Three Persons are seen as almost peripheral to a foundational doctrine of God. When we begin from a tradition that sees a non-Trinitarian divine essence as the starting point for a doctrine of God, it is no surprise that the integration of the Three Persons becomes a genuine theological difficulty. It also is no surprise that it creates exegetical difficulties.

Whether the New Testament authors had an exegetical method that is either possible or desirable to imitate is a matter that seems to attract more and more discussion. However, it is worth noticing the way these Trinitarian distinctions are detected, even assumed, as the New Testament authors exegete the Hebrew Scriptures. Let us note just one obvious example.

The first chapter of Hebrews is a compilation of Hebrew Scriptures indicating the relationship of the Son to the Father, particularly in contrast to the angels. Now, if this book is written to a Hebrew audience and the writer is attempting to prove the character of Jesus to them, it might strike some modern readers as strange that all these Scripture quotations are listed as *manifestly* showing those relations between the Son and the Father that we now label Trinitarian. They are not intricately explained, nor are they seen as having acquired 'a new meaning' (whatever *that* might mean!), but they are simply quoted as if the reader was expected easily to see the Trinitarian import of each Scripture.

The Scriptures quoted interweave Ps. 2.7, 2 Sam. 7.14, Ps. 104.4 and Ps. 45.6–7. Is this an example of faithful exegesis of those Scriptures, or is it an imposed 'Christian' eisegesis, claiming to find (whether by the Spirit or a new perspective) a 'meaning' that the original authors knew nothing of? If the writer of the book of Hebrews were engaged in a theologically driven eisegesis we must ask to what extent this would have been persuasive to his original audience. If these Scriptures were *not* recording the Father's declarations concerning his divine Son, then what value would they have to the Hebrew readers who were struggling to understand the identity of Jesus?

The 'Development' of the doctrine of the Trinity

This raises a deeper question about theological assumptions. The standard 'story of the doctrine of the Trinity' that I was taught cast the first generation of post-Pentecost believers as people in theological crisis. They were portrayed as committed to the 'monotheism' of the Hebrew Scriptures, but faced with the 'problem' of the obvious divinity of Jesus. Therefore, they had to 'revise' or 'reconstruct' their doctrine of God to cope with a second divine person. No sooner had they begun to do this than they were faced with a similar problem with the Spirit! Now they had to 'revise' further their doctrine of God until after much discovery and crisis they arrived, out of breath, three hundred years after Pentecost at 'a doctrine of the Trinity'. This 'story', I grant, is a little simplified here, but I hope it is a recognizable account.

The fundamental problem with this common narrative is that it does not do justice to the New Testament documents nor to the theological writings of the second century. The New Testament never *struggles* to speak of Jesus as divine. It never indicates a tension between a Hebrew doctrine of Yahweh and any affirmations of the full divinity of Jesus. In fact, the constant and repeated assumption of the New Testament is that the Hebrew doctrine of God includes and demands a whole-hearted confession of the divinity of the Father, Son and Spirit.

Margaret Barker's work in accounting for this overwhelming feature of the New Testament contains much fascinating material, even if I struggle to accept all her methods and conclusions. Her rejection of the notion that Israel originally worshipped some divine monad in isolation has reminded the modern church of many of the assumptions that we find scattered through the writings of Philo, Justin, Tertullian and Irenaeus:

> The Trinitarian faith of the Church had grown from the older Hebrew belief in a pluriform deity, and so the earliest Christian exegetes had not been innovators when they understood the LORD of the Hebrew Scriptures as the Second God, the Son of El Elyon. The One whom they recognized in Jesus had been the LORD, and so they declared 'Jesus is the LORD'.[4]

We will examine the exegesis of Justin later, but for now we need to note that when we study the thought of the biblical scholars of the first century BC through to the second century AD we do not find a theological crisis about describing the Second God, the Great Angel, Jesus the divine Messiah. We *do* find this crisis in Augustine, and Colin Gunton has done much to trace the reasons for this.[5]

What we find developing in these early centuries is not the *concept* of the biblical God who is Father, Son and Spirit, but rather the development of an arsenal of terms and formulae to be used against heretics such as Arius and Sabellius, heretics that the church so instinctively opposed.

When we read the pre-critical exegesis of Puritan scholars,[6] as well as the great Jonathan Edwards, we still find the general assumption that the doctrine of God in the Hebrew Scriptures is Trinitarian, either fairly well-formed or at least present in principle:

> When we read in sacred history what God did from time to time towards his church and people, and what he said to them, and how he revealed himself to them, we are to understand it especially of the Second Person of the Trinity. When we read of God's appearing after the Fall, from time to time, in some visible form or outward symbol of his presence, we are ordinarily, if not universally, to understand it of the second Person of the Trinity.[7]

Critical biblical scholarship brought a definite change. The reasons for this are too complex for us to trace here (though all our minds are certainly reaching for Hegel right now), but we should certainly note the assumption of a progression of the doctrine of God through human history from animism, to polytheism, to monotheism and finally (for the Christian exponents of this perspective) Trinitarianism. Under such a theological understanding of history, it is anachronistic to recognize a Trinitarian faith in the early stages of Hebrew thought, for it would identify the final stage of the progression at a time when the Hebrew theologians were still (allegedly) struggling out of polytheism!

This understanding of history would certainly need to be re-examined if the Hebrew Scriptures were to be given a chance to speak in the way that we find in the exegesis of the first chapter of Hebrews or in the writings of those second-century scholars.

When we read Justin's own account of the doctrine of God found in the Hebrew Scriptures we find a very robust account of the Trinitarian God. For Justin, the Jews who reject Jesus as the divine Messiah were rejecting the explicit and intentional theology of Moses and the prophets.

Justin's understanding of history turns upside down the modernist understanding of history. For Justin, Moses is automatically more trustworthy, profound and truthful because he is *older* than the Greek philosophers! 'I will begin, then, with our first prophet and lawgiver, Moses . . . that you may know that, of all your teachers, whether sages, poets, historians, philosophers, or lawgivers, by far the oldest, as the Greek histories show us, was Moses, who was our first religious teacher.'[8] We find this same attitude to the antiquity of the Hebrew theologians in the New Testament. When Paul wishes to establish the truth of his claims his preference is to go right back to Abraham and Moses—see Rom. 4.1, Acts 26.22–3 *et al.*

We note this simply in order to challenge the assumptions that so often seem unexamined in many aspects of contemporary biblical studies. As long as we assume that the doctrine of the Trinity is the summit of a long process of development, there is no possibility of arriving at the exegetical results that we find in writers like Philo or Justin, or even the New Testament itself.

The Appearing of the LORD God

I would like to explore one of the most obvious and foundational features of the Hebrew doctrine of Yahweh-Elohim, focusing on the writings of Moses. While not an exhaustive study, it will highlight reasons why the biblical scholars of the second century were able to pose the kind of theological challenge that they did.

The question of the visibility of the Living God is a key issue within the Bible. *Seeing* the Living God is taken very seriously. We see this in Exod. 33.18–23. Moses speaks to the LORD who hides himself in the thick darkness, and requests that he may see the Most High.[9] This request is very firmly rejected. However, within the Pentateuch we find that there is a divine Person whose face may be seen, a divine Person who appears to a variety of people, Moses included. We need only look back earlier in Exodus 33 to see an example of this, in vv. 7–11.[10]

Exodus 24.9–11 provides an intense and specific example of the visibility of the LORD God. This crucial Scripture acknowledges the significance of *seeing* the LORD. Far from being an isolated aberration within the Pentateuch, the *appearing* of the LORD is perhaps one of the most consistent features of this doctrine of God. At least seven passages in Genesis alone feature God's appearing—Gen. 12.7, 16.13, 17.1, 18.1, 26.2, 26.24, 32.30 and 35.9. An unmistakable feature of this Pentateuchal doctrine of God is that the LORD God can *appear* even though it is also stated that the Most High God may not be seen. At face value this would naturally lead to the confession that one of the divine Persons can be seen and one of the divine Persons cannot be seen. Surely, only on the strange assumption that the Living God must only be a single divine Person would we see any tension or difficulty here.

Justin Martyr's Exegesis

When we see the way in which Justin Martyr deals with this strand in the Hebrew doctrine of God, we can see how the doctrine of the Trinity was understood to be an obvious feature of Moses' theology. However, before we focus specifically on Justin Martyr, we must note that the exegesis we find in him is shared by the other theologians of the era.[11]

For example, against the Gnostics, Irenaeus saw the Old Testament as the revelation, not of another being than the Father revealed in Christ through the Spirit, but the very same God, known by the faithful:

> the law never hindered them from believing in the Son of God; nay, but it even exhorted them so to do, saying that men can be saved in no other way from the old wound of the serpent than by believing in Him who, in the likeness of sinful flesh, is lifted up from the earth upon the tree of martyrdom, and draws all things to Himself, and vivifies the dead.[12]

Moreover, this was no opaque revelation of a distant, deceitful or unknown God. On the contrary, to take just one example, Irenaeus conceives of Moses as having been explicitly aware of the passion and name of Jesus.[13] The content of the apostolic proclamation in Acts was new to Jewish audiences in but one respect: that the same Word known by the patriarchs had now come in the flesh. This Irenaeus saw as equally true for Jewish proselytes such as the Ethiopian eunuch that Philip encountered in Acts 8: 'For nothing else (but baptism) was wanting to him who had been already instructed by the prophets: he was not ignorant of God the Father, nor of the rules as to the (proper) manner of life, but was merely ignorant of the advent of the Son of God.'[14] That the faithful of the Old Testament could have had such complete knowledge of the apostolic gospel was possible because of Irenaeus' belief that the one Father always reveals himself through his one Word: 'the Spirit shows forth the Word, and therefore the prophets announced the Son of God; and the Word utters the Spirit, and therefore is Himself the announcer of the prophets, and leads and draws man to the Father'.[15] Therefore, it was this Word, Jesus Christ, who had spoken with Adam in the garden, with the patriarchs, the prophets, the faithful in exile in Babylon, and even less salubrious characters such as Balaam.[16] A common designation of the Word for Irenaeus is, simply, 'the one who spoke with Moses'.[17] In what resembles a primitive confession, he writes:

> With regard to Christ, the law and the prophets and the evangelists have proclaimed that He was born of a virgin, that He suffered upon a beam of wood, and that He appeared from the dead; that He also ascended to the heavens, and was glorified by the Father, and is the Eternal King; that He is the perfect Intelligence, the Word of God, who was begotten before the light; that He was the Founder of the universe, along with it (light), and the Maker of man; that He is All in all: Patriarch among the patriarchs; Law in the laws; Chief Priest among priests; Ruler among kings; the Prophet among prophets; the Angel among angels; the Man among men; Son in the Father; God in God; King to all eternity. For it is He who sailed [in the ark] along with Noah, and who guided Abraham; who was bound along with Isaac, and was a Wanderer with Jacob; the Shepherd of those who are saved, and the Bridegroom of the Church; the Chief also of the cherubim, the Prince of the angelic powers; God of God; Son of the Father; Jesus Christ; King for ever and ever. Amen.[18]

Justin Martyr is just as careful in delineating the divine Persons in the Godhead in his exegesis of the Hebrew Scriptures:

> Moses, then, the blessed and faithful servant of God, declares that He who appeared to Abraham under the oak in Mamre is God, *sent with the two angels in His company to judge Sodom by Another who remains ever in the supercelestial places, invisible to all men,* holding personal intercourse with none, whom we believe to be Maker and Father of all things; for he speaks thus: 'God appeared to him under the oak in Mamre, as he sat at his tent-door at noontide . . . I shall attempt to persuade you . . . that there is, and that there is said to be, another God and Lord subject to the Maker of all things; who is also called an Angel, because He announces to men whatsoever the Maker of all things . . . wishes to announce to them.[19]

Justin picks up another feature of the Hebrew doctrine of God here in order to elucidate the nature of the LORD who appears. The title 'Angel of the LORD' is clearly favoured by Moses, though it is also found in Judges, the Psalms and Isaiah. It is of great significance because it means 'the One sent from the LORD'—that is to say it refers to a divine Person who sends the One who bears the title. It is a title that contains within itself the Father and the Son.[20] The title is first given to the appearing-LORD in Gen. 16, where the nature of the Angel of the LORD is defined for us by Hagar's confession—Genesis 16.7-13.

The divine character of the Angel of the LORD is spelled out again in Gen. 22.11-18; notice especially vv. 11 and 12. Jacob's own confession of faith at the end of his life sets out his doctrine of God in clear terms. His faith is in the God who is the Angel of the LORD, the God who appears to him, the One who mediates the Unseen God Most High:

> [Israel] blessed Joseph and said, 'May *the God* before whom my fathers Abraham and Isaac walked, *the God* who has been my shepherd all my life to this day, *the Angel* who has delivered me from all harm—may he bless these boys. May they be called by my name and the names of my fathers Abraham and Isaac, and may they increase greatly upon the earth.' (Gen. 48.15–16)

When Jacob explicitly identifies the God of Abraham and Isaac as the *Angel* of the LORD, we see how problematic it is to suggest that a theological crisis occurred in the first century AD. when the divinity of Jesus was confessed. If Jacob could so confidently and self-consciously confess the divinity of the God who is sent by God, why would it be so traumatic to do this in the first century AD?

The heart of Justin's argument about the Hebrew doctrine of God revolves around his careful analysis of the details of the various encounters that the patriarchs had with the appearing-LORD:

> It is again written by Moses, my brethren, that He who is called God and appeared to the patriarchs is called both Angel and LORD, in order that from this you may understand Him to be minister to the Father of all things . . . Moreover, I consider it necessary to repeat to you the words which narrate how He who is both Angel and God and LORD, and who appeared as a man to Abraham, and who wrestled in human form with Jacob, was seen by him when he fled from his brother Esau . . .[21]

Naturally, Justin also examines the account in Exodus 3 when the Angel of the LORD commissions Moses from within the flaming bush.

We have studied Justin's argument simply to show that his exegesis of the Hebrew Scriptures has a similar character to the pattern that we saw in Hebrews 1 (the confident recognition of Trinitarian distinctions within the Hebrew text). For Justin it is manifestly plain that the One God of Israel is not a single person, but a transcendent, invisible Father, an appearing, sent LORD, and the Spirit of the LORD. It is quite true that Justin does not formulate his findings in the language of the fourth century, but his assumptions and exegesis give us a vivid insight into the patterns of theological thinking that existed among the second-century biblical scholars.

Non-Trinitarian Approaches to Exegesis

Different strategies have been suggested for dealing with the Scriptures to which we have referred. So much biblical scholarship, without any theological explanation or defence, speaks of the God of the Hebrew Scriptures in a way that can only be described as Yahweh-Unitarian. That is to say, the Scriptures are handled as if it were a self-evident truth that the God of the Hebrew Scriptures were a single person! Given even the small number of Scriptures we have referred to, such a claim would require a very thorough proof!

Such a theological proof is quite hard to find. Very few Hebrew exegetes actually take the time to explain and defend theologically a non-Trinitarian approach to these Scriptures. However, the great Augustine takes a great deal of care to explain why he departs from the exegetical tradition that has gone before him, beginning in bk 2, ch. 7 of his mighty work *On the Trinity.*

He begins by posing this key question—how are we to explain the appearances of the LORD in the Hebrew Scriptures? As a Christian theologian Augustine knows that in the incarnation the LORD God is visible, but what of the time before the incarnation? Augustine gives himself two basic options in answering these questions:

> In the perplexity of this inquiry, the LORD helping us, we must ask, first, whether the Father, or the Son, or the Holy Spirit; or whether, sometimes the Father, sometimes the Son, sometimes the Holy Spirit; or whether it was without any distinction of persons, in such way as the one and only God is spoken of, that is, that the Trinity itself appeared to the Fathers by those forms of the creature.[22]

So, are the appearances of God to be understood in a Trinitarian way (as one particular Person, or a combination of the Persons), or are the appearances of God to be understood as non-Trinitarian such that 'the Trinity itself' appeared, indirectly mediated through creatures? When Augustine speaks of 'the Trinity itself', we should note that he does not mean 'all three Persons together' but 'the divine substance' that is shared by the three Persons.

In order to make a choice between his two options Augustine surveys much of the Hebrew Scriptures. Augustine seems genuinely confused throughout this whole section as to how he might decide which member of the Trinity is speaking or visible at any time in the Hebrew Scriptures. He seems to think such judgements are somehow arbitrary. Augustine argues that it is *essentially* impossible for God to be seen, so all 'appearances' must be through creaturely intermediaries. The viewer sees only a specially prepared creature through which the divine substance ('the Trinity itself') is mediately encountered. To allow any Trinitarian distinctions at any point in his analysis of the Hebrew Scriptures would mean that Adam, Abraham, Jacob or Moses encountered a divine *person* rather than the mediated divine *substance*. Therefore, Augustine takes great pains to find ways of explaining why 'the LORD appearing' cannot refer to any specific member of the Trinity. Gunton's analysis of this aspect of Augustine's doctrine of God is a real theological treasure.[23] Most of us simply stand in awe of Augustine, and yet Gunton's ability to expose the inner workings of Augustine's doctrine is profoundly valuable. When Gunton pinpoints Augustine's understanding of mediation, we then see why his doctrine of God must take the shape that it did.

Because Augustine's doctrine of God began with the divine substance rather than the three Persons, his understanding of the divine substance controls his understanding of the possible roles and actions of the three. The nature of the divine essence determines what the three persons can or cannot do, rather than a specific examination of what the three persons *actually* do or do not do.

Thus, when Augustine deals with Moses' request to see the Unseen LORD in Exodus 33, Augustine imagines that Moses is asking to view the divine substance rather than a specific divine Person!

> Who sees God the Father with the eyes of the body? And that Word, which was in the beginning, the Word that was with God, the Word that was God, by which all things were made, who sees Him with the eyes of the body? And the spirit of wisdom, again, who sees with the eyes of the body? Yet what is, 'Show me now Thyself plainly, that I may see Thee,' unless, Show me Thy substance?[24]

For Augustine, to see 'the face of God' is to see 'the divine substance', and not with the eyes of the body, but with spiritual eyes. Professor Gunton showed that Augustine translated the text of Exodus into the language of Neo-Platonism, losing in the process the primacy of the Persons over the divine substance. How can God be encountered other than encountering one or more of the Persons? God is nothing other than these Three Persons.

Again, because Augustine imagines that any appearance of God must be in the form of created intermediaries there is no reason to prefer one member of the Trinity over another. If none of them are seen directly and personally then there is no reason to think that any particular 'sign of the presence of God' indicates a particular member of the Trinity. Consequently, Genesis 18 creates more difficulties for Augustine:

That place of Scripture demands neither a slight nor a passing consideration. For if one man had appeared, what else would those at once cry out, who say that the Son was visible also in His own substance before He was born of the Virgin, but that it was Himself? Since it is said, they say, of the Father, 'To the only invisible God.' And yet, I could still go on to demand, in what manner 'He was found in fashion as a man', before He had taken our flesh, seeing that his feet were washed, and that He fed upon earthly food? (Gen. 18.4–8) How could that be, when He was still 'in the form of God, and thought it not robbery to be equal with God'?[25]

Augustine's concern here is that any attempt to see the Son as performing a mediatorial role throughout the Hebrew Scriptures would undermine the reality and significance of the incarnation. If the Word of God, through whom all things were made and were pronounced to be very good, was so directly involved in the creation before his incarnation that he ate food and washed his feet, is this tantamount to saying that the incarnation had occurred at the beginning of the world?

However, the Scriptures make it clear that the Son began his work of mediation in the work of creation itself. We need only recall Genesis 1 or Proverbs 8 to see how the great mediatorial work of the Son was written into the very character of the creation itself. The incarnation was not the moment when the Son became directly involved in his creation, his inheritance. Rather, the incarnation marks a particular kind of involvement. He becomes one of us, a human subject to the consequences of the fall (yet without sin), a human subject to pain and hunger and even death. That is what 'becoming flesh' refers to.[26]

Augustine very helpfully places his cards on the table. He explains why he makes the exegetical decisions that he does. When we understand the structure of his doctrine of God, we can fully understand why he refuses to acknowledge the Trinitarian distinctions in the Hebrew Scriptures that the previous generations had done. If we allow the three Persons who *actually are* the Living God to define their essence, roles and activities, then we are free to return to the earlier patterns of exegesis.

Conclusions

When we adopt the theological convictions of exegetes such as Justin, Irenaeus, Luther, Owen, Edwards, and moderns like Colin Gunton, we are able to follow the careful detail of the Hebrew text in its delineation of the identity and roles of the divine Persons. When we start with the truth that the God of Israel is a unity of God Most High, his Son, and his Spirit, then we are free to give full exegetical weight to the distinctions between the three Persons made in the text, through its careful descriptions of divine titles and roles. God Most High sends his Angel with his Spirit to accomplish his work of creation, revelation, judgement and redemption. When we reject the assumptions of one such as Harnack and acknowledge this Hebrew doctrine of God, beginning in the book of Genesis, it enables us to read the Psalms and the Prophets from the same theological vantage point—that is to say, we can understand and imitate the Trinitarian exegesis of the New Testament and the second-century scholars.

The contemporary growth in Trinitarian thought cannot be sustained unless it finds its deep roots in the Hebrew Scriptures. The great Trinitarian theologians of the past were exegetes of these Scriptures, and it is as we sit and learn from that most brilliant and careful Trinitarian theologian, Moses, that we can go further and deeper into the God of Israel who is the Most High, the appearing LORD, and the Spirit.

Notes

1   Jürgen Moltmann, *The Trinity and the Kingdom of God* (London: SCM Press, 1993), pp. 16–17.

2   Colin E. Gunton, *The Promise of Trinitarian Theology* (Edinburgh: T&T Clark, 1991), p. 32.

3   Thomas Watson, *A Body of Divinity* (Edinburgh: Banner of Truth Trust, 1965), p. 39.

4   Margaret Barker, *The Great High Priest* (Edinburgh: T&T Clark, 2003), p. xi. See also her book *The Great Angel: A Study of Israel's Second God* (London: SPCK, 1992).

5   Gunton, *The Promise of Trinitarian Theology*, ch. 3.

6   See especially John Owen's brilliant tenth introductory essay in vol. 1 of his commentary on Hebrews, entitled 'Appearances of the Son of God under the Old Testament': John Owen, *Hebrews*, 7 vols (Edinburgh: Banner of Truth Trust, 1991). For example: 'He by whom all things were made, and by whom all were to be renewed that were to be brought again unto God, did in an especial and glorious manner appear unto our first parents, as he in whom this whole dispensation centred, and unto whom it was committed. And as, after the promise given, he appeared "in human form" to instruct the Church in the mystery of his future incarnation, and under the name of Angel, to shadow out his office as sent unto it and employed in it by the Father; so here, before the promise, he discovered his distinct glorious person, as the eternal Voice of the Father.'

7   Jonathan Edwards, *A History of the Work of Redemption* (Edinburgh: Banner of Truth Trust, 2003), p. 23.

8   Justin Martyr, *Hortatory Address to the Greeks* 9, in *Ante-Nicene Christian Library* (ANCL), I, ed. James Donaldson and Alexander Roberts (Edinburgh: T&T Clark, 1867), p. 277.

9   I use the title 'Most High' here to refer to the LORD, who refuses all visual contact, simply because it is one of the most common Hebrew titles that is reserved for God

the Father. I know that the title is not used by Moses in Exodus 33, but I wanted to introduce the title in order to clarify exactly what is happening in Exodus 33–4. I do so in much the same way that I would use the word 'Father' to indicate the meaning of the first use of 'God' in the Gospel of John (1.1).

[10] ANCL, I, ed. James Donaldson and Alexander Roberts. See Irenaeus, in *Adversus Haereses* 4.20.9 (Edinburgh: T&T Clark, 1867), p. 490.

[11] See especially Juan Ochagavía, *Visibile Patris Filius: A Study of Irenaeus' Teaching on Revelation and Tradition* (Rome: Pont. Institutum Orientalium Studiorum, 1964), pp. 85–7.

[12] Irenaeus, *Adversus Haereses* 4.2.7, (cf. 4.2.3); *ANCL* I, p. 464.

[13] Irenaeus, *Adversus Haereses* 4.10.1; *ANCL* I, p. 473.

[14] Irenaeus, *Adversus Haereses* 4.23.2; *ANCL* I, p. 495.

[15] Irenaeus, *The Demonstration of the Apostolic Preaching*, tr. J. Armitage Robinson (London: SPCK, 1920), 5, p. 74.

[16] Irenaeus, *Adversus Haereses* 3.6.2, 3.18.1, 4.5, 5.5.2; Fragments 23; *Dem.* 43 *et passim*. In reference to Gen. 3.8, Irenaeus refers to Jesus not just as the Word, but also as the 'Voice of God' (*Adversus Haereses* 5.15.4, 5.16.1, 5.17.1; cf. 4.16.3–4).

[17] Irenaeus, *Adversus Haereses* 3.15.3, 4.5.2, 4.9.1, 4.10.1; *Dem.* 40.

[18] Irenaeus, *Frag.* 53; cf. also *Frag.* 54, *Fragments from the Lost Writings of Irenæus* (Edinburgh: T&T Clark, 1867), p. 577. These Christophanies were provided out of God's mercy, for Irenaeus holds that without such a sight of the object of their faith, not only would the faithful themselves fall into despair, but mankind as a whole would 'cease to exist' (*Adversus Haereses* 4.20.7). I am grateful to Dr Mike Reeves for pointing out these references in Irenaeus.

[19] Justin Martyr, *Dialogue with Trypho* 56; *ANCL* I, p. 223.

[20] It is of course no accident that in John's Gospel Jesus defines Himself so consistently as 'the One sent from the Father'.

[21] Justin Martyr, *Dialogue with Trypho* 58; *ANCL* I, p. 225.

[22] Augustine, *On the Trinity* 2.7, in *Nicene and Post-Nicene Fathers* (NPNF), III, ed. James Donaldson and Alexander Roberts (Edinburgh: T&T Clark, 1890), p. 43.

[23] Gunton, *The Promise of Trinitarian Theology*, ch. 3.

[24] Augustine, *On the Trinity* 2.16; *NPNF* III, p. 50.

[25] Augustine, *On the Trinity* 2.11; *NPNF* III, p. 47.

[26] I have been asked the question, 'If the Trinity is known in the Old Testament, then what is the point of the incarnation?' For a long time I did not understand this question at all. Surely, the point of the incarnation is to fulfil all that the Divine Mediator promised he would do since the beginning of the world. He is born of the virgin, as promised, and makes atonement for the whole creation, as promised. To imagine that the Living God is essentially unknown before the incarnation seems to wander suspiciously close to a kind of Marcionism.

4

The Trinity: The Significance of Appropriate Distinctions for Dynamic Relationality

Peter M. B. Robinson

The recent surge of interest in the doctrine of the Trinity has left some theologians wondering what is going on and what will be the long-term contribution of this revival.[1] It is right to be cautious of any movement or theological trend that reflects such a broad interest and has acquired such a sudden popularity. Colin Gunton, one of the pre-eminent theologians in the recovery of the doctrine of the Trinity, wryly acknowledged this popularity: 'Suddenly we are all Trinitarians, or so it would seem.'[2] The danger, of course, is that a theological revival may be used to support *a priori* ideals. This is particularly true when it comes to the doctrine of the Trinity, which, with its focus on the being of God, has often tended towards abstract idealism. Given that the revived interest is largely fuelled by attention to the concepts of persons and relations witnessed to across a broad range of philosophical and scientific fields, there is a danger of an idealism of relations preconditioning our understanding of the doctrine of the Trinity. This danger does not discredit the revival, but can and should prompt us to examine closely the arguments being made.[3] The key to such an examination is to establish the grounds within which the discussion must take place.[4] An important qualification for keeping the doctrine of the Trinity properly grounded is the distinction between God *ad extra* and God *ad intra*.[5] In this paper we will affirm that the recovery and development of the notion of dynamic relationality rooted in the doctrine of the Trinity is both an appropriate and critical foundation for theological development. We will also establish that maintaining an appropriate balance in the distinction between God *ad extra* and God *ad intra* is fundamental to ensuring that a dynamic relational notion of the doctrine of the Trinity remains theologically realistic and constructive.

Eastern and Western Approaches

At the heart of the doctrine of the Trinity lies the paradox of the three persons, Father, Son and Spirit, who are one God. In the recent revival in Trinitarian theology, discussion commonly begins by speaking about the traditional difference between the approaches of the Eastern and Western churches. Father de Regnon describes the different approaches: 'Latin philosophy first considers the nature in itself and proceeds to the agent; Greek philosophy first considers the agent and afterwards passes through it to find the nature.'[6] Certainly one of the perceived differences between the Eastern and Western approaches to the doctrine of the Trinity has been that the East focuses on the three persons while the West focuses on the one nature, or essence, of God.

The different approaches have been reflected in the respective analogies. While the East, following the Cappadocians, has tended to emphasize the relational analogy, the West has preferred the psychological analogies, which Augustine developed in his writings on the Trinity.[7] What makes the neat comparison between East and West problematic is that in the West, over the past thirty years, there has been a swing or even a stampede towards the relational analogy.[8]

Any exploration of the different analogies must be conducted within an understanding of the use of analogies and, in particular, of the limits to what we might say about God. One of the results of the stampede toward the relational Trinity has been the extremes to which a notion of relationality is used to license or affirm various doctrines of being. This tendency raises perhaps the biggest danger with regard to the revival in Trinitarian theologies; the difficulty happens when analogies concerning the being of God are used to support a notion of ontology, which can then be abstracted from God's action in the world. Understanding the limits to the use of analogies in speaking about God is vital given the way in which these analogies have shaped our theology.

Limits to the Use of Analogies

In both East and West, theologians have been careful to affirm that while we use analogies to speak about God, the limitations to analogies must be respected.[9] Any analogy has limitations. Analogies provide a way of articulating a reality that cannot be fully defined. '"Analogy" thus does not provide a neat alternative between univocity and equivocity that solves problems. It is, Aquinas admitted, itself a type of equivocation.'[10] The limits this places upon us do not inhibit a discussion on the doctrine of the Trinity or theology proper but raise questions concerning our epistemological framework.

What inevitably shapes or distorts our discussions regarding the nature or being of God is the epistemological framework in which we ask our questions. Recognizing the limits to analogies does not force us to make a choice between apophatic or cataphatic approaches to God, although as Stanley Grenz suggests, it does challenge strictly rationalistic approaches: 'The acknowledgement that theological language is metaphorical alters our understanding of the task of the theologian. Rather than a scientist who discovers truths about God waiting to be discerned, the theologian is a poet who crafts meaningful pictures about our world and our relationship to the transcendent.'[11] Properly understood, analogies provide a vital tool in exploring the nature of the God who is revealed in Jesus Christ. Analogical language enables us to speak about God without suggesting that our descriptions or depictions are comprehensive.

It is significant that the two most prominent analogies used to describe the Trinity, the psychological and the relational, are both based on the human person or persons. While this seems obvious and appropriate given the 'personal' agency of God it invariably leads to complications. The most obvious of these is the danger of anthropomorphism, but the more significant complication has to do with the way in which the Trinity is formative for theological anthropology. In other words, the particular danger of using analogies based on human persons to speak about the Trinity is that the Trinity clearly has implications for how we understand human person: first, in the incarnation, the God-man allows us to speak of God as revealed or reflected in a particular human person and therefore to a degree in human persons; second, God's engagement with us as Father, Son and Spirit clearly shapes who we are; finally, there are implications for the doctrine of the image of God.[12] The close connection between the doctrine of the Trinity and theological anthropology is not a problem to be overcome, nor does the connection inhibit our use of analogies based on human persons, but it must be taken into account in the way we use these analogies. Failure to account for these issues leads to the danger of conflating language about God with language about ourselves and to a resulting inability to maintain the limits of an analogy.[13]

The dangers inherent in failing to maintain the limits to an analogy point us towards the necessity of an epistemological framework that is itself established by who God is. Given the theological framework within which analogies may be used, it is not enough to affirm the limits inherent in the use of analogies. When speaking about the Trinity we must also affirm, with the Church Fathers, that every analogy about God is limited because God always remains greater than anything we can say about him.[14] It is not enough to believe that the limitation to our knowledge of God has to do with the human capacity for knowledge. Instead it must be affirmed that because of who God is, God is not confined to human terms or human understanding. The danger with the former perception is that God can be perceived as an object which is not comprehended because 'it' is not yet fully visible to the human eye.[15] Inevitably that perception fosters the belief that the key to a clear understanding of God is to overcome our human limitations either through the development of human language or through a transcendence of reason. When it comes to the doctrine of the Trinity, the limits inherent in human language are not the issue; rather we must maintain that our language is limited because of who God is, and that brings us to the distinction between God *ad intra* and God *ad extra*.

Theologia and Economia

When speaking of the distinction between God *ad intra* and God *ad extra*, the Church Fathers used the terms *theologia* (that which pertains to the nature of God in himself) and *economia* (that which pertains to the work of salvation).[16] The distinction between *theologia* and *economia* was developed in order to maintain several key affirmations, including: that God remains greater than but not distinct from the revelation in Jesus Christ (with the affirmation that God is truly God as he has shown himself to us in Jesus the Christ); and that the unity in diversity of the Trinity is a mystery, in so far as God's being is not subject to human logic.

The Fathers began from the context of revelation; they did not begin by attempting to describe God *ad intra*. Their concern was primarily to explain how we might speak of the God who is revealed in Jesus Christ, rather than to offer a philosophy of being.[17] The distinction is meant to ensure that God's being remains greater than that which has been revealed—not distinct from, nor removed from that which has been revealed.

Unfortunately, the distinction which the Fathers insisted on has been identified as one of the causes of the abstraction of theological discourse. Karl Rahner called into question the distinction between *theologia* and *economia* by affirming in his 'Rule' that the economic Trinity is the immanent Trinity and the immanent Trinity is the economic Trinity.[18] The trouble with positing a distinction between *theologia* and *economia*, or God *ad intra* and God *ad extra*, combined with the affirmation of the mystery of God's being, is that it might suggest that God's essence is beyond and even disconnected from God *ad extra*. Rahner's bold declaration that most theologians in the West were mere 'monotheists' suggests that discussions on the doctrine of God have often been concerned with identifying the essence of God lying beyond the economy of God.[19] Meanwhile 'Rahner's Rule' overturns the assumption that, while the three hypostases are true to God *ad extra*, God *ad intra* is a simple undifferentiated essence or *ousia*.

To explore the implications of this rule, we return to Father de Regnon's thesis regarding the difference between Eastern and Western approaches to the doctrine of the Trinity. What is somewhat misleading about de Regnon's thesis is the suggestion that the choice is between moving from the nature to the agent or from the agent to the nature, as though the issue is how we make sense of three *hypostases* who are one *ousia* or how one *ousia* can be three *hypostases*. A result of this type of approach is that the doctrine of the Trinity becomes a mathematical formula attempting to account for how the three are one or the one is three. Neither emphasizing the three persons (or agents) at the expense of the one *ousia* (or nature) nor emphasizing the one *ousia* at the expense of the three persons is acceptable. The peril is in either describing the unity of God and then allowing that the unity in some way includes a distinction of the three persons, or emphasizing the distinction of persons and continuing to describe their unity as one aspect of their personhood.[20] When the emphasis is placed primarily upon either the unity or the persons within the Godhead our descriptions of the Trinity inevitably mislead us. T. F. Torrance, acknowledging the problem with Western treatments of the essence as a static 'object', notes the danger for the East in undermining the *ousia* of God to the point that it is perceived as generic:

> the one Being of God refers not to some impersonal essence, which has often been the problem of the Latin West, nor to some abstract generic notion of being, which has been a tendency in the Greek East, but to the living dynamic 'I am' of the One God, the eternal living Being which God has of Himself.[21]

The tendency has been to affirm that either the *ousia* or the *hypostases* are the true or ontological foundation of the Godhead. However, to accept either alternative is to overturn the creedal affirmation that

God is both three and one and that God must always be spoken of as both three and one at the same time.[22]

Drawing on the arguments of the Cappadocian Fathers, John Zizioulas argues that the debates following the council of Nicaea and culminating in the council of Constantinople resulted in an affirmation that the three *hypostases* and the one *ousia* are terms which are not synonymous; yet both refer to the being *qua* being of God. These two ways of speaking of the 'being' of God are not mutually exclusive options which we must choose between, nor are they comprehensive in their own right; they must both be held together at the same time. Held together, they enable us to balance more carefully our discussions of the mystery of the Triune God.

In many ways, Rahner's Rule forced us to recognize the way in which the Trinitarian affirmation of the One and the Three became confused with the distinction between *theologia* and *economia*, confusion which in turn resulted in abstract speculation regarding the essence of God *ad intra*. Yet that confusion does not rule out the need for some kind of distinction between God *ad extra* and God *ad intra*. The danger of speculation regarding God's being *ad intra* was one of the reasons for the distinction between *theologia* and *economia* in the first place.

It is vital to be able to speak about the nature of the unity of the persons as long as we do not suggest that by doing so we have solved the problem of the mystery of the One and the Three. It is the distinction between God *ad extra* and God *ad intra* which enables us to say that, while we know that God is Trinity in his operation towards us, we cannot fully define or understand how God is Trinity *ad intra*. Maintaining the limits to our understanding of 'how' God is Trinity enables appropriate discussion regarding the unity of the three persons on the basis of God's economy. In other words, we may speak about the ways in which the three are united, not so as to establish the oneness of God, but as a result of the affirmation of the oneness of God.[23] While the Trinitarian statement of one *ousia* and three *hypostases* confirms that God is one and three, the distinction between God *ad extra* and God *ad intra* confirms that we cannot 'solve' the paradox but must affirm it as true to God *ad extra* and true to God *ad intra*. Thus, while we may affirm with Rahner that the economic Trinity is true to the immanent Trinity, we would agree with Yves Congar (against Rahner), who insists that we cannot say the immanent Trinity is wholly encompassed by the economic Trinity.[24]

Disjuncture Between God's Being and Action

Catherine LaCugna identifies another concern regarding the patristic distinction between *theologia* and *economia*. LaCugna, who begins with acknowledging Rahner's Rule concerning the unity of the economic and immanent Trinity, continues by suggesting that the distinction between *theologia* and *economia* was the cause not only of abstract speculation on the essence of God but also of the understanding of a God who is not intimately involved with the world:[25]

> Indeed the ultimate theological error, the ultimate non-orthodoxy or heresy or untruth about God, would be to think of God as living in an altogether separate household, living entirely for Godself, by Godself, within Godself. This is what the Church tried to overcome in Arianism and Eunomianism, but to some degree this 'heresy' is incipient even in Trinitarian theologies that make divine self-sufficiency absolute.[26]

To reiterate, LaCugna maintains that one must reject any distinction between God *ad intra* and God *ad extra* to affirm a dynamic understanding of God's engagement with the world. In contrast to LaCugna, we would argue that the solution is not to deny this distinction but rather to affirm that it is an epistemological rather than an ontological distinction. That epistemological distinction then maintains the limits of what we might say of or about God. It does not affirm that God's true 'being' remains other than his involvement with the world. On the other hand, the distinction of *creatio ex nihilo* is the ontological distinction which maintains freedom for God and freedom for humanity.[27]

One of the reasons why the distinction between God *ad extra* and God *ad intra* has been perceived as an ontological distinction has been the desire to safeguard the immutability of God. Theologians in both the East and the West have attempted to safeguard divine immutability by positing a distinction between the being of God and his action in the world. In the East, following Gregory Palamas, this has resulted in a distinction between the essence and energies of God, while in the West it has resulted in a distinction between the essence and action of God. Recent theologies of the Trinity have attempted to address this issue in different ways. Rahner and LaCugna attempt to deal with it by collapsing the 'Trinity *ad intra*' into the economic Trinity. In contrast, Colin Gunton emphasizes the doctrine of *creatio ex nihilo* as the ontological distinction which affirms God's freedom. Gunton insists that affirming God's relationality *ad intra* enables God's engagement with that which is other than himself without in turn changing God's being.[28] The doctrine of *creatio ex nihilo* affirms the difference between the being of God and his creation. It establishes that creation is free rather than necessary, while the distinction between God *ad extra* and God *ad intra* allows us to say that 'because God is, "before" creation took place, already a being-in-relation, there is no *need* for him to create what is already other than himself'.[29] The distinction between God and the world is not that God 'exists' somehow beyond the world but that in existing before the world he is not inseparably joined to the world; God's relation to the world is a free rather than a necessary and pantheistic relation. Or as Zizioulas suggests, the doctrine of *creatio ex nihilo* shows 'that God existed *before* and *regardless of* the world, and thus that it is imperative to be able to refer to God without implicitly or explicitly referring at the same time to the world'.[30] The confusion arises when the doctrine of *creatio ex nihilo* is conflated with the distinction between God *ad intra* and God *ad extra*; such a conflation would suggest that the essence of God, what God truly 'is', remains other than his engagement with the world. When these distinctions are held together appropriately, it enables us to acknowledge that God's being is not encompassed by his engagement with the world.

The intention of the Greek patristic distinction between *theologia* and *economia* was not to suggest that God was disengaged from the world but to acknowledge that God in God's self is the ultimate category of being rather than a category derived from or dependent upon human conceptions of being. In making a clear distinction between the world and God and yet affirming that God is the source of all being, the Fathers were implicitly challenging how 'being' could be defined or understood. Unfortunately, as LaCugna has clearly noted, the distinction between *theologia* and *economia* has not been correlated with a revision of the understanding of ontology in much of the tradition. As a result, God has been understood as ultimately removed from or disengaged from the world. When theology has been aligned with the traditional philosophical paradigms that identify being or essence with that which lies behind a particular existent, the quest for the essence of God or the oneness of God has begun with God *ad intra*. Focusing on God *ad intra* without reference to God *ad extra* allowed a speculative focus on the essence of God, where the being of God was perceived in static terms.[31] The understanding of the being of God was shaped by philosophical presuppositions or ideals concerning the nature of God rather than by the revelation of God. Thus, the issue in utilizing a distinction between *economia* and *theologia* is not, as LaCugna suggests, that it has produced an abstract doctrine of a God totally uninvolved with the world but that the philosophical paradigms which were called into question by the doctrine of the Trinity were still used to interpret the being of God.

Comparing Analogies

That brings us back to considering the different analogies for understanding the Trinity. The test of the adequacy or appropriateness of an analogy is seen in the theology it produces. In the recent revival of Trinitarian theology, the psychological analogy has come under frequent criticism for this reason. The primary problem is that the analogy's inward direction affirms the tendency to look for the essence or ontological foundation within or behind the three persons. The tendency to look inward became further distorted when 'image' language was used to posit a coherence between human intellect or *nous* and the being of God. Participation in the being of God became identified with a conscious or unconscious union of minds. LaCugna suggests that it was Augustine's psychological model that began the process of abstract speculation about the being of God.[32] She goes on to note that although Rahner sought to advance the discussion by distinguishing between the essence of God and the existence of God, he failed to establish that the distinction between God in God's self and God for us was not about an essence/existence distinction because he used the psychological analogy.[33]

Meanwhile, the relational analogy has often been rejected in the West because it does not fit with traditional philosophical categories of being. Given traditional categories, this analogy inevitably suggests tritheism. Proponents of the relational analogy have recognized that it can only make sense if it calls into question our standard ontological models. One of the greatest dangers with the relational analogy is to see in human community a simple mirror of the divine community. While we may speak of the persons of the Trinity in communion with one another, or *perichoretically* united to one another, such unification cannot be equated with human concepts of unity because we know that God is one in a way that humans cannot be.[34] Therefore, while human community may be in some ways analogous to divine communion, it is always intrinsically different. Looking for a notion of communion or community which can be applied equally to both God and humanity results in the same problems that are seen with the psychological analogy, where the emphasis is on a shared ontological basis found in both divine and human being.

Conclusion

The recent renewed interest in the relational analogy is a result of the way in which it enables us to speak of God's intimate involvement with the world. One of the greatest benefits of the relational analogy, if not the greatest benefit, is that it directs us to look outward rather than inward. Whereas the psychological analogy points us inward to examine the inner being of God, the relational analogy points us outward to understand God in his engagement with us. The relational analogy helps us to make sense of the way in which God engages with us as Father, Son and Holy Spirit. As a result, it enables us to work with the distinction between God *ad extra* and God *ad intra* in a way that invigorates our theology rather than rendering it abstract, speculative and unconstructive.

At the heart of the recent revival in Trinitarian theology has been the recovery and development of a dynamic and relational understanding of the being of God. This recovery has helped to overturn the static notion of a distant and disengaged God that developed as a result of the separation between God's being and action. The notion of a static, disengaged God resulted from the failure to understand properly the epistemological distinction between God *ad extra* and God *ad intra* as well as the corresponding failure to hold that distinction together with both the ontological distinction between God and creation, grounded in the doctrine of *creatio ex nihilo*, and the ontological affirmation of the Trinity as both three and one. The contribution offered by the revival in Trinitarian theology will be determined in significant ways by how well we maintain a healthy understanding of the distinction between God *ad extra* and God *ad intra*. For it is this distinction which enables us to speak with confidence about God's being and action by keeping the focus on his economy, while at the same time, avoiding the danger of *a priori* ideals shaping our theology by maintaining appropriate limits to our understanding of God *ad intra*.

Notes

1   Thomas Weinandy provides an extensive list of works published on Trinitarian theology during the past century in *The Father's Spirit of Sonship* (Edinburgh: T&T Clark, 1995), p. 1.

2   Colin E. Gunton, *The Promise of Trinitarian Theology*, 2nd edn (Edinburgh: T&T Clark, 1997), p. xv.

3   'The social model, especially insofar as it speaks of God as subsisting in three subjective centers of action, has met not only remarkable applause but also rigorous

critique': Stanley J. Grenz, *The Social God and the Relational Self: A Trinitarian Theology of the Imago Dei* (Louisville: Westminster John Knox Press, 2001), p. 4.

4 'The less clear the ground of the doctrine of the Trinity and the warrant for our affirming it become, the more arbitrary and irrelevant the doctrine appears in its relation to the actuality of this world': Andreas Loos, 'Divine Action and the Trinity: A Brief Exploration of the Grounds of Trinitarian Speech about God in the Theology of Adolf Schlatter', *International Journal of Systematic Theology* 4 (2002), p. 257.

5 In this paper, we will use the term 'God *ad intra*' to speak of God's being in himself. Alan Torrance highlights the difficulty with the term 'immanent', 'which is a theologically weak term implying a static conception of God "as he remains in himself". The phrase Deus *ad intra* is a much healthier one, in that it implies that God conceived independently of his relation towards that which is not God, still remains a relational being': Alan J. Torrance, *Persons in Communion: Trinitarian Description and Human Participation* (Edinburgh, T&T Clark, 1996), p. 279.

6 Théodore de Regnon, *Etudes de théologie positive sur la Sainte Trinité*, p. 433; quoted in Vladimir Lossky, *The Mystical Theology of the Eastern Church* (Cambridge: James Clarke, 1957), pp. 57–8, and John Meyendorff, *Byzantine Theology: Historical Trends and Doctrinal Themes* (Crestwood, NY: St Vladimir's Seminary Press, 1974), p. 181.

7 I prefer the term 'relational analogy' to 'social analogy' for two reasons: first, because the latter term is often associated with Jürgen Moltmann, who has often been accused of failing to maintain appropriate limits to analogy in his doctrine of the Trinity; and second, because the focus in the Eastern understanding of the Trinity is on the relations, not the sociality of the Trinity.

8 '[T]he stampede to the relationality inherent in the social model of the Trinity has crossed traditional and confessional divides': Grenz, *The Social God and the Relational Self*, p. 5.

9 Gregory Nazianzen, 'Fifth Theological Oration'; see also Augustine, *De Trinitate* 8.2. Cf. Colin E. Gunton, *The Promise of Trinitarian Theology*, 1st edn (Edinburgh, T&T Clark, 1991), pp. 44–5. Gunton suggests that Augustine himself fails to maintain appropriate limits to analogies.

10 William C. Placher, *The Domestication of Transcendence* (Louisville: Westminster John Knox Press, 1996), p. 31.

11 Grenz, *The Social God and the Relational Self*, p. 8.

12 See Stanley Grenz's discussion in Ch. 7 of this volume.

13 By maintaining an emphasis upon God *ad extra* as the dynamic engagement of God with us we avoid the tendency to look for a parallel between God *ad intra* and human imaging of God.

14 'Setting rules for Christian language, Aquinas never claimed too much for what language can tell us about God: What it signifies in God is not confined by the meaning of our word but goes beyond it': Placher, *The Domestication of Transcendence*, p. 31.

15 Eunomius suggested that it was sin that prevented the human mind from fully comprehending God. See Jaroslav Pelikan, *Christianity and Classical Culture: The Metamorphosis of Natural Theology in the Christian Encounter with Hellenism* (New Haven: Yale University Press, 1993), p. 51. This approach leads to the view that ultimately the fullness of God can be comprehended if and when sin is dealt with.

16 Catherine M. LaCugna, *God For Us: The Trinity and Christian Life* (New York: HarperCollins, 1991), p. 211.

17 'The basis of Eastern triadology is found in soteriology, in that its fundamental goal is to maintain the christological and pneumatological presuppositions that (a) the

incarnate Logos and Divine Spirit are met and experienced first as divine agents of salvation; and (b) only then are they discovered to be essentially one God': Gregory Havrilak, 'Karl Rahner and the Greek Trinity', *Saint Vladimir's Theological Quarterly* 34 (1990), pp. 61–77.

[18] Karl Rahner, *The Trinity*, tr. J. Donceel (London: Burns & Oates, 1970), p. 22. Stanley Grenz suggests that Roger E. Olsen was the originator of the term 'Rahner's Rule': *The Social God and the Relational Self*, p. 38.

[19] Rahner, *The Trinity*, p. 10.

[20] 'It is often assumed that perichoresis and the oneness of the divine substance are two complementary ways of conceiving the unity of God. Perichoresis is "the exact reverse of the identity of *ousia*," writes G. L. Prestige in *God in Patristic Thought* (London: SPCK, 1956), p. 298': Miroslav Volf, *After Our Likeness: The Church as the Image of the Trinity* (Grand Rapids: Eerdmans, 1998), p. 210.

[21] T. F. Torrance, *Trinitarian Perspectives* (Edinburgh: T&T Clark, 1994), p. 19.

[22] As John Zizioulas clearly states, 'the identification of God with the Father risks losing its biblical content unless our doctrine of God includes not just the three persons, but also the unique *Ousia*': *Being as Communion: Studies in Personhood and the Church* (London: Darton, Longman & Todd, 1985), p. 89.

[23] According to Grenz, 'Pannenberg notes that *perichoresis* was never intended to account for the unity of the divine essence (the use to which Moltmann puts it) but presupposes that unity on the basis of the origin of the Son and the Spirit in the Father.' Grenz, *The Social God and The Relational Self*, p. 49.

[24] Yves Congar, *I Believe in the Holy Spirit: The River of Life Flows in East and West*, iii, tr. D. Smith (New York: Seabury Press, 1983), pp. 11–18.

[25] Building upon Rahner (*The Trinity*), LaCugna says, 'no adequate distinction can be made between the doctrine of the Trinity and the doctrine of the economy': LaCugna, *God For Us*, p. 211.

[26] LaCugna, *God For Us*, p. 383.

[27] 'A God who has to have a world around him is a miserable godlet, a pagan projection, and not the omnipotent God of Christian confession': Colin E. Gunton, *The Christian Faith: An Introduction to Christian Doctrine* (Oxford: Blackwell, 2002), p. 187.

[28] Gunton, *The Promise of Trinitarian Theology*, 1st edn, p. 147.

[29] Colin E. Gunton, 'Relation and Relativity', in Christoph Schwöbel (ed.), *Trinitarian Theology Today: Essays on Divine Being and Act* (Edinburgh: T&T Clark, 1995), p. 97, italics in original.

[30] John Zizioulas, 'The Doctrine of God the Trinity Today: Suggestions for an Ecumenical Study', in *The Forgotten Trinity: The Report of the BCC Study Commission on Trinitarian Doctrine Today*, ed. Alistair Heron (London: British Council of Churches, 1991), pp. 19–32. Zizioulas notes Rahner's failure to appreciate the need to maintain a distinction between the economic and immanent Trinity.

[31] 'The significance of this interpretation lies in the assumption that the ontological "principle" of God is not found in the person but in the substance, that is, in the "being" itself of God. Indeed the idea took shape in Western theology whereby that which constitutes the unity of God is the one divine substance, the one divinity; this is, as it were, the ontological "principle" of God': Zizioulas, *Being as Communion*, p. 40.

[32] LaCugna, *God For Us*, p. 44.

[33] LaCugna, *God For Us*, p. 222. LaCugna says, 'Rahner was not entirely able to resist making use of the Cartesian conception of a person as a discrete self-consciousness but in such a way that it is the divine "essence", not the three divine persons which is made the referent of that self-consciousness.'

[34] '[The] dynamic in God is such that the question as to which is more fundamental between union or communion is inappropriate and fundamentally anthropomorphic or, indeed, cosmo-morphic—deriving, that is, from a failure to think out of the unique form which the divine communion takes *ad-extra*': Torrance, *Persons in Communion*, p. 257.

5

Towards a Trinitarian Reading of the Tradition: The Relevance of the 'Eternal' Trinity[1]

Colin E. Gunton

Towards a Narrative Definition

We now approach an answer to the question of what our doctrine of the immanent or eternal Trinity, God in himself, might have to teach us about the attributes. The distinction between the doctrines of the economic and eternal or immanent Trinities is important. It is not suggesting that there are two Gods, two Trinities, but that two different things have to be said about the Triune God if we are to do justice to Scripture: that he is triune as he presents himself to us in our time, and that this tri-unity is eternal. We need to know and say this because we need to know that we can rely on what God reveals: that what he seems to be, that he truly is. Otherwise, how could we rely on his always being loving, holy, merciful, powerful, and the rest?

The doctrine of the Trinity performs, among other things, the function of identifying God—indicating what makes him distinctively who he is. It is a kind of definition. Now, to be sure, when that is said, questions will begin to be raised. Is God the kind of being who can be defined? Is not such an enterprise as this precisely what the negative theology was rightly devised to prevent? The answer is that the definition comes in a number of forms. It can be logical – a real essence, in Locke's terms – and claim a measure of completeness, as when we define a triangle as a plane figure consisting of three straight lines in a certain relation to one another; or as when Eunomius defines God *a priori* in terms of a certain conception of simplicity. A definition can also be ostensive, definition by indication, as we say to a child who is learning to identify colours, that and that and that are red. Again, a definition can be open, in the sense of indicating some of the things characteristic of a person or thing, but never exhaustive—Locke's nominal essence. Thus, speaking of someone's character, we can only begin to list the salient characteristics, knowing that the mystery of the person always eludes final definition. It is something of this kind with which we are concerned here. We know from—for example—a good biography that we can learn a great deal about another human being. A biography is a kind of definition by narrative, yet the narrative is not the whole. In an adequate biography it will constitute also the grounds for an account of character, by which is meant something impressed by the life on the basic material, which was given at birth, so that, at the end we can make an at least provisional judgement on the kind of person with whom we are dealing. Giving us the freedom to make such a judgement about God is the function of the doctrine of the immanent Trinity.

Is God defined in Scripture, and how? Can we attempt generalizations? The point of Paul's account of the divine wisdom in 1 Corinthians 2 is that in the cross of Jesus God defines himself by a particular form of action and that self-definition is apprehensible by the Spirit's gift. Generalizing, we can say that in Scripture God is presented both narratively and creedally: in narratives of actions and in creedal summaries of the meaning of those actions, summaries which were developed and systematized in the early centuries of the church's life. To neglect the first is to risk taking the definition out of its historical placing; to neglect the second is to risk losing any account of the being of God. The foregoing account of the struggle which has taken place in the history of theology between abstract and narrative versions of the doctrine of the attributes is designed to recommend a more strongly narrative approach to the topic, seeking to save theology from an *a priori* definition in the interests of a doctrine in which being and act are brought into a more successful harmony than appears often to have been the case. It is in that light that we can understand the disaster represented by the distinction drawn by Wollebius: '"God" . . . is known in himself absolutely in his essence, relatively in the persons.'[2] Do we not see drawn here in sharpest lines one of the symptoms of Western modalism? The essence of God is known pre- and extra-trinitarianly; once that is sketched in, we treat the attributes deriving from the persons. (If Bannach is right, something like that had already been pointed out by Scotus some centuries earlier.)

In recent times, the struggle to develop a more narratively based account of God's attributes has often centred on the doctrine of impassibility, which appears to rule out some of the things done by God, for example genuinely suffering on the cross and being genuinely compassionate with those who suffer. For consideration of this 'contentious attribute', see chapter 7 of *Act and Being*. Here we will develop our more general theme by a visit to the thought of one who has been claimed to have reintegrated act and being in a way that goes back to near the roots of Trinitarian theology in Athanasius.[3] As Eberhard Jüngel has shown in his recently retranslated *Gottes Sein ist im Werden—God's Being is in Becoming*—Barth uses the concept of divine becoming to show that there is no breach between God's action and his being. In the incarnation God demonstrates his freedom 'to become unlike Himself and yet to remain the same',[4] and it is this revelation of himself which ought to be the source of any conclusions we draw about what he is in eternity. That is the order of knowing: we know God (by his ostensive self-definition) from and in his acts. We know *who* God is from what he does. The other aspect of our response to the same divine self-presentation in time is that the order of being grounds the order of knowing, so that what God does in time is shown to be a function of what he is in eternity. The outcome is that historical revelation and eternal being correspond to one another: 'The self-relatedness of God's being makes possible God's self-interpretation (his self-definition, we might say). God reveals himself *as* Father, Son, and Spirit because he *is* God *as* Father, Son, and Spirit.'[5]

Barth certainly distinguishes God's 'essence as the One who works and reveals himself' from the 'essence of God as such'. But this distinction has no other purpose than to establish the fact that God reveals himself 'not constrained by His essence', but 'in a free decision grounded in His essence'. But the essence of this one who works is now thought strictly from the point of view of revelation, and so not as substance, but as the 'unity of Father, Son and Spirit among themselves' to which 'their unity *ad extra*' corresponds.[6]

Barth's project to bring revelation and being together is an implicit, and often explicit, reproach to much of the tradition. It establishes an important principle: that treatments of the being or essence of God must be Trinitarian from the outset and that it must be a Trinitarianism which is based in, and a drawing out of the implications of, the economic Trinity: of how God reveals himself to be in the narratively identified economy of creation, reconciliation and redemption.

In this light, we move to sketch the main lines of the way in which this Trinitarian construal comes to shape Barth's own discussion of the divine perfections.[7] Beginning with the claim that 'God is means God loves', Barth proceeds to give an account of the divine perfection in the light of the kind of love that is revealed in Scripture.[8] It is love that is given freely to those who are and cannot but be unworthy of it. This unconstrained love for the unworthy other provides in turn the basis of a polarity or dialectic of love and freedom which forms a matrix within which the discussion of the attributes is formed. Barth begins with a polar account of God's being: God loves, but he loves freely, so that each of the perfections is to be understood as characterized as a perfection either of love or of freedom, but in such a way that perfections of God's loving are understood in the light of freedom, perfections of his freedom in the light of his love. God's attributes are thus treated dialectically as functions of the freedom in which God is love and loves the world. Barth is insistent that this is not a division of a kind that suggests that while love is the seeking of fellowship, freedom is God's transcendence over against the created world. Rather, all the perfections are an expression at once of God's love and freedom: 'God is not first the One who loves, and then somewhere and somehow, in contradistinction to that, the One who is also free. And when He loves He does not surrender His freedom, but exercises it in a supreme degree.'[9]

There are twelve perfections, the first six being three perfections of the divine loving (grace, mercy and patience) which are dialectically paired with and whose meaning is therefore controlled by the perfections of the divine freedom (holiness, righteousness and wisdom). An example of the integration of act and being is Barth's account of grace and holiness:

> Grace is the distinctive mode of God's being in so far as it seeks and creates fellowship. . . . We are not [Barth qualifies six pages later] . . . making any crucial change of theme when we go on to speak of God's holiness . . . As holy, [grace] is characterized by the fact that God, as He seeks and creates fellowship, is always the Lord. . . . He condemns, excludes and annihilates all contradiction and resistance to it.[10]

After the six perfections of love that is free, there follow three perfections of the divine freedom (unity, constancy and eternity), which are in their turn balanced and controlled by their 'love' counterparts (omnipresence, omnipotence and glory). What this enables Barth to do is, on the one hand, to give priority to what can be called the personal and biblical attributes, those, that is, primarily revealed in the economy of divine action as narrated in Scripture—mercy, patience and so on; but, on the other, to engage in their light with the traditional treatment of the attributes by giving due account of the more metaphysical and philosophical terms, like eternity and omnipresence. That is to reverse the order found in so much of the history of the topic, where the *a priori*, abstract and impersonal—attributes deriving from the analogy of causality—provide a foundation—an essentially contradictory one, as it has turned out—for the personal.

Some brief examples will show how Barth's Trinitarian dialectic shapes the doctrine. If we first refer to the classical definition of omnipotence, as found in Aquinas, and virtually a scholastic commonplace, we shall notice the difference: 'Therefore everything that does not imply a contradiction in terms, is numbered among those possible things in respect of which God is called omnipotent'.[11] Barth is wary of anything that might suggest a deification of power in itself—not that that is necessarily the implication of Aquinas' definition—and argues that it is necessary to begin rather where God's power is seen paradigmatically at work, in the cross of Jesus: 'Power in itself is not merely neutral. Power in itself is evil.'[12] That does two things: it grounds a conception of divine and ordered power in the biblical narrative; and it produces a conception of unlimited divine power which is controlled by the doctrine of the incarnation, which is an action, we must note. In a later volume, Barth picks up a saying of Gregory of Nyssa which makes a similar point, that the Son's 'descent to humility which took place in the incarnation of the Word is not only not excluded by the divine nature but signifies its greatest glory: περιουσια τις εστιν της δυναμεως (an overflow of power).'[13] He realizes that Trinitarian control is necessary:

> Already in the creed the *omnipotentem* is not to be separated from the *Deum patrem* nor is the latter to be explained by the former. The omnipotence of which the creed speaks is the omnipotence of God the Father, the omnipotence of the God and Father who reveals Himself to be God and Father in accordance with the remaining content of the creed, and is therefore of one essence with the Son and the Holy Spirit.[14]

Similarly revealing is the treatment of immutability,[15] which Barth seeks to personalize and moralize, preferring to speak of the divine constancy. Rejecting one treatment of this attribute in the Protestant scholastics, according to which God is the pure *immobile*, he comments: '[W]e must not make any mistake: the pure *immobile* is—death. If, then, the pure *immobile* is God, death is God. That is, death is posited as absolute and explained as the first and last and only real.'[16]

The spelling out of Barth's concept is made by appeal to the continuity of God's action in creation, reconciliation and redemption.

> [I]t is by the incarnation that God has revealed His truly immutable being as free love in the perfection in which, on the basis of the incarnation, we recognize it again and find it confirmed in His acts as Creator, Reconciler, and Redeemer. God is 'immutably' the One whose reality is seen in His condescension in Jesus Christ, in His self-offering and self-concealment.[17]

Characteristically, these developments, though founded in the Trinity, are largely Christological in orientation, and it is in the last words of the latter citation, 'self-offering and self-concealment', that we shall find the key both to the structure of Barth's treatment of the attributes and to its chief weakness.

The structure of Barth's discussion of the attributes corresponds precisely with that of the doctrine of the Trinity in the previous volume of the *Church Dogmatics*. There, the dialectic is of revelation and hiddenness, the former expressing God's making himself known in the world, the latter the freedom of his self-revelation in time. The programmatic statement, 'Revelation in the Bible means the self-unveiling, imparted to men, of the God who cannot be unveiled to men', though thrice repeated, is fundamentally twofold in structure, with the weight thrown on the contrast of 'self-unveiling' and 'cannot be unveiled'. Corresponding to the Son's revelation is the Father's hiddenness and freedom. '[E]ven in the form He assumes when He reveals Himself God is free to reveal Himself or not to reveal Himself. . . . God's self-unveiling remains an act of sovereign divine freedom.'[18] This is clearly a reference to the fatherhood of God: 'God's fatherhood, too, is God's Lordship in His revelation.'[19]

In sum, the polarity of love and freedom in the doctrine of the divine perfections corresponds to the Son–Father duality in the preceding volume. That it is in a twofold pattern that Barth takes up the theme of the divine perfections is therefore not an accident and suggests that the doctrine of the Spirit is not determinative for the treatment of the attributes. That raises a question. What might happen to our topic if we were to introduce a more explicitly pneumatological element? The Holy Spirit is the perfecting Spirit, breaking in from the eschaton to perfect first the humanity of Jesus and through him that of those for whom he died. What implications might it have for our understanding of the being of God that he is Spirit as well as Father and Son? John Zizioulas has famously argued that God's being is communion. Communion, too, is an eschatological reality, because all true human communion with God and between human beings is an anticipation of the fellowship of the life to come. May we say—taking up a hint supplied by Basil—that the Spirit perfects the life of the eternal Trinity by so relating the Father and Son that together the three are one being in communion?[20] In that case, how might our understanding of the one who *makes perfect* affect our doctrine of the *divine perfections*? Let us try to think fully Trinitarianly about one contentious attribute, the freedom of God.

The Freedom of God

A dialectic of revealedness and love, on the one hand, and of hiddenness and freedom, on the other, is central to the shaping of Barth's doctrine of God. The question must be whether this leads to an overly-voluntaristic understanding of freedom; that is, one oriented to absolute rather than ordered freedom. The reason is something like this. We do need a doctrine of the absolute freedom of God, in the respect that God's actions are not necessary: he does not have to create a world, nor, having done it, to perfect it. It follows that the being of the creation as creation and not as the outflow of God's being is what gives it its own distinct reality, and this distinct particularity of the creation as creation derives from God's freely making it what it is. The doctrine of the Trinity is essential to the mainte-nance of such a teaching, showing that God is both self-sufficient in himself—the doctrine of the divine *aseity*—and creates and remains in relationship with the world that is other than he. Thus, we do need a doctrine of divine freedom, which corresponds to what we might consider to be a 'natural' understanding of freedom: God creates, but is not bound to.

However, without a fully Trinitarian construal of the divine freedom, we shall be in danger of being left with a mere voluntarism, a *potentia absoluta* which appears to give God no reason to create except sheer arbitrariness. On such an account, he creates by sheer will, and not by a will formed by love. We shall also break the analogy between divine and human freedom, or, perhaps better, in Scotist terms, the elements of univocity in the uses of the word 'freedom' of God and of ourselves that enable us to understand both God and ourselves more satisfac-torily. Let us pause to consider the matter of freedom. In relation to God, human freedom comes from the divine action that graciously creates, upholds, and redeems the creature who has preferred slavery to freedom. To be free is to be set free by the Spirit of the Father who is the Spirit of freedom. That is to say, true freedom is realized in communion with God, for unfreedom is, essentially, the loss of a right relationship to God. In terms of the way that freedom, which is given, works itself out in the world, we must say that freedom is a function of communion at the human level also. Our freedom is what we each make of our own particularity, and none of us are truly the particular persons we are created to be except in love and fellowship with our neighbour. In sum, both freedom and its loss are a function of our relation to the other, and especially the divine other, the creator. To be out of true communion is to be unfree; to be free is to be for and with the other, both the divine and the human other. Accordingly, freedom is never absolute, but always structured and ordered, either wrongly or rightly—as a matter of fact, always, this side of eternity, a combination of both.

In what sense may we speak of an ordered or structured freedom both within God's being and in his relations *ad extra*? What reason, for example, might there be, other than sheer arbitrary will, for God's creation of the world? Might there be something within his eternal being which grounds what he does? John Zizioulas has located the basis of all God is and does in the person of the Father, who freely, though timelessly, begets the Son and breathes the Spirit, thus constituting an eternal communion which is the source of created communion.[21] While there is much to be said for the Cappadocian teaching that the Father is the source of both the being and the divinity of the other two persons, there must be some doubt about the rather voluntarist terms in which this freedom is expressed. A more pneumatologically structured concept of freedom might mitigate such a tendency. If the Spirit is sent by the Father through the Son to perfect the creation, what place might he be conceived to have in structuring the being of the Triune God, and particularly the freedom of the Godhead? Robert Jenson has made an attempt to do this, basing his argument on that of Luther's *De Servo Arbitrio*. 'God is freedom antecedent to himself as determinate free will. He can intelligibly be said to be this as the Father is the source of the Son and both are freed in the Spirit. God is rapt by another without dependence on an other than God.'[22] Similarly, he suggests that 'the Spirit liberates God the Father from himself, to be in fact fatherly, to be the actual *arche* of deity; and so is indeed otherwise originated from that source than is the Son'.[23] If the only freedom for creatures is freedom that is given, freedom for and with the other (God first and then the creaturely other); if freedom is only freedom in relation, might not the same be true of God? Economically speaking, God's free creation is free because it is ordered through the Son and perfected by the Spirit. Similarly, his gracious reconciliation is free because it is achieved by the Son through the Spirit's perfecting of his free life of obedience. What might this mean for the eternal Trinity? May we say that the triune life is free by virtue of the free but ordered perichoresis— the *taxis*—of Father, Son, and Spirit in which there is constituted a communion in which each of the hypostases is what he is from and through the others? Thus, whether or not we put it precisely in the way that Jenson does, we might say that divine freedom is that which consists at once in the Father's breathing of the Spirit through the Son, and the

Spirit's reciprocal perfecting of the love which God is through the Son? On such an account, freedom is indeed a function of that holy love, of that love which is the essence of God.

That leads us into a concluding point about the nature of freedom. If freedom is like love, indeed, a function of love, then it is not an absolute possession, an attribute construed *a priori*. In chapter 2 of *Act and Being*, it was suggested that the will is not a thing, a hypostasis, but refers to a mode of action of a person-in-relation. So it is with God: freedom is a mode of personal action. In that case, God's freedom is a form of unconstrained and yet determined action which is determined because personally shaped by the relations of Father, Son, and Spirit, and yet unconstrained because it is a form of love. Perhaps we have now reached a stage when we should not attempt to speculate any further, but make a point which is taken up in chapter 7 of *Act and Being*. Is freedom an attribute or a form or mode of God's action? Indeed, what kind of distinction should we draw between the two? We have seen that attribute is best understood in terms of action, in God's case the action in which God is who he is as Father, Son, and Holy Spirit.

Notes

[1] [Editor's note] This essay was originally published as ch. 6 of Colin E. Gunton's *Act and Being: Towards a Theology of the Divine Attributes* (1st edn London: SEM Press; 2nd edn Grand Rapids: Eerdmans, 2003). I have made a few minor revisions for this volume.

[2] See *Act and Being*, pp. 88–9.

[3] T. F. Torrance, *Karl Barth: An Introduction to his Early Theology* (London: SCM Press, 1962).

[4] Karl Barth, *Church Dogmatics*, I/1, *The Doctrine of the Word of God*, ed. G. W. Bromiley and T. F. Torrance (Edinburgh: T&T Clark, 1975), p. 320.

[5] Eberhard Jüngel, *God's Being is in Becoming: The Trinitarian Being of God in the Theology of Karl Barth*, tr. John Webster (Edinburgh: T&T Clark, 2001), p. 42.

[6] Jüngel, *God's Being is in Becoming*, p. 47.

[7] As a matter of fact, Barth's very creativity in this one of the finest sections of his dogmatics has brought a number of problems in its train, at the extremes threatening to collapse the orders of time and of eternity rather than relating them positively.

[8] Karl Barth, *Church Dogmatics*, II/1, *The Doctrine of God*, ed. G. W. Bromiley and T. F. Torrance (Edinburgh: T&T Clark, 1957), p. 283.

[9] Barth, *Church Dogmatics*, II/1, pp. 344–5.

[10] Barth, *Church Dogmatics*, II/1, pp. 353–9.

[11] Aquinas, *Summa Theologiae* 1.25.3.

[12] Barth, *Church Dogmatics*, II/1, p. 524.

[13] Karl Barth, *Church Dogmatics*, IV/1, *The Doctrine of Reconciliation*, ed. G. W. Bromiley and T. F. Torrance (Edinburgh: T&T Clark, 1956), p. 192, citing Gregory of Nyssa, *Catechetical Oration* 24.

14 Barth, *Church Dogmatics*, II/1, p. 524.
15 See ch. 4 of *Act and Being* for consideration of this theme.
16 Barth, *Church Dogmatics*, II/1, p. 494.
17 Barth, *Church Dogmatics*, II/1, p. 517. Jaroslav Pelikan, *The Christian Tradition: A History of the Development of Doctrine*, 5 vols (Chicago and London: Chicago University Press, 1971–89), I, p. 22, states that in Judaism 'the immutability of God was seen as the trustworthiness of his covenanted relation to his people in the concrete history of his judgment and mercy, rather than as a primarily ontological category'. I owe this reference to Demetrios Bathrellos.
18 Barth, *Church Dogmatics*, I/1, p. 321.
19 Barth, *Church Dogmatics*, I/1, p. 324.
20 That would be a version, though a rather different one, of Augustine's conception of the Spirit as the bond of love between the Father and the Son. In this case, the Spirit is not the bond but the agent (mediator?) of love as a third person, a hypostasis with his own particular being.
21 John D. Zizioulas, *Being as Communion: Studies in Personhood and the Church* (London: Darton, Longman & Todd, 1985), pp. 87–9, but, in a sense, *passim*.
22 Robert W. Jenson, 'An Ontology of Freedom in the *De Servo Arbitrio* of Luther', *Modern Theology* 10 (1994), p. 250.
23 Robert W. Jenson, *Systematic Theology*, I, *The Triune God* (New York and Oxford: Oxford University Press, 1997), p. 158.

6

Triune Creativity: Trinity, Creation, Art and Science[1]

Stephen R. Holmes

Finding Room

'Make yourself thoroughly, intuitively, aware of the difficulty of admitting a one Ground of the Universe (which however *must* be admitted) and yet finding *room* for anything else'.[2] So wrote Coleridge in a quotation I first heard from Colin Gunton, but which became a crucial interpretative key for my own writings on that great poet-theologian.[3] As Gunton saw,[4] Coleridge's own solution to this problem was to appeal to a doctrine of the Trinity; his Trinitarian theology, however, although suggestive, was idiosyncratic, and contained problems that affected the way he conceived of the 'room' that was found.[5] This chapter is an attempt to construct a more adequate answer than Coleridge's, and to explore some of the implications of the 'room' that is found.

What, first, is the problem? Coleridge's insight is that the creation needs what we might call a 'relative independence' from God if it is to be what God calls it to be. If God is present immediately or directly to the universe, and God is personal and volitional, then the universe will be overwhelmed: nothing will possibly prevent God's will being done instantly and without opposition. Creation is not able to have its own life, its own freedom, to grow and develop in its own way—there is no 'room' for creation to be. This might not be seen as a problem: a thoroughly deterministic account of the being of the world is neither inconceivable nor incoherent, as far as I can see. However, as I shall explore in the second section of this chapter, it removes any possibility of an account of human culture, of artistic endeavour, or of scientific understanding. There is no space for creativity of whatever sort. Only, I will suggest, a thoroughly triune doctrine of creation can provide room for created creativity.[6] Let us return, however, to the problem of finding room, and to its solution in the doctrine of the Trinity.

The story begins with what I regard as the first great patristic articulation of how the gospel differed from (all schools of) Greek philosophical thought: the doctrine of creation *ex nihilo*, out of nothing. Although this doctrine was developed before the Imperial recognition of Christianity, and so before the possibility of cementing it in conciliar declaration arose,[7] it seems to me just as crucial an insight as the Nicene *homoousion to Patri*, the Ephesian *theotokos*, or the Chalcedonian *homoousion ton hemin*. Greek myths of origin (as indeed almost all myth-systems of which I am aware) postulated only two possible beginnings for this world: either it was ultimately made out of the same 'stuff' as the divine (so the Neoplatonism of Plotinus) or it was made out of 'stuff' that was ultimately foreign to the divine (so Plato's *Timaeus*). One may have a monistic pantheism, or a dualism, or some complex development or confused mixture of the two; nothing more.[8]

The first encompasses 'primitive' myth-systems which suppose that some divine principle gives birth to the world, or dies and thus provides the matter out of which the world is created; it also includes sophisticated philosophical pantheisms and emanationist accounts, where the world is held to be identical to God (Spinoza), or somehow to be an overflow of divine power or fecundity. The second presumes that there is some eternal entity that is not divinity, whether the 'unformed matter' of Plato or the 'darkness' of Manichaean dualism. In Coleridge's day, the one was represented by the Romantic pantheism that had so excited him and Wordsworth in early days, and that seems to inform the conversation poems (and Wordsworth's *Prelude*), the other by the sub-Newtonian[9] mechanistic deism that he saw (fairly or not) in Paley and others.[10] In either case it is central to Coleridge's complaint that there is not room for human freedom. On the one hand, humanity is swallowed up in God: if God is volitional, then human volition will necessarily be overwhelmed. On the other, humanity is reduced to a mechanism among other mechanisms, or (better) a sub-mechanism within the world machine. All is cogs and levers, and freedom is necessarily excluded.

In the early church, the enemies were not pantheism and deism, and not even (particularly) the various schools of Greek philosophy (although there is something of this in the Apologists of the second century); rather it was the various attempts to assimilate the nascent Christian movement to the prevailing philosophical-religious thought-world of the day that tend to be lumped together under the heading

'Gnosticism'.[11] Through all the diversity of Gnostic teachings, strands not dissimilar to those Coleridge found in his own day can be discerned, or at least were discerned by the greatest of the anti-Gnostic fathers, Irenaeus of Lyons. The first book of Irenaeus's magisterial work *Against All Heresies* is devoted to a taxonomy of Gnosticism, tracing lines of descent, agreements and divergences. In the complex Valentinian mythology of the Aeons comes a cosmic fall, which produces matter through a malformed emanation. Matter is thus at once from God and also somehow opposed to God. Marcion, by contrast, is accused of teaching that matter is simply evil[12] ('the body, because it is taken from the earth, cannot possibly partake of salvation'[13]), the product of some other being than the Father of Jesus. On the one hand there is a monism, albeit a confused one; on the other a dualism.[14]

Irenaeus will not accept either position. Against Marcion and the dualistic tinge within Valentinian Gnosticism, he urges the goodness of the one God, the creator of all, and the final material glory of the world in the millennial reign of Christ.[15] Against the monistic aspect of Gnosticism, he urges the genuine otherness of the created order. Both points may be established through consideration of the incarnation:[16] on the one hand, matter cannot be alien to God because God the Son was able to make his home in matter; on the other hand, as Augustine later argued, if the material (or indeed spiritual) world is created out of God's own being, it is impossible to differentiate it from the divine Son, who is precisely *ek ton Patri* and *homoousion to Patri*. Trinitarian reasons for looking beyond the impasse of either dualism or monism are already in evidence.

What else, however, may be said? The distinctive Christian claim formulated around the time of Irenaeus, is that God creates out of nothing, *ex nihilo*.[17] Against the monists, the created world is something genuinely other than God, not an extension or emanation of his own being; against the dualists, the world is not dependent on some principle that stands eternally in competition over against God. The 'stuff' that is other than he is 'stuff' that God has brought into being. Just so, it can be called 'good', as all that God has made is good. Irenaeus constantly links this claim to an account of omnipotence.

I recall Colin Gunton warning me that an appeal to omnipotence is almost always the mark of a bad theological argument. If by 'omnipotence' one means nothing more than a vague notion of an ability to do anything, the point is both perceptive and right. But Irenaeus's appeals are not like that. Rather, he qualifies what he means by omnipotence with some care. God's own life contains all the resources he needs to accomplish his purposes. Therefore, *inter alia*, God can create that which is genuinely not God without the need for any further resource—*ex nihilo*. This line of argument becomes particularly interesting when he applies it to the question of the mediation of creation.

Irenaeus appears to accept without comment the argument/assumption of his opponents that there is a need for the creation to be mediated, although I presume that his reasons for accepting this differ from theirs in at least some respects. The endless procession of mythical Aeons so characteristic of the Valentinians, and of many other Gnostics, was in part an attempt to preserve the idea (indeed worth preserving!) that one divine principle is the source of all that is, while also offering a vision of the material world as sufficiently removed from that divine *arche* that it may be described as sullied, fallen or evil. Precisely because he will not admit that the material world is evil, Irenaeus has no need to postulate such a complex system of mediation depending on that which is outwith God; instead, God can be personally present to the world. However, Irenaeus will not conceive of this personal presence as immediate presence. His reasons for this are obscure to me; I suspect they have something to do with a philosophical argument that regards creation as an act touching at once God and the world, and so claims the act is a different thing from God, and hence a mediation. This resonates with the clear biblical tradition—already present in the Old Testament—of seeing the Word of God and the Spirit of God (and also the arm of God, the wisdom of God, and the Angel of the Lord) as standing in a complex relationship to God himself. They are at once God's act and beings that seem to have an existence that stands alongside God's own. The development of such themes during the intertestamental period, and its relationship to early Christian Trinitarianism, is of course endlessly studied; for my purposes I need only note that this was commonly read back into Genesis 1, so that God's creative act was mediated by his word.

Nonetheless, God is personally present to the creation on Irenaeus's account: God, we might say, gets his hands dirty by having direct contact with the world—or rather, as Irenaeus argues, the whole point is that contact with the world will not dirty God's hands. God's two hands, in the bishop's memorable phrase, are the Son and Spirit;[18] God thus mediates his presence to the world through himself. Thus the connection with Irenaeus's account of omnipotence and his vision of God's creation *ex nihilo*: if Irenaeus's core doctrinal claim is that God contains within his own life all the resources that he needs to accomplish his creative act, then this must include the resources to mediate that act, if it must be mediated. Thus, God's personal presence is mediated to the world, but it is mediated by the act of God himself, and not by another. Irenaeus does not, of course, solve the conundrums of how one can adequately describe the triune life of God, but he depends on an assumption that these can be solved, in that to make sense of his theology he needs an account of the Son and Spirit as at once mediating God's presence and existing within God's own life. This notion of the 'mediated immediacy' of God's presence will become important in addressing Coleridge's problem of 'finding room'.

Coleridge's development of a Trinitarian alternative focuses on the notion of 'alterity', the distinction-without-division that he found exemplified in the relationship of the Son with the Father, a relationship that is upheld and eternally preserved by the Spirit, who in classical Augustinian style is identified as the 'bond of love' shared by the Father and Son. Coleridge saw the possibility, the 'room' for all else to be held in existence by God, and yet to preserve its genuine otherness from God, as contained in this one primal relationship between Father and Son guaranteed by the Spirit. In the Son, there is 'room' for the world to be. This is a distinctively different account of the 'mediated immediacy' of God's relationship to the world than that of Irenaeus; I have argued elsewhere that it is less adequate, and leads to real problems when Coleridge comes to discussing the freedom of creation.[19]

Yet a third Trinitarian account of the mediation of creation is available, in a profoundly suggestive exegesis of Genesis 1 advanced by Francis Watson. Watson notes that God creates in three distinct ways: through direct divine *fiat* ('God said, "Let there be light"; and there was light', Gen. 1.3); through his own purposeful activity ('God said, "Let there be a dome . . ." So *God made* the dome . . .', Gen. 1.6–7; my emphasis); and through a giving of the creation to have its own fecundity ('God said, "Let the earth bring forth . . ." and it was so. The earth brought forth . . .', Gen. 1.11–12). Watson suggests that these three different modes of divine action may be read as an affirmation that 'God as creator is triune'.[20] Of course, a more traditional exegesis of Genesis 1 (which, however, Watson identifies with post-modern concerns[21]) focuses in on the repeated 'and God said . . .', and so argues for the Father mediating creation through his Son, the Word.[22] Some writers extend this to suggest that the speaking forth of a word is dependent upon breath, and so the Christological mediation of creation is enabled by the presence/action of the Spirit.

It is not my purpose here to decide between these ways of describing the mediation of creation in Trinitarian terms. No doubt, there are strengths and weaknesses to each, and perhaps one is more adequate than the others. In each case, however, there is an attempt to describe how the mediation of God's presence to the world can take place without the invocation of entities other than God, and this is the core point for my argument here. Because there is genuine mediation, it is at least possible to claim that the necessary 'room' can be found; because that mediation does not depend on entities other than God, the true connectedness of God to creation is preserved. Only a Trinitarian account can possibly meet both these conditions.

Still, however, only 'possibly'. So long as an orthodox doctrine of the Trinity is maintained, I see no problem in the fulfilment of the 'true connectedness' condition; it is not obvious, however, that mediation through Son and Spirit (however that is described) provides enough 'room' for creation to have its own being. If the unmediated presence of God is overwhelming, why not the presence of God mediated through Son and/or Spirit?[23]

The answer, I think, is found in accounts of divine action. The particular ways in which God has chosen to be present to the world as Son and Spirit are ways which, in God's sovereignty, do not overwhelm the world; because as Father God remains transcendent from the world, these 'kenotic', or perhaps better 'self-limiting', modes of presence do not threaten his existence as God. So the presence of the Son, understood through the incarnation, is a particular presence that permits, and indeed perhaps establishes, the possibility of (Coleridge's point) other particular presences. The presence of the Spirit is not particular in the same way,[24] but it seems in the Scriptures that it is the particular economic act of the Spirit to establish created beings in their relative independence: the life of creatures is maintained by the Spirit (Ps. 104.29–30); the Spirit enables agency and Christian life within the church; and so on.

It is not, then, that any account based on three terms, or even on a generic triunity, is adequate to solving this problem; those modern theologians who (following, I suppose, Hegel) wish to claim that the doctrine of the Trinity teaches us to look for the third term in any supposed binary opposition seem to me to be making the error of which Augustine is generally (if unfairly) accused, of finding triads everywhere and thinking they have something to do with the life of God.[25] Rather, it is the particular biblical narrative of the activity of Father, Son, and Spirit—and the doctrine of the Trinity that seeks to express in propositional form the underlying relationships that make that narrative possible—which offers a particular vision of triunity which is adequate to the task. If God is as he is described in the biblical narratives, if Father, Son and Spirit relate as we are told there that they do, then there is room for the world to have its relative independence, 'to be itself to the praise of its creator' (to borrow another phrase from Colin Gunton).

Science and Culture

I have argued, then, that a triune doctrine of creation uniquely offers an account of God's relationship with the world that affirms both his close activity with the world and the world's relative independence from God. Why might this matter? I offer two examples relating to human culture, one focusing on the fine arts, and one on natural science. In both, the argument is of a similar form: the world's relative independence from God allows space for there to be genuine creativity in these areas, while the affirmation of God's close connection to the world allows the assertion that this creativity is of ultimate value. An account of the world which asserts its separation from God might well leave room for all sorts of mundane/secular activity, but will not be able to ascribe any value to such activity; this world is of no theological interest, so neither can this-worldly activity be.

The argument in relation to natural science is easier to make, because historians of science have mapped the territory very adequately over the past century. Beginning with Michael Foster,[26] a series of writers have explored the reasons for the sudden discovery of the methods of natural science in late medieval Europe.[27] Living in an age when the methods of science are assumed, it is difficult for us to realize how counter-intuitive they were originally, but the historical fact that only one culture has developed these methods indicates the truth of the proposition. To do science, one needs to make a series of assumptions about the nature of the world, assumptions that are very far from being 'common sense'. Some of these are relatively easy to grasp: as David Hume famously pointed out, the entire programme of induction needs convincing foundations before it may be accepted. That is (to take one of Hume's own examples), the fact that the sun has been observed to rise every morning since time immemorial is, of itself, no good reason to suppose that it will rise again tomorrow morning. Only if we introduce further premises can there be a convincing argument: at the very least, we need to believe that the world is possessed of some order, regularity or trustworthiness, leading to the presumption that what has happened in the past will happen in the future unless something has changed. We also need reason to believe that our observations of the world are accurate, or at least accurate enough that they can be held to correspond in some uncomplicated way to reality.

Once it is recognized that science can only begin in a culture where certain assumptions about the world are in place, the historical question becomes pressing: why did the right assumptions happen to be in place in late medieval Europe, and not elsewhere? At the time, after all, the Islamic civilizations of North Africa, the Chinese cultures, and probably several others, were more 'advanced' in the common meaning of that term; Europe was almost the last place one would have expected to find such an intellectual breakthrough. The answers given by historians tend to turn on the particular accounts of creation given by the nominalist theologians of the day.

Without going into too much historical detail, we can say that William of Ockham and other representatives of the *via moderna* were stressing the impossibility of any logical arguments linking God and the world.[28] One result of this was the radical suggestion that the logic that lay behind the being of the world (theistic philosophies tend to have reasons to suppose that the world is in fact logical) is immanent to the world: the world can be made sense of without reference to theology, metaphysics, astrology or any other external system.[29] Thus, the practice of science, the study of the world with reference only to itself, becomes a possible, imaginable enterprise.

Coupled with this was the nominalist position on universals. Instead of believing, with Plato and the earlier medieval theologians, that for each class of things (dogs, say) there exists a perfect mental/spiritual archetype ('the idea of dogness'), Ockham and his colleagues held that universals ('dogness') were merely abstractions we construct for our own convenience.[30] This encourages the method of natural science, in that it forces the enquirer after truth to pay attention to particulars, rather than always attempting to abstract away from the (allegedly imperfect) particulars to focus on some ideal archetype. Thus, one studies dogs by studying particular dogs, rather than by attempting to purify the characteristics of all the various dogs one has encountered in an attempt to reduce the idea to its essence.

This is, of course, only a cursory sketch of some fairly complicated historical discussions, but the point should be clear: natural science becomes an imaginable activity precisely because of an account of the being of the world that is at once broadly theistic but also able to stress the relative independence of the world from its deity. There are, I believe, problems with the account of creation offered by Ockham, but my historical survey makes the point that precisely those ideas that are safeguarded by a Trinitarian doctrine of creation are necessary axioms for the practice of natural science.[31]

Turning to the fine arts, it is easy enough to construct a similar argument which allows the ascribing of value to the arts; the more difficult issue concerns their diversity. Taking music as the example, not only is no particular musical form privileged—there is nothing that makes an opera necessarily better aesthetically than an art song, for instance—but neither is any particular musical logic to be preferred. Modal jazz in a pentatonic scale is just as valid as twelve-tone serialism or traditional Western octave-based harmony. There is a proper cultural relativism to be applied: not refusing to make judgements, in this case aesthetic, but recognizing that there are many standards to judge by, and so that many different perfections are possible. The ideal towards which Van Gogh was striving in painting a cornfield was different from the ideal towards which Constable was reaching when painting his haywain: it is not that one is better or worse; they are merely incommensurate. If, however, culture is theologically interesting, then even given the agnosticism just described, there is an apparent logical, or theological, problem: how can there be many different perfections, many different rationalities, within God's good ordering of the world?

In answering this, I would turn first to the witness of Scripture. In the miracle of Pentecost, where the text pointedly asserts not that all nations can now hear God's word in Hebrew (or Aramaic, or Greek), but that God's word can be heard in every language, and in the visions of the final consummation in Revelation, where people from every nation and tribe, speaking every tongue, make up the redeemed, there is a strong witness to God's valuing of the diversity of human culture. A rich diversity of varied, but not opposed, human cultures would seem to be God's will for the world, perhaps mirroring the unity-in-plurality which is his own triune life. If this is an adequate reading of the text, there are indeed many cultural perfections permissible within God's good purposes in creation.

There is still a need to account for this diversity theologically; this can be done, I think, by using the notion of contingency. As I have indicated, with the linked doctrines of divine omnipotence, self-sufficiency, and creation *ex nihilo*, the patristic theologians of creation refused to accept that God needed or gained anything from the creation. His perfection was complete without a world; he had no need for this world or any other, and so creation was an utterly gratuitous act. The world is free to be itself to the praise of its creator, and so is free to have its own inner rationality, unconstrained by any need to be something particular for God. There is nothing, so far, in the argument to suggest that this rationality is unitary.

The theological reason to insist that the inner rationality of the world is single is its ontological homogeneity. This must be decisive for physics—the supracelestial realm must, as Galileo saw, operate according to the same laws as the mundane realm—but it is at least not obvious that such an argument applies, or at least not with the same force, to aesthetics. Physical realities are simply created by God; cultural realities are, under God, made by men and women. As such, while there is an ontological component to their rationality, in that music does finally depend on the modes of vibration of catgut scraped by horsehair, or of a reed attached to a valved brass column, there is a component which is not straightforwardly ontological, and so which does not need to be homogeneous, for any of the reasons so far discussed. Thus, within certain proper limits to do with physicality, there is space for a plurality of cultural rationalities and so perfections.

Which all, finally, brings us to the point of being able to talk about artistic activity in theological terms. There is theological space for a proper plurality of art forms and visions of perfection in this account, which we might compare to the space opened up for the practice of science within a proper Christian doctrine of creation—and so there is no need to insist on the superiority of any one tradition of aesthetics, or to seek spurious theological or biblical reasons for opposing artistic change. That there are laws of motion, regularity and order in the universe is theologically demanded; what these laws of motion actually state is, in contrast, dogmatically indifferent, and so must be investigated by a different science. Similarly, while this account will resist any attempt to derive cultural norms from theological or biblical data, it will impose certain boundary conditions: there is no one uniquely Christian aesthetics (or indeed economics, or politics) but certain particular descriptions of the beautiful (or polities or economies) might conceivably be demonstrably anti-Christian. The devil might have his music, although I suspect it is not rock and roll (pure evil would be far more banal than that . . .); all other music, however, can be Godly by being beautiful in its own terms, whether it be an improvised jazz solo, an electric guitar riff, a gamelan ensemble, or an opera by Mozart. This is a necessary derivation from the doctrine that the world is free to be itself, which in turn depends on a belief that the creator is triune.

Notes

[1] In view of the dedication of this volume, it is worth noting that my first serious thought about the doctrine of creation came as a result of team-teaching a course on the subject with my mentor and friend Colin Gunton, an immensely rich experience.

[2] Samuel Taylor Coleridge, *Letters*, ed. E. L. Griggs (Oxford: Clarendon Press, 1959), IV, p. 849.

[3] See my 'Samuel Taylor Coleridge', in *The Nineteenth Century Theologians*, ed. Colin E. Gunton & Christoph Schwöbel (Oxford: Blackwell Publishers, forthcoming), and 'Of Neoplatonism and Politics', in my *Listening to the Past* (Carlisle: Paternoster Press, 2003).

[4] See e.g. Colin E. Gunton, *The Triune Creator* (Edinburgh: Edinburgh University Press, 1998), pp. 137–8.

[5] For a defence of this charge, and a demonstration of how the problems play out in relation to political theory, see again my 'Of Neoplatonism and Politics'.

[6] Or rather, only a doctrine of creation that affirms certain positions that have historically only ever been affirmed within the context of a robust doctrine of the Trinity. It might be possible to imagine an equally useful doctrine based on some novel metaphysic, but that is not my concern. (I owe this clarification to a conversation with Dr Randal Rauser.)

[7] Within the Latin tradition, of course, it is dogmatically defined at the Fourth Lateran Council (1215), presumably in part as a response to the Aristotelian teaching of the eternity of the world.

[8] Coleridge, in *On the Prometheus of Aeschylus*, describes these as the 'Phoenician' system, according to which 'the cosmogony was their theogony and vice-versa' and the 'Greek' system, under which '[t]he corporeal was supposed co-essential with the antecedent of its corporeity': Samuel Taylor Coleridge, *Works*, IV, ed. W. G. T. Shedd (New York: Harper, 1853), pp. 353–5.

[9] Newton himself probably did not think in purely mechanistic ways, although some of the implications of his work (notably the necessary assumption that space is a transcendental metric) undoubtedly encouraged the development of such ways of thinking. For Newton, see *Newton's Philosophy of Nature*, ed. H. S. Thayer, (London: Collier-Macmillan, 1953); for the implications of Newton's scientific theories on accounts of nature see T. F. Torrance, *Space, Time and Incarnation* (Oxford: Oxford University Press, 1969) and *Divine and Contingent Order* (Edinburgh: T&T Clark, 1981).

[10] Of course Paley, and indeed the self-denominated deists of Coleridge's day, would have affirmed their belief in God's creation of the world; Coleridge identifies them with the error of Plato in the *Timaeus* (which explicitly teaches that matter exists eternally alongside God) because he sees the effect of their account of providence as the exclusion of God from the world, and so the making of matter to be something foreign to God. In this, he was probably right—see the two works by Torrance cited in the previous note.

[11] On Gnosticism, and particularly the recent realization of the sheer diversity of the movement, see M. A. Williams, *Rethinking Gnosticism* (Princeton: Princeton University Press, 1996).

[12] Much modern scholarship would try to distance Marcion from Gnosticism, accepting an influence but suggesting that his thought lacks some of the defining features (the procession of Aeons, for instance). Particularly in the light of the work on the

diversity of Gnosticism noted above, this seems to me merely a question of how 'Gnostic' is defined. It suited Irenaeus's polemical purposes to broaden the definition so as to lump Marcion in with his other, more straightforwardly Gnostic opponents. Modern scholarship is helped by narrowing the definition so as to identify the differing religious options of the day more precisely.

13 Irenaeus, *Adversus Haereses* 1.27.3, my translation.

14 Although we lack Marcion's own writings, the polemics directed against him are united in reading him as a dualist, and there is evidence that most of the Marcionite communities that survived to the end of the third century had been absorbed into Manichaeism, which again suggests that the movement had a broadly dualist bent.

15 As Eric Osborn has shown in his *Irenaeus of Lyons* (Cambridge: Cambridge University Press, 2001), millennialism is not a slightly strange and alien accretion, but is thoroughly bound up within Irenaeus's theology. See esp. pp. 139–40.

16 Irenaeus constantly hints at an incarnational defence of the first point—matter must be good, because God dwelt in material flesh—without ever (to my knowledge) really developing it.

17 There is a certain amount of debate as to where the phrase is first used, and where the concept is first articulated. See Gerhard May, *Creatio ex nihilo* (Edinburgh: T&T Clark, 1994); F. M. Young, 'Creatio ex nihilo', in *Scottish Journal of Theology* 44 (1991), pp. 139–51. In *Irenaeus* (pp. 65–8) Osborn suggests that Justin Martyr has the concept but lacks the phrase; however, in arguing this he depends on an assertion that Justin nowhere denies the concept, which seems open to challenge (see, for instance, *1 Apol.* 10, where God is held to create 'out of unformed matter', or *1 Apol.* 59, where Justin argues that 'Plato borrowed [from Moses] his statement that God . . . altered matter which was shapeless': *The Writings of Justin Martyr and Athenagoras*, tr. M. Dods, G. Reith and B. P. Pratten, in *Ante-Nicene Christian Library*, II (Edinburgh: T&T Clark, 1867)). Osborn further suggests, more convincingly to my mind, that although Basilides uses the phrase, he does so without any clear grasp of the concept it came to represent (pp. 68–9), and so Osborn accords Athenagoras and Irenaeus the accolade of having first asserted *ex nihilo* creation and meant by that what the church has meant ever since.

18 See Irenaeus, *Adversus Haereses* 4.20.1, 5.1.3.

19 See again my 'Of Neoplatonism and Politics'.

20 Francis B. Watson, *Text, Church and World* (Edinburgh: T&T Clark, 1994), pp. 140–53; quotation from p. 144.

21 Watson, *Text, Church and World*, pp. 137–40. Watson's concern is not with the Christological point (Christology not being a common feature of post-modern philosophy), but the exclusive focus on the role of speech in creation.

22 So, for example, Basil of Caesarea, *Homilies on the Hexameron* 3.2, or Karl Barth, *Church Dogmatics*, III/2, *The Doctrine of Creation*, ed. G. W. Bromiley and T. F. Torrance (Edinburgh: T&T Clark, 1960), pp. 114–17.

23 One of the (very few) defects I find in Gunton's *The Triune Creator* is his failure to address this question.

24 The biblical text seems to suggest both that there is a genuine particularity about the presence of the Spirit within the church (Acts 2, Romans 8), and that the Spirit fills and upholds the whole created order and maintains all life in its existence (Gen. 1.2; Ps. 104.29–30).

25 Augustine, as I understand *De Trinitate*, is not merely looking for random triads; rather he is exegeting Gen. 1.26, and assuming that if humanity is made in God's image, and God is triune, then it is proper to look for images of the Trinity in

humanity. Whether the second half of *De Trinitate* does this adequately is a moot point, but it is not merely an exercise in natural theology.

26 Michael Foster, 'The Christian Doctrine of Creation and the Rise of Modern Natural Science', *Mind*, n.s., 43 (1934), pp. 446–68.

27 For example, John Headley Brooke, *Science and Religion* (Cambridge: Cambridge University Press, 1991); P. Harrison, *The Bible, Protestantism and the Rise of Science* (Cambridge: Edinburgh University Press, 1998); R. Hooykaas, *Religion and the Rise of Modern Science* (Edinburgh: Scottish Academic Press, 1972). There are many others.

28 The reasons for this stress are not important to my argument, but have to do in part with an acceptance of Duns Scotus's critique of Thomas Aquinas's doctrine of analogy (which offered a way of connecting God and the world in the same argument, classically in the Five Ways), coupled with a dissatisfaction with Scotus's own suggestion (which involved an assertion that there are things that can be said univocally of God and creatures). Linked to this were other discussions concerning the nature of universals (see the next paragraph in the text below) and the relative importance of intellect and will in the life of God.

29 Basil of Caesarea had made a similar point in his criticism of astrology.

30 Again, Scotus had held a complex mediating position, the details of which are not important to my argument.

31 I do not see a direct link between Trinitarian doctrine and Ockham's nominalism, although I am aware that others do.

7

The Social God and the Relational Self: Toward a Trinitarian Theology of the *Imago Dei*[1]

Stanley J. Grenz

The Fluid Self Lost in Cyberspace

In the mid-1990s, airwaves across North America were monopolized by Canadian pop diva Alanis Morissette's 'All I Really Want'. The lyrics ramble through a hodgepodge of seemingly disconnected preferences and competing desires that the singer finds present within and around her. Morissette bemoans life in a world populated by superficial people; she desperately yearns for a soul-mate, a kindred spirit, someone who truly understands.

Like many others of her generation, sixteen-year-old Aminah McKinnie of Madison, Mississippi, spends much of her non-school waking hours on the Internet. She lives in a strangely paradoxical realm in which the opinions of peers and relationships are crucial, and yet social groups are fluid, friendships change over a period of months or even weeks, and the possibility of lifelong 'best friends' is not even on the radar screen.[2] The fluidity characteristic of the contemporary ethos is epitomized by the Internet chatroom. Here participants are able to be whomever they want, to try on new identities with ease, even to the point of becoming a different person with each foray into cyberspace.

Do the resources of Christian anthropology have anything to offer in the realm described by Alanis Morissette or inhabited by Internet devotees and chatroom dwellers? The goal of this chapter is to explore how the traditional Christian anthropological concept of the *imago Dei*, understood as God's intention for humankind from the beginning, embodied in Jesus Christ, and finding its fullness in the eschatological new creation, might provide a point of engagement with the realm described by Alanis Morissette or inhabited by Aminah McKinnie. By connecting the *imago Dei* to contemporary developments in Trinitarian theology and social psychology, the following paragraphs propose the ecclesial self, constituted in relation to the Triune God, as the model for forming the self in the face of the fluidity endemic to the current cultural situation.

The Biblical-Theological Resource: The Concept of the *Imago Dei*

Throughout much of Christian history, the link made in Scripture between humans and the divine image (*imago Dei*) has served as the foundation for the task of constructing a Christian conception of the human person or the self. Bringing this theological concept into conversation with the contemporary demise of the self begins, therefore, with a return to the biblical texts that explicitly refer to the concept of the *imago Dei*.

From Humankind to the True Human

The Hebrews likely did not invent the concept of humans as the divine image. Rather, the background for the idea lies in the kingship ideology of ancient Near Eastern cultures. In the ancient world, images were viewed as representatives of the entity they designated. The representational motif was especially strong when an image was designed to depict a deity. The god's spirit was believed actually to indwell the image (or idol). In addition, images were often thought to represent and even mediate the presence of one who is physically absent, whether this absent reality be the conquering king whose throne is in a distant city or a deity whose abode is on the remote mountain of the gods. By extension, the concept of the *imago Dei* indicates that humankind somehow mediates within creation the immanence of the transcendent Creator. Viewed from this perspective, Gen. 1.26–7 stands at the pinnacle of the biblical creation narrative that posits a God who creates a world external to God's being and then places humankind within that creation as a creaturely representation of the transcendent deity.

The story of the creation of humankind as the *imago Dei* was included in the Genesis narrative for the purpose of undermining the exclusivity of the royal ideology out of which the biblical concept emerged. By extending the divine image to humankind, the first creation story—in a manner akin to Psalm 8—declared that humankind, and not merely the king, is the representation of and witness to God on earth. In this way, the first creation narrative effects a universalizing of the divine image.

Although Gen. 1.26–8 suggests that as the divine image humans are to resemble their Creator, the question as to *how* humans are to fulfil the role of being the divine image leads beyond this text to the full sweep of the biblical narrative. Because the wider narrative centres on Jesus as Israel's Messiah, the open-ended character of Gen. 1.26–7 clears the way for a move from a creatiocentric to a Christocentric anthropology. Three New Testament verses explicitly sound this theme.

In 2 Cor. 4.4–6, Paul links Christ directly to the *imago Dei*. For the apostle, being the divine image means that Christ radiates the very glory of God. Rather than speculating about the ontological nature of Christ, however, Paul's statement evidences a narrative focus. It embodies an implicit allusion to the creation of humankind in the image of God narrated in Gen. 1.26–7 as understood through the lens of Christ as the Second Adam.

The narrative focus is even more pronounced in Col. 1.15–20, in which Paul incorporates what some scholars suggest is an edited version of a previously formed hymn that not only emphasizes Christ's pre-eminence over all things but also extols his centrality in creation and redemption. Crucial for understanding the nature of the *imago Dei* in the Colossian hymn is the twofold assertion that Christ is the 'first-born' (*prototokos*), a motif that brings together the themes of the two strophes into which the hymn is divided. The one who is the *eikon tou theou* is the 'firstborn of all creation' (v. 15 NRSV) and, reiterating a theme found elsewhere in the New Testament, the 'firstborn from the dead' (v. 18 NRSV). The repetition of the term links the 'beginning' with the 'new beginning', and draws the entire creation/salvation-historical narrative into its proper centre, Jesus, who as the final embodiment of God's saving action toward the world is the pre-eminent one and the *imago Dei*.

Similar to the great Johannine declaration, 'the Word became flesh and lived among us' (John 1.14 NRSV), Paul draws together into a single whole the entire life of Jesus as it converges on his resurrection as the prolepsis of the *eschaton* (v. 18) and on his death as God's great act in reconciling all creation (v. 20). The apostle's intent is to declare that this historical life is the dwelling place of the fullness of deity, understood in accordance with the wisdom tradition and as the fulfilment of the creation story. Alternatively, stated in the opposite manner, the entire narrative of the invisible God's self-disclosure through the divine wisdom, together with the Genesis story of humankind being created in the divine image, can only be rightly understood when viewed in the light of Jesus, who as the pre-eminent Christ is the *eikon* of God.

By declaring that Jesus is the reflection of God's glory and the imprint of God's being, the opening verses of the epistle to the Hebrews fuse glory and image language to declare what it means to say that as the one who is 'Son', Jesus Christ is the *imago Dei* (even though the phrase is not explicitly used in the text). Jesus manifests who God is, but not by being a passive reflector of the divine reality, similar to a mirror that can only reflect the light issuing from another source. Rather, Jesus *is* this light. He is the pattern according to whom those who are stamped with the divine image are conformed. The high-water mark toward which the author moves comes with the declaration of Jesus' historical work of making 'purification for sins' (v. 3). The point of Heb. 1.1–3, therefore—indeed the point of New Testament Christology in general—is that Jesus Christ fully reveals God, and thereby is the *imago Dei* in fulfilment of Gen. 1.26–7, as he redeems humankind.

From Eschatological Hope to Ongoing Task

The witness of the New Testament is that Jesus is the divine image. Yet, this witness adds another chapter to the narrative of the *imago Dei*. Jesus is also the head of the new humanity destined to be formed according to the image of God in fulfilment of God's intent for humankind from the beginning.

In Rom. 8.29, Paul articulates this theme in Christocentric language reminiscent of Gen. 1.26–7. According to the apostle, God's intention is that those who are in Christ participate in his destiny and thereby replicate his glorious image. The eschatological orientation of the text is confirmed by the prefix *sym-* in the word *symmorphous*, which carries overtones of a central theme of Paul's theology, the idea of being 'in Christ'. In Rom. 8.29, Paul declares that his readers will be caught up in the Christ event and become copies of God's Son. Above all, however, the eschatological focus is evident in the crucial phrase 'image of his Son', with its overtones of the Son-Christology found repeatedly in the pages of the New Testament. By declaring that they are destined for conformity to the *eikon tou huiou autou*, Paul is reminding his readers of God's purpose to imprint them with the very qualities of Christ, who as the image of God is the divine Son.

The climax of the verse comes in the subordinate clause that follows, 'that he might be the firstborn', which expresses the Christological intent of God's foreordination, namely, the pre-eminence of Christ among those who participate in the eschatological resurrection. The designation of these as Christ's *adelphoi* indicates the communal interest of the text, which marks Rom. 8.29 as the final exegesis of Gen. 1.26-7. Although in his risen glory Jesus Christ now radiates the fullness of humanness that constitutes God's design for humankind from the beginning, God's purpose has never been limited to this. God's goal is that as the Son, Jesus Christ be pre-eminent within a new humanity stamped with the divine image. Consequently, humankind created in the *imago Dei* is none other than the new humanity conformed to the *imago Christi*, and the *telos* toward which the Old Testament creation narrative points is the eschatological community of glorified saints. In this manner, the narrative of the emergence of the new humanity provides the climax to the entire salvation-historical story and becomes the ultimate defining moment for the Genesis account of the creation of humankind in the *imago Dei*.

The question as to the exact nature of conformity to Christ leads beyond Rom. 8.29 to its 'essential commentary',[3] 1 Cor. 15.49. Here Paul connects the *imago Christi* with the resurrected new humanity by means of an Adam–Christ typology with its correlate last-Adam Christology. To set forth Jesus' resurrected body as the paradigm for all who will bear his image, Paul introduces an antithesis between the *psychikon soma* and the *pneumatikon soma*, and then draws a contrast between Adam and Christ as the representations of these two corporate realities. Involved here is a type of midrashic reflection on Gen. 2.7. Paul's Christological reading of this Old Testament text yields the conclusion that the advent of the spiritual body was in view at the creation, yet not as an aspect that was inherent within human nature from the beginning but as the eschatological destiny of the new humanity in Christ. Paul's Adam–Christ typology, therefore, indicates that the creation of Adam did not mark the fulfilment of God's intention for humankind as the *imago Dei*. Instead, this divinely given destiny comes only with the advent of the new humanity, consisting of those who participate in the *pneumatikon soma* by means of their connection to the last Adam. In this manner, Paul paints Christ as the true image of God who imparts his supernatural characteristics to his spiritual progeny in a manner similar to Adam passing on his natural traits to his physical offspring.

The biblical narrative of the *imago Dei* that climaxes with the glorified new humanity sharing in the divine image leads back to the present. The new humanity already shares in the divine image by means of being 'in Christ'. This is explicitly stated in 2 Cor. 3.18, which comes as the climax to Paul's midrash on Exod. 34.29–35. In this verse, the apostle declares that 'the essence of the Christian life' entails unity with Christ.[4] At the heart of the verse is a contrast between believers, who now see the Lord's glory, albeit indirectly, and Israelites, who in Moses' time could not look upon God's splendour and who in Paul's day remained veiled. The apostle declares that those who behold the divine glory are participants in a process of transformation into that image, a process that is gradual and progressive. In commenting on this text, Margaret Thrall notes the ethical orientation of the process of transformation: 'assimilation to Christ as the image of God produces a visibly Christ-like character, so that the divine image becomes visible in the believer's manner of life'.[5] Moreover, this building of character occurs through the new narrative that is inaugurated at conversion and reaches its climax at the eschatological resurrection. Yet envisioned here is no mere private beholding, leading to an individualistic 'me-and-Jesus' ethic. Rather, the metamorphosis involves the reformation of relationships and the creation of a new community of those who share together in the transforming presence of the Spirit and who thereby are, as A. M. Ramsey notes, 'realizing the meaning of their original status as creatures in God's image'.[6]

In Colossians and Ephesians, the apostolic author takes the ethical dimension of the *imago Dei* a step further. Those who are destined to be the new humanity, and therefore are already in the process of being transformed into the divine image, are to live out that reality in the present. The declaration in Col. 3.9–11 that through conversion/baptism into Christ, believers have put off the 'old human' and have put on the 'new', evidences an underlying Adam–Christ typology. For Paul, being 'in Adam' and being 'in Christ' not only designate two orders of existence, but also the way of living that characterizes each. In this text, the apostle uses the imagery of changing garments to signify an exchange of identities. The old and new human designate two frames of reference from which participants in each realm not only gain their identity, but also out of which, on the basis of which, or in keeping with which, they conduct their lives. The text concludes with a grand declaration that the way of living—the ethic—that belongs to the realm 'in Christ' entails what is appropriate to life in the new community. The new humanity not only does not emerge from the distinctions that separate humans into competing communities, but can give no place whatsoever to such peculiarities,[7] because 'Christ is all and in all'.

The Colossians text finds echo in Eph. 4.17–24. Although the *imago Dei* is not explicitly mentioned here, it comes to the fore in the final infinitive of the passage, the apostle's declaration that believers put on the 'new human' (v. 24). In Eph. 2.15, the writer asserts that Christ has created in himself 'one new human' out of the formerly warring groups of Jew and Gentile. In Eph. 4.24, this corporate focus emerges again. Rather than referring to the new self in an individual sense, the term designates the new form of human life, the new communal ethic, that results from redemption, namely, 'life patterned after God's' life[8] (cf. Eph. 5.1). This new realm is stamped by the qualities that reflect God's own character as it is revealed in the biblical narrative.

The Application: Toward a Reconstruction of the Self

The Christocentric, eschatologically focused anthropology of the New Testament interprets the Old Testament idea of humankind as *imago Dei* reaching its fulfilment in the new humanity headed by Jesus Christ. In so doing, the New Testament anthropology leads inevitably back to Gen. 1.26–7. Following this hermeneutical journey from new creation back to creation provides the basis for a Trinitarian ontology of the person-in-community that can facilitate the reconstruction of the self-in-relationship in the contemporary context.

The *Imago Dei* and Sexual Differentiation

Two anthropological themes stand at the heart of Gen. 1.26–7—the creation of humankind in the divine image and the creation of humans as sexually differentiated and hence relational creatures. The enumeration of these two themes sparks the query as to the connection between them, a query that can only be answered by reading this text together with the second creation story and ultimately within the biblical narrative as a whole.

Claus Westermann points out that the central concern of the Genesis 2 narrative is not the creation of the woman as such, or even the origin of the mutual attraction of the sexes, but the creation of humankind. The making of woman completes the creation of humankind, Westermann argues, because 'God's creature is humankind only in community'.[9] But why? The answer leads back to the perspective on sexuality suggested by the story. Adam's cry of delight as the presence of the woman rescues him from his debilitating solitude, with which the second creation story reaches its climax, suggests that individual existence as an embodied creature entails a fundamental incompleteness, or, stated positively, an innate yearning for fellowship. Sexuality, in turn, is linked not only to the incompleteness each person senses as an embodied, sexual creature, but also to the potential for wholeness in relationship with others that parallels it.[10] Sexuality comprises the dynamic that forms the basis of the uniquely human drive toward bonding. For the narrator, the drive toward bonding finds expression in marriage, which in turn leads to the establishment of the broader human community.

Reading the Genesis creation accounts canonically suggests that the creation of sexual creatures in the image of God is most clearly understood in light of the eschatological goal of God's creative work. When viewed from the perspective of the new humanity as God's intent from the beginning, the ultimate goal of sexuality (and hence of the impulse toward bonding) is participation in the fullness of community, that is, life together as the new humanity in relationship with God and all creation. Although the anticipated fullness of community is a future reality, a partial, yet genuine foretaste of the eschatological fullness may be enjoyed prior to the eschaton. The focus of the prolepsis of the future reality is the community of reconciled people in fellowship with God through Christ.

The relational 'self', therefore, is sexual. This 'self' consists of the person-in-bonded-community. But how does sexuality relate to humankind as the *imago Dei*, if at all? This question takes us back to the plural address found in the first creation narrative: 'Let us make humankind in our image' (Gen. 1.26 NRSV). Although the narrator surely did not intend this as a reference to the Trinitarian persons, viewing the *Wortbericht* from the vantage point of the post-Cappadocian hermeneutical trajectory facilitates Christians in seeing the Triune God at work in the creation of humankind as male and female. This, in turn, raises the possibility that creation in the *imago Dei* endows human sexual differentiation with significance as reflecting something about the Creator. But what about the Creator could the creation of humans as male and female represent? The most promising possibility is divine relationality.

Dietrich Bonhoeffer may have been the first theologian to propose that the image of God be interpreted by means of a relational analogy in which the duality of male and female is the defining human relationship.[11] Yet Karl Barth was responsible for the wide influence the idea has enjoyed.[12] In setting this forth, Barth draws from I–Thou relationality, which he claims is grounded in the Triune God, was disclosed in Christ, and remains evident in both divine and human life. For Barth, sexuality is theologically crucial, because of the I–Thou relationship that the creation of humans as male and female facilitates. According to his interpretation of the second creation narrative, the fashioning of the woman is crucial in that it facilitates in the created realm the kind of I–Thou relationality that characterizes the eternal Trinity.

Barth correctly finds in the story the idea that the male–female bond involves the recognition of sameness and difference. The man sees in the woman a creature like himself, in contrast to the animals who are unlike him, but acknowledges as well that the two are different, for he is male and she is female. For the narrator, this sameness and difference—this mutuality within a plurality—explains the mystery of the two forming the unity of 'one flesh', for this unity is held together by the attraction they sense as male and female for each other. Read in the light of Genesis 2, Genesis 1 suggests that the interplay of sameness and difference is present in a prior way in the Triune God.

Barth goes astray, however, when he exchanges the dynamic of sexuality, understood as the sense of incompleteness that gives rise to the drive toward bonding, for the paradigm of I–Thou relationality. In spite of his concern to draw deeply from the creation of humankind as male and female, in the end Barth leaves human sexuality behind. Sexuality, however, simply cannot be left behind. Marriage and genital sexual expression are limited to this penultimate age, of course. But sexuality is not. To leave sexuality behind is to undercut the significance of the resurrection. This central Christian doctrine indicates that sexuality is not eradicated en route to eternity. Instead, after the manner of the risen Jesus, humans participate in the transforming event of resurrection as the embodied persons—male or female—they are.[13] Above all, however, to relegate sexuality to the temporal is to undermine the basis for community in eternity. Even though genital sexual expression is left behind, the dynamic of bonding continues to be operative beyond the eschatological culmination, for this dynamic is at work in constituting humans as the community of the new humanity within the new creation in relationship with the triune God.

The reminder that the human destiny as the *imago Dei* is linked to the new humanity leads to the other debilitating difficulty posed by the appropriation of I–Thou relationality. This approach leads theologians like Barth to move directly from the male–female relationship to the divine prototype. Reading the Genesis creation narratives in the light of the *telos* of the *imago Dei*, i.e. the establishment of the new humanity, indicates, however, that an intermediate step is required.

The New Testament writers declare that ultimately the *imago Dei* is Christ and, by extension, the new humanity, consisting of those who through union with Christ share in Christ's relationship to God and consequently are being transformed into the image of God in Christ. For this reason, the church emerges in the New Testament as an even more foundational exemplar of the *imago Dei* in this penultimate age. In the final analysis, then, the *imago Dei* is not simply the I–Thou relationship of two persons standing face to face. Instead, it is ultimately communal. It is the eschatological destiny of the new humanity as the representation of God within creation. For this reason, the pathway between humankind as male and female and the *imago Dei* leads inevitably through the church as the prolepsis of the new humanity, and the relational self is ultimately the ecclesial self.

The Relational Self as the Ecclesial Self

The image of God does not lie in the individual per se, but in the relationality of persons in community. This assertion calls for a relational ontology that can bring the divine prototype and the human antitype together.

The philosophical genesis of the contemporary idea of the social self begins with William James's distinction between the 'me' (the objective, empirical person, the 'empirical self') and the 'I' (the subjective consciousness of the *me* as continuing in time). The American social psychologist[14] George Herbert Mead, in turn, postulated that the individual experiences oneself only indirectly by means of the reflected standpoints of the social group.[15] The 'me' emerges within a dialogue, as it were, between the 'I' and the social context. In so doing, Mead also opened the door to viewing the self as an ongoing process, rather than as a given that exists prior to social relationships.[16] This self may be said to have both a past and a future that taken as a whole forms a 'narrative'.

The trajectory of social psychology inaugurated by Mead opens the way for a reintroduction of an alternative understanding of the construction of the self-in-relationship that enjoys a long pedigree within the Christian tradition but was overshadowed by the Augustinian inward turn. Beginning with John of Damascus, the patristic thinkers appropriated the Christological concept of *perichoresis* (mutual indwelling) to express the dynamic of the divine life. This term, which had been invoked to speak about the interdependence of Christ's deity and humanity,[17] provided a ready way of describing the relations among the Trinitarian persons. The three persons 'mutually inhere in one another, draw life from one another, "are" what they are by relation to one another', to cite Catherine LaCugna's insightful description of *perichoresis*.[18] Hence, the word indicates that the personhood of the three is relationally determined; each is a person-in-relationship to the other two. By avoiding any hint of dividing God into three and yet maintaining the personal distinctions within God, the appeal to *perichoresis* preserved both the unity of the one God and the individuality of the Trinitarian persons. Colin Gunton voices the importance of this aspect of the Christian conception of the Trinity:

> an account of relationality that gives due weight to both one and many, to both particular and universal, to both otherness and relation, is to be derived from the one place where they can satisfactorily be based, a conception of God who is both one and three, whose being consists in a relationality that derives from the otherness-in-relation of Father, Son and Spirit.[19]

The link between the insight of social psychology regarding the formation of the self and the biblical anthropology is forged by the concept of being 'in Christ', which lies at the heart of the New Testament conception of spirituality. Both perspectives agree that personal identity arises *extra se* (outside oneself). Social psychology relates the *extra se* character of the construction of the self to the dynamic of self-consciousness, in which one's sense of self is dependent on the 'generalized other'. The *extra se* advanced by Christian theology, in turn, speaks of the self as arising 'in Christ'. The insight regarding the social character of the self articulated by Mead and other social psychologists suggests that being 'in Christ' is a social phenomenon and that the Christian self is ultimately what we might call the 'ecclesial self'. That is to say, the self emerges *extra se* in that participation 'in Christ' constitutes the identity of all participants in the new humanity and constitutes their identity together.

Yet, this connection between being 'in Christ' and the ecclesial self must be given its full Trinitarian-theological cast. A crucial consideration in this process is the Pauline understanding of the role of the Spirit in believers' lives. Paul links the prerogative of addressing God as 'Abba' explicitly to the presence of the indwelling Spirit, whom the apostle identifies as 'the Spirit of [God's] Son'. Furthermore, according to Paul, the Spirit who leads those who are 'in Christ' to address God as 'Abba' likewise constitutes them as 'heirs of God and joint heirs with Christ' (Rom. 8.17). Taken together, these Pauline observations imply that by incorporating the new humanity into Christ, the Spirit gathers them into the dynamic of the divine life. Yet the Spirit does so in a particular manner, namely, specifically and solely 'in the Son'. Through the Spirit, those who are 'in Christ' come to share the eternal relationship that the Son enjoys with the one whom he called 'Father'. Because participants in this new community are by the Spirit's work co-heirs with Christ, the Father of Jesus bestows on them by virtue of their being 'in Christ' what he eternally lavishes on the Son.

Being 'in Christ' by the Spirit means as well that in the Son, they participate in the Son's act of eternal response to his Father. In this manner, those who by the Spirit are in the Son participate in the very *perichoretic* dynamic that characterizes the eternal divine life. This participation constitutes the self-in-community of all who are 'in Christ', thereby transforming the relational self into the ecclesial self.

Personhood, then, is bound up with relationality, and the fullness of relationality lies ultimately in relationship with the Triune God. Creating this relational fullness is the work of the Spirit, who places humans 'in Christ' and thereby effects human participation in the dynamic of the divine life. Moreover, being 'in Christ' entails participating in the narrative of Jesus, with its focus on the cross and the resurrection (cf. Rom. 6.1–14). This identity-constituting narrative, I would add, is a shared story—a communal narrative. Consequently, being-in-relationship with the Triune God not only inherently includes, but is even comprised by, being-in-relationship with those who participate together in the Jesus-narrative and thereby are the ecclesial new humanity. As the indwelling Spirit proleptically comprises the new humanity as the *imago Dei* after the pattern of the *perichoretic* life of the Triune God, the Spirit constitutes continually the 'self' of the participants in Christ's ecclesial community and, by extension, the 'self' of the world.

This relational and ecclesial self, whose identity and longevity emerges from its centredness in Christ, in whom all things find their interconnectedness, offers hope in the face of the loss of self articulated in Alanis Morissette's poignant song and experienced by sixteen-year-olds such as Aminah McKinnie. Against this backdrop, each year at Advent, we celebrate the coming of the one who alone can bestow true selfhood in every age, including our own—the age of cyberspace.

Notes

1   This essay is based on the author's longer work, *The Social God and the Relational Self: A Trinitarian Theology of the Imago Dei* (Louisville: Westminster John Knox Press, 2001). Previous versions of the essay have been published 'The Social *Imago*: The Image of God and the Postmodern (Loss of) Self', in *The Papers of the Henry Luce III Fellows in Theology*, VI, ed. Christopher I. Wilkins (Pittsburgh: Association of Theological Schools, 2003) and 'The Social God and the Relational Self: Toward a Theology of the *Imago Dei* in the Postmodern Context', *Horizons in Biblical Theology* 24:1 (June 2002), pp. 33–57.

2   For this report on the millennial generation, see Sharon Begley, 'A World of Their Own', *Newsweek*, 8 May, 2000, pp. 54–5.

3   Brendan Byrne, *Romans*, vol. VI of *Sacra Pagina*, ed. Daniel J. Harrington (Collegeville, Minn.: Liturgical Press, 1996), p. 268.

4   Jan Lambrecht, 'Transformation in 2 Cor 3.18', *Biblica* 64 (1983), p. 254.

5   Margaret E. Thrall, 'A Critical and Exegetical Commentary on the Second Epistle to the Corinthians', in *The International Critical Commentary*, eds J. A. Emerton, C. E. C. Cranfield and G. N. Stanton, II (Edinburgh: T&T Clark, 1996), p. 285.

6   A. M. Ramsey, *The Glory of God and the Transfiguration of Christ* (London: Longmans, Green & Co., 1949), p. 151.

7   James D. G. Dunn, *The Epistles to the Colossians and to Philemon*, New International Greek Testament Commentary (Grand Rapids: Eerdmans, 1996), p. 223.

8   Andrew T. Lincoln, *Ephesians*, Word Biblical Commentary 42 (Waco, Tex.: Word Books, 1990), p. 287.

9   Claus Westermann, *Genesis 1–11: A Commentary*, tr. John J. Scullion (London: SPCK, 1984), p. 192.

10 James B. Nelson and Sandra P. Longfellow, 'Introduction', in *Sexuality and the Sacred: Sources for Theological Reflection*, eds James B. Nelson and Sandra P. Longfellow (Louisville: Westminster John Knox Press, 1993), p. xiv.

11 Phyllis A. Bird, '"Male and Female He Created Them": Genesis 1.27b in the Context of the Priestly Account of Creation', *Harvard Theological Review* 74 (1981), p. 132 n. 8.

12 Bird, 'Male and Female He Created Them', p. 132 n. 8.

13 For a fuller explication of this view, see Stanley J. Grenz, *Sexual Ethics: An Evangelical Perspective*, 2nd edn (Louisville: Westminster John Knox Press, 1997), pp. 24–7.

14 For this descriptor, see Charles W. Morris, 'Introduction: George Herbert Mead as Social Psychologist and Social Philosopher', in George Herbert Mead, *Mind, Self, and Society, From the Standpoint of a Social Behaviorist*, ed. Charles W. Morris (Chicago: University of Chicago Press, 1932), pp. xi–xii. For a discussion of the genesis of Mead's move to social psychology, see Gary A. Cook, *George Herbert Mead: The Making of a Social Pragmatist* (Urbana, Ill.: University of Illinois Press, 1993), pp. 43–7.

15 Mead, *Mind, Self, and Society*, p. 138. For a similar characterization of Mead's position, see Paul E. Pfuetze, *The Social Self* (New York: Bookman Associates, 1954), p. 79.

16 Mead, *Mind, Self, and Society*, pp. 222–6.

17 For what may have been the initial use of this term as a Christological descriptor, see Gregory of Nazianzus, Epistle 101, in *Nicene and Post-Nicene Fathers*, 2nd Series, vii, ed. Philip Schaff (1894; repro. Peabody, Mass.: Hendrickson, 1995), pp. 439–43.

18 Catherine Mowry LaCugna, *God For Us: The Trinity and the Christian Life* (San Francisco: HarperSan Francisco, 1992), pp. 270–1.
19   Colin E. Gunton, *The One, the Three and the Many: God, Creation and the Culture of Modernity*, The Bampton Lectures 1992 (Cambridge: Cambridge University Press, 1993), pp. 6–7.

8

Sin and Grace

R. N. Frost

C. S. Lewis in *Perelandra*—a study of the Fall in the guise of a science fiction novel—conceived a temptation scene on paradisiacal Venus. An Eve-like first woman is invited to realize her individuality. The tempter is a demonic man who intrudes on virgin Venus to bring a wisdom already embraced on Earth. He gives her a small mirror to view herself. Self-love, he tells her, is necessary to build mature relationships among equals. The view of herself startles her: 'a fruit', she responds, 'does not eat itself, and a man cannot be together with himself.' The tempter has a ready reply:

'A fruit cannot do that because it is only a fruit,' said the Un-man. 'But we can do it. We call this thing a mirror. A man can love himself, and be together with himself. That is what it means to be a man or a woman—to walk alongside oneself as if one were a second person and to delight in one's own beauty. Mirrors were made to teach this art.'[1]

The temptation scene engages a critical metaphysical question in our study of sin and grace in a Trinitarian context: How does sin subsist in the soul? Is human self-love a critical feature of sin as Lewis suggests here? By adapting the story of the Fall to the myth of Narcissus he portrays sin as egoism in individuals and, implicitly, as anthropocentrism in society. Is he accurate? However that question is answered a second concern remains. Sin is the problem, but what of its solution? The Bible regularly treats sin and salvation in tandem, and the symmetry of Rom. 5.20—'but where sin increased, grace abounded all the more'—guides us to ask the correlative question as well: How is sin engaged and overcome by grace?

101

Evil and the Evil One

That evil exists is one of the great empirical realities of life. Sin as the applied expression of evil also serves as the pervasive context for the entire canon of Scripture, from Genesis 3 through Revelation 21. Yet the Christian axiom that God is neither the cause nor source of sin led theologians to dismiss any version of dualism as a solution to the twin questions of 'Whence and why sin?'

The fourth-century description of sin offered by Augustine of Hippo that holds it to be a privation of good has been the main answer to the problem of theodicy until now. In his conversion Augustine rejected the Manichaean belief in an eternal dualism of good and evil that once satisfied him. In its place he used the Christian axiom of divine impeccability as the basis for a syllogism. God's goodness and his role as creator of all that exists precludes any true existence of evil.[2] Sin, therefore—as the rejection of God's goodness—can only exist as a distortion rather than as substantial reality. Gluttony, for instance, is eating deprived of its proper function. Sin, then, is a reality based on distortion rather than on the basis of actual being:

> When all good is completely taken away, there will remain not even a trace—absolutely nothing. All good is from God; therefore no kind of thing exists which is not from God. Hence that movement of turning away, which we agree to be sin, is a defective movement, and a defect comes from nothing. Notice, then, what is its source and be sure it does not come from God. Yet, since the defect lies in the will, it is under our control. If you fear it, you must simply not desire it; if you do not desire it, it will not occur . . . But, though man fell through his own will, he cannot rise through his own will . . .[3]

However, as much as this solution allowed Augustine to avoid the Manichaean dualism of an eternal ontology of good versus evil, or, alternatively, of making God the author of evil, it did so by conceding relative autonomy to the human will.[4] In turn, it led to Augustine's most famous controversy when his solution was taken up by Pelagius. G. R. Evans notes the dilemma for Augustine that came from making the human will capable, of choosing the good: 'Grace need not come into the picture. Here lay the source of Augustine's embarrassment in later years. The Pelagians were able to point to the *De Libero Arbitrio* as a step on Augustine's part in their direction.'[5]

Augustine's early *privatio* theology implied that grace is an enabling gift that supports the viable will. Grace, in this view, is an intermediary feature in the divine–human event of salvation. Augustine, in holding to his view of original sin, recognized that this arrangement clashed with his deeper understanding that grace is actually God's *immediate* disclosure of his love that transforms the will. The will is viable only in response to God's revealed love. We will return to this critical feature below, but our review of Augustine's response to the Pelagians needs some additional development.

Augustine's revision took him back to the question of the will, which, in turn, offered a positive expression of sin, namely, a disposition to depart from God because of self-love (*amor sui, cupiditas*).[6] When Pelagius cited Augustine's *De Libero Arbitrio* in support of his own position, Augustine responded by writing *De Natura et Gratia*. This work displays two important aspects of Augustine's mature effort to explain God's solution to sin. First, he set out his case in favour of a real union with Christ. Second, he defined the cooperative relationship of nature and grace in affective terms—as God's compatibilistic solution to sin.

The doctrine of a real union with Christ was a necessary obverse in his solution to the Pelagian claim that nature and sin were qualitatively unrelated. That is, Pelagius argued, on the basis of Augustine's early doctrine of *privatio*, that because sin does not have any substance—it is merely a lack of goodness—then human nature must be free from any taint of material evil. An 'un-reality' is not transmitted from generation to generation and, by extension, there is no ontic basis for Adam's original sin to be passed on to his progeny. Each person is affected only by the evil of his or her individual sins.

Pelagius thus forced Augustine to enlarge his early position in light of the latter's belief, from Romans 5, that Adam's original sin had spread to all of humanity as moral death. Augustine re-examined the relations of nature and grace. Grace, he had always believed, is not 'in opposition to nature' but is that which 'liberates and controls nature'.[7] The question he was now forced to answer is how grace 'liberates and controls' nature when, in earlier writings, he had, indeed, affirmed that the will is free and sin is without substance. Thus, in an effort to clarify (if not to alter) the implications of *privatio*, he adopted an argument that affirmed sin as present within nature as a material distortion, without denying his earlier point that sin is alien to God's creation of nature.[8] He did this by affirming God's substance—which for him did not denote a concrete or material ontology—and the need for God's substance to sustain the human soul. He used the analogy of physical health: if a body is deprived of food, it fails; so in the Fall Adam and his progeny are deprived of God's presence and substance, and their spirituality fails.

> In the same way sin is not a substance; but God is a substance, yea the height of substance and only true sustenance of the reasonable creature. The consequence of departing from Him by disobedience, and of inability through infirmity, to receive what one ought really to rejoice in, you hear from the Psalmist, when he says: 'My heart is smitten and withered like grass, since I have forgotten to eat my bread.'[9]

The human free will is able to depart from God, but, in doing so, the sinner dies toward God as does his or her ability to return to God: 'He has need of a vivifier because he is dead.'[10]

More recent expositions of evil continue to view sin as a privation of good—a theology of evil as nothingness. Colin Gunton saw two main options in recent theology that seek, among other issues, to engage theodicy. He preferred Karl Barth's solution in contrast to the process theology of Charles Hartshorne, and I will follow Gunton's lead in looking to Barth as an initial conversation partner.[11]

Barth's discussion in the *Church Dogmatics* of *das Nichtige*—nothingness—adopts paradoxical language in order to avoid treating evil as if it were part of the creation.[12] That nothingness is a reality, yet without any being, is explained in the context of the privative tradition.[13] For Barth, evil does not exist except negatively and parasitically as a denial of God's grace, but within that context evil is a true reality beyond what some other privative theologians allow for. He rejects, for instance, the language of privation as it was offered by Leibniz, who in his *Theodicy* characterized evil as mere deficiency—the non-divinity of the creature—and thus not a 'positive' reality. This position, Barth argues, is a confusion of 'nothingness with the intracosmic antithesis or negative side of creation'. And as a result it offers no clear demarcation between the positive and the negative.[14] Barth, against Leibniz, points out the distinction in Augustine's original exposition of *privatio* between evil as a mere lack of goodness and evil as an active malignancy: 'For Augustine privation is *corruptio* or *conversio boni*. It is not only the absence of what really is, but the assault upon it.'[15] Barth similarly challenges Schleiermacher's antithetical consciousness of sin and grace as inadequately defining the reality of grace for it is set in a symmetrical opposition against a subjectivized consciousness of sin.[16] Grace, Barth argues, must be established in its own right, and it depends on a more profound understanding of Christology than Leibniz accepted or Schleiermacher developed.

How, then, does Barth explain the origin of evil in his own privative scheme of *das Nichtige*? He points to the realm beyond the boundaries of God's electing will as a region where evil finds freedom to exist. This realm of counter-reality has 'its own being, albeit malignant and perverse'.[17] Barth was thus led to criticize Schleiermacher for creating an implicit equivalence of sin and grace— 'It includes sin in the same category as grace, and thus esteems, justifies and even establishes it as the counterpart and concomitant of grace.'[18] Grace is an eternal reality, not a mere counterweight to evil. It is, of course, in the contrast of sin and grace that we experience grace as sinners, but grace does not rely on sin to exist. Nor is Schleiermacher's sphere of human subjectivity an adequate arena for grace:

> In this sphere [of Schleiermacher's religious consciousness], therefore, the threat of sin, the nullity of nothingness and the glory of grace could not be seen in their reality, i.e., in their encounter and history, but only in a peace, which is really spurious, and not the peace of God that passes all understanding.[19]

Barth's own sphere, in which nothingness 'is real', is not simply in the subjective realm but, in a greater way, within the reality of God's creative and elective purposes: 'God elects, and therefore rejects what He does not elect. God wills, and therefore opposes what He does not will.'[20] This evil-being is God's *opus alienum*, subject to his 'jealousy, wrath and judgment' because it is 'adverse to grace, and therefore without it'. It exists as sin, evil and death.[21]

However, Barth's paradoxical language of 'sin as the concrete form of nothingness'[22] emphasizes evil in its tangible expression—as the behaviour of those who are adverse to grace. Here it is useful to return to the underlying privative paradigm that Augustine adopted after the Pelagian controversy exploded. God's saving work is conceived by Augustine in relational terms, so that his anti-Pelagian treatise *On Grace and Free Will* emphasized the social features of the soul as the crucial context for examining sin and salvation. For him sin is a loss of love for God—the 'hardened heart'—and grace is God's love brought to the soul by the Spirit himself.[23] The question of how the soul sins and comes to righteousness, then, does not begin with human behaviour— matters of law, law-breaking and law-keeping—but with motivations that exist in the context of community, first in responding to God and then in loving others.[24] It is the adultery of the heart, the lust for human glory, the idolatry of greed, and the careless self-absorption of pride that Jesus condemns. The behavioural dimensions of sin are merely barometric indications of the hurricane of death that destroyed and destroys human hearts through their desire to be like God.

How, then, does God's own being, existing as an eternal communion of three persons, reveal the nature of sin and grace? Sin, if viewed in terms of a relational Trinity, points to a more pervasive sort of violation than is usually recognized by theologians who embrace some form of substance theology, and with it, a preference for moralistic spirituality. The antithesis of substance metaphysics and relational metaphysics is a central insight of Trinitarian theology—and the basis for identifying evil. David Cunningham properly speaks of the enthusiasm among Trinitarian scholars for the 'category of "relationality"'. Relationality is pitted against the Greek perception of God as an essence or as an 'isolated, passionless monad', which is common in Western theology.[25] In this view, to use Robert Jenson's description, we perceive the self as 'a monadic entity, a self-possessed, closed unit'. Jenson addresses this substantialist version of self as it applies to God by pointing to the perspectival distinctions that must apply to God's relational existence as person and as persons. Any notion that an 'identity and personality are correlated one to one' undermines the relational reality of Trinitarianism. 'But when the Trinity is regarded as in *one way* personal, and Father, Son, and Spirit as in variously *other ways* personal, then Father, Son, and Spirit can be fully acknowledged as persons and also interpreted as poles in the Trinity's personal life.'[26]

The importance of these distinctions to our discussion of sin is revealed in God's purpose for creation, and subsequently in the manner in which evil seeks to deprive that purpose from its proper application. The matter rests on how God offers himself to us in relationship, and that depends in turn on who God is in himself. If, as in substance metaphysics, he is a singular essence with either three modes or three personal centres of expression, then as those created as the *imago Dei* we must engage him symmetrically, as singular, self-possessed, closed units. If, on the other hand, 'God is not personal in that he is triunely self-sufficient' but 'he is personal in that he triunely opens himself',[27] we are then called to engage him in the relationship he offers. Sin rejects that call. It is the refusal to engage him in terms of who he is and how he loves—the denial of his grace.

Helmut Thielicke's Trinitarian critique of Western theology extends the antithesis of substance versus relationship metaphysics, but he shifts it from the realm of ontology to that of epistemology, an argument that he adopts and enlarges from Barth.[28] Rather than accept the conventional rhetoric of his day that pitted liberal theology against conservative theology, he held instead that Christian theology is divided by Cartesian and non-Cartesian theologies. His historical analysis creates strange bedfellows—from the pietist Spener to the demythologizing Bultmann—whom he holds together as Cartesians, as those who believed that theology is the task of engaging God as individuals who are finding a way to the Person of God, as centres of rational consciousness—as *cogito*, *ego*, or the *autos* of autonomy—coming to him as the ultimate rational being. Their common quest is to seek God as distinct individuals, with an ambition for subjective assurance and to appropriate the benefits God offers. Their starting point is the human subject and their desire is to appropriate from God whatever God allows, 'whether in a very lofty, profound, and unintentional way the kerygma is put under man's control, so that in the last analysis theology is reduced to a mere chapter in anthropology.'[29]

The non-Cartesians, on the other hand, are those who find God seeking them in the Word: 'The Spirit's testimony does not just point us away from the self and its pre-conditions and activities.' Theology shifts its direction from anthropocentrism so that 'The Spirit orients us to Christ'.[30] Furthermore, it is God's intrinsic relationality that 'kindles fervent love within us' as the Spirit reveals God to us 'as a lovable object'.[31]

The essence of sin, then, is a privation of relationship rather than a particular behaviour or even a breach of covenant between 'individuals' in the fashion of a self-concerned Cartesian contract. It is, instead, to reject God's love as revealed in Christ and as witnessed by the Spirit. Luther concluded 'that this is the sin of the world that it does not believe on Christ. Not that there is no sin against the law besides this; but that this is the real chief sin, which condemns the whole world even if it could be charged with no other sin.'[32]

Luther, by his placing all of sin, and any moral laws, within a single relational context, reflects a basic consensus among the Trinitarian theologians we have considered. For Augustine, Barth and Thielicke, with Luther included, sin is defined relationally. The essential ontology of God and humanity—the *imago Dei*—is relational in the sense that it is characterized by the bond of mutual love. As such there is no qualitative or quantitative ontic gap between the Creator and the creation as there must be if a metaphysic of substance is used. Augustine's—and Barth's—guiding premiss in defining evil as privation is that it must be viewed relationally. If, for instance, we restate Augustine's clarification of his *privatio* doctrine (after he encountered the Pelagian response) in terms of the antithesis 'substance versus relational metaphysics', we can identify his consistent insight to be this: evil is the loss of God's Spirit-presence in the soul, with particular sins consisting in the expression of that autonomy. Sin, in other words, is human 'freedom' from God's loving rule. So, too, the 'nothingness' of Barth's *das Nichtige* expresses the assertion of Jesus in John 15.5 as *the* ultimate moral absolute: 'for apart from me you can do nothing'.

A relational review of the status of spiritual 'death'—a perpetual conundrum—will sharpen the point being made by certain Trinitarian theologians. Various seemingly disparate salvation traditions, including Pelagians, Arminians and Reformed, all differ over the status of human initiative in the event of salvation while still sharing the basic Cartesian axiom. That is, some human disability or limitation is affirmed by all groups, and in practical terms, the strongest of these is a belief in the total incapacity of death. If humans somehow have a hand in choosing God in an 'act' of faith, some capacity for initiative must be present prior to salvation. Solutions that have been used hold that sin's 'death' is resolved or mitigated by common grace (e.g. the Pelagians); by baptismal grace (the Catholic tradition); and/or by 'created' or 'effectual' grace that is infused before the act of faith. These all, in effect, presume a hypostatic addition to the rational-volitional soul—a view rooted in substance metaphysics. The result is a set of cooperative versions of salvation that vary only over the question of whether the enabling hypostatic grace is given conditionally or gratuitously.

If, on the other hand, the Spirit himself is the full expression of God's grace—by his coming to the soul to re-establish the broken love relationship—we discover salvation to be the very life of God entering the spiritually 'dead' soul, i.e. our being 'born of the Spirit'. This was a central issue at the beginning of the Protestant Reformation and remained so until theologians of both the Lutheran and the Reformed traditions—in large numbers—reacquired the pre-Reformation concepts of hypostatized grace and/or the anthropology of substance based on an individual free will.[33]

Sin and the Grace of God

The death–resurrection symmetry of sin and salvation thus required a restoration by the presence of God's very life, the foundation for a doctrine of real union. Augustine's solution was twofold, juridical *and* ontological: God justifies the ungodly *and* frees the person from an absolute enslavement to sin.[34] This transformation represents God's relational presence yet without it being a presence of fused-ontology, a matter reinforced by Augustine's caveat that his solution is not a deification of nature.[35] Yet the creature, while incommensurate to the creator in essence, may still be united with him on the basis of a relational metaphysic of mutual love. This is achieved by the Spirit, who is 'poured out' into the believer's life to save and transform.

Human relationality, then, is brought to birth on the basis of God's 'being as communion',[36] a notion that needs to be engaged, if only in outline. Recent discussions of human ontology, such as that offered by Oliver Davies, have traced a number of competing ontologies. The relational ontology we have traced so far is best described in terms of an 'I-and-other' relationality—aligned with Davies' category of an ontology of being as accessed through both the self and the other.[37] The Trinity, for instance, requires the Father to have another—the Son—in order to exist as Father, and vice versa. The Spirit consists in his relation of communication and communion as he 'searches' and expresses the depths of the persons in whom he resides. The bond of these 'economic' relations requires both their distinctions—sustained 'otherness' as in the Father always existing as Father—and their basis of union in love. Augustine, for instance, spoke of the Father as 'lover', the Son as the 'beloved', and the Spirit as the 'love' that binds the Father and the Son as one. Each is engaged, biblically, with the qualities of a person, but only as persons-in-relation, rather than as separate centres of individual identities. So, then, Adam and Eve were created in God's image as the male–female unit. And before the Fall, their common bond was God's very presence in them by his own Spirit. In the Spirit's departure at the moment of their rebellion they lost the presence of the one who is 'life' and were, therefore, truly dead towards God. Their bond of love was broken, with God and in some measure with each other.

The question of how life is to be lived in grace, then, must centre on our love: whether or not we have become lovers of God or remain autonomous agents. It is only in the restoration of relationship with God through his initiative of bonding love in the Spirit that 'grace' exists. A single Bible text, Rom. 5.5, was used repeatedly by Augustine to make this point, and to establish the framework for an affective solution: 'For the love of God has been poured out in our hearts through the Holy Spirit who was given to us.'[38]

But, in order to clarify the historical claims being made in this chapter, what should be made of Augustine's continued use of the language of the individual will, God's enablement, and human cooperation even after he confronted Pelagius? In Augustine's exposition of these points, he frequently used the language of enablement and cooperation, which did much to foster the subsequent claims that he espoused a cooperative model of salvation and sanctification. Yet, his repeated application of Rom. 5.5 dispels any notion that it was in terms of a free will in purely volitional terms. Instead, it was a compatibilistic view of nature controlled by grace through the revival of the affections. That is, the continuing impact of the Spirit's love enables believers to live in response to God—reciprocating God's love:

> Thus the beginning of love is the beginning of righteousness; progress in love is progress in righteousness; great love is great righteousness; perfect love is perfect righteousness . . . Yet wherever and whenever it becomes complete, in such a way that nothing can be added to it, it is certainly not 'poured forth in our hearts' by the powers of nature or the will that are within us, but 'by the Holy Spirit who is given to us', who both helps our weakness and cooperates with our strength. For this is the very 'grace of God by Jesus Christ our Lord', to whom, with the Father and the Holy Spirit belong eternity and goodness, for ever and ever. Amen.[39]

Conclusion

In the story of *Perelandra* Lewis captured an aspect of the Trinitarian theology of relations. The temptation of the Eve-like first mother of Venus was to be invited to a theology of individualism—to be a person who related by means of equivalence and cooperation rather than in absolute dependence. The contemporary obsessions of Western civilization suggest that the 'gift' of a mirror may well be the best metaphor for sin—as in the apparent account of the satanic fall in Ezek. 28.17—'Your heart was proud because of your beauty; you corrupted your wisdom for the sake of your splendour.' The gaze of faith can only be on one who exists as our eternal 'other'—on Jesus, the author and finisher of our faith—so that the solution to the Fall is found not in a mirror but in magnifying the Other, who in turn reveals his Father to us; and all of this by the presence of the Spirit, who is our life and love.

Notes

1 C. S. Lewis, *Perelandra* (New York: Macmillan, 1944), p. 137. The function of a mirror-image, as in the myth of Narcissus, is a common metaphor for evil self-absorption. See e.g. Marguerite Shuster, *The Fall and Sin: What we have Become as Sinners* (Grand Rapids: Eerdmans, 2004), p. 34. She, in turn, cites the work by the seventeenth-century English bishop Jeremy Taylor, *Holy Living* (Oxford: Clarendon Press, 1989), p. 91.

2 See e.g. Augustine, *Confessions* 7.12–13.

3 Augustine, *De Libero Arbitrio* 2.20.54, in Augustine, *The Problem of Free Choice*, tr. Dom Mark Pontifex (London: Longmans, Green & Co., 1955), p. 137.

4 The notion of privation, as we shall see below with Barth, is widely held. Cf. G. C. Berkouwer's position that 'Sin is not "material" but is parasitic on creaturely reality' and a 'deformation' of God's good creation: *Sin* (Grand Rapids: Eerdmans, 1971), p. 261.

5   G. R. Evans, *Augustine on Evil* (Cambridge: Cambridge University Press, 1982), p. 113.

6   G. Vandervelde, *Original Sin: Two Major Trends in Contemporary Roman Catholic Reinterpretation* (Amsterdam: Rodopi N.V., 1975), p. 27; cf. Evans, *Augustine*, p. 95. Vandervelde's introduction, pp. 1–54, includes a survey of this development. See, concerning the affections and the will, Augustine's discussions of sin in his *Confessions* in which love shapes the will by its desires, e.g. 8.5, 'I was quite sure that it was better for me to give myself up to your love [*tuae caritati me dedere*] than to surrender to my own lusts [*cupiditati*].' Cf. *The Problem of Free Choice*, 1.16.34.

7   Augustine, *Retractions* 2.42, tr. P. Holmes, in *Nicene and Post-Nicene Fathers* (*NPNF*), 1st series, v, ed. James Donaldson and Alexander Roberts (Edinburgh: T&T Clark, 1886), p. 116. Cf. Evans, *Augustine*, p. 128.

8   Augustine, *On Nature and Grace* 80, tr. P. Holmes in *NPNF*, 1st series, V; p. 67.

9   Augustine, *Nature and Grace* 21–22; pp. 19–20.

10 Augustine, *Nature and Grace* 25; p. 23.

11 Colin E. Gunton, *Becoming and Being: The Doctrine of God in Charles Hartshorne and Karl Barth* (Oxford: Oxford University Press, 1978). A broader but overlapping review of ontological traditions is offered by Paul S. Fiddes, *The Creative Suffering of God* (Oxford: Oxford University Press, 1988), pp. 13–15.

12 Karl Barth, *Church Dogmatics*, III/1, *The Doctrine of Creation*, ed. G. W. Bromiley and T. F. Torrance (Edinburgh: T&T Clark, 1958).

13 See Oliver Davies, *A Theology of Compassion: Metaphysics of Difference and the Renewal of Tradition* (Grand Rapids: Eerdmans, 2001), pp. 49–55.

14 Karl Barth, *Church Dogmatics*, III/3, *The Doctrine of Creation*, ed. G. W. Bromiley and T. F. Torrance (Edinburgh: T&T Clark, 1960), pp. 316–17.

15 Barth, *Church Dogmatics*, III/3, p. 318.

16 Barth, *Church Dogmatics*, III/3, pp. 320–4.

17 Barth, *Church Dogmatics*, III/3, p. 352.

18 Barth, *Church Dogmatics*, III/3, pp. 332–3.

19 Barth, *Church Dogmatics*, III/3, p. 334.

20 Barth, *Church Dogmatics*, III/3, p. 351.

21 Barth, *Church Dogmatics*, III/3, pp. 353–4.

22 Barth, *Church Dogmatics*, III/3, pp. 308–10.

23 Augustine, *On Grace and Free Will* 30–1, tr. P. Holmes, in *NPNF*, 1st series, V, pp. 30–1. Augustine engages Ezek. 36.26–7, representing God as speaker, promising that the human 'heart of stone' will be replaced by 'my Spirit within you'.

24 Augustine, *On Grace and Free Will* 33 (p. 17), speaks of martyrs as those who displayed 'great will', which Augustine immediately restates to be a 'great love'. This launches a six-chapter excursus (34–9) on the Spirit's love as God's transformative agency in the salvation of the elect.

25 David S. Cunningham, *These Three are One: The Practice of Trinitarian Theology* (Oxford: Blackwell, 1997), p. 25.

26 Robert W. Jenson, *Systematic Theology*, I, *The Triune God* (Oxford: Oxford University Press, 1999), p. 123; italics in original .

27 Jenson, *Systematic Theology*, I, p. 124.

28 Helmut Thielicke, *The Evangelical Faith*, I, *Prolegomena: The Relation of Theology to Modern Thought-Forms*, tr. Geoffrey W. Bromiley (Grand Rapids: Eerdmans, 1974), pp. 53–4. Barth's discussion is in *Church Dogmatics*, I/1, *The Doctrine of the Word of God*, ed. G. W. Bromiley and T. F. Torrance (Edinburgh: T&T Clark, 1975),

pp. 197, 214–27; cf. Geoffrey W. Bromiley, *Historical Theology: An Introduction* (Grand Rapids: Eerdmans, 1978), ch. 30.

[29] Thielicke, *The Evangelical Faith*, I, p. 53.

[30] Thielicke, *The Evangelical Faith*, I, p. 132.

[31] Thielicke, *The Evangelical Faith*, I, p. 134.

[32] Martin Luther, *Sermons of Martin Luther: The Church Postils*, III (Grand Rapids: Baker, 1983), p. 139.

[33] For recent studies that trace these shifts, see R. N. Frost, 'Richard Sibbes' Theology of Grace and the Division of English Reformed Theology' (unpubl. Ph.D. diss., University of London, 1997) and Gregory B. Graybill, 'The Evolution of Philipp Melanchthon's Thought on Free Will' (unpubl. D.Phil. diss., University of Oxford, 2002).

[34] Augustine, *On Nature and Grace* 29, p. 26.

[35] Augustine, *On Nature and Grace* 37, p. 33.

[36] For an exposition of the Nicaean Trinitarian tradition and the Cappadocian ontology of relations, see John D. Zizioulas, *Being as Communion: Studies in Personhood and the Church* (Crestwood, NY: St. Vladimir's Seminary Press, 1985). Zizioulas, however, arguably overstates the evidence offered by the Cappadocians. A stronger case may be made that Augustine's relational ontology is the basis for this view. On Augustine's contribution see J. N. D. Kelly, *Early Christian Doctrines*, 5th edn (London: A. & C. Black, 1977), p. 274, and Fiddes, *The Creative Suffering of God*, p. 139 n. 105.

[37] Davies, *A Theology of Compassion*, p. 49.

[38] Augustine, *On Nature and Grace* 49 (p. 42); 67 (p. 57); 70 (p. 60); 77 (p. 64); 79 (p. 66).

[39] Augustine, *On Nature and Grace*, 84; p. 70.

9

The Sinlessness of Jesus:
A Theological Exploration in the
Light of Trinitarian Theology[1]

Demetrios Bathrellos

The ruler of this world is coming, and he has nothing in me. (John 14.30)

Introducing the Problem

Until the early nineteenth century, the sinlessness of Jesus had generally been a self-evident certainty, implicitly or explicitly asserted by virtually all forms of Christian theology in all Christian Churches.[2] It was then that Edward Irving put forward the view that Christ bore a fallen, sinful humanity. As a result, Irving was condemned for heresy and excommunicated by the Presbyterian Church of his day.

Irving was at that time a lonely voice. His view, however, was to be adopted by some of the most reputable theologians of the twentieth century, for instance Karl Barth and Dietrich Bonhoeffer. The way in which the latter formulated his views concerning the humanity of Christ is remarkable. For Bonhoeffer,

> liability to sin and self-will are an *essential* part of our flesh. Christ became involved in the predicament of the whole flesh. . . . He is man as we are; he is tempted on all sides as we are, indeed far more dangerously than we are. In his [Christ's] flesh, too, was the law that is contrary to God's will. He was not the perfectly good man.[3]

Are the views expressed by Irving, Barth, Bonhoeffer and others justified? In this article, I will attempt to tackle this question in the light of Trinitarian theology as it pertains to Jesus' personal identity and his place in the Trinity.

113

The Personal Identity of Jesus

The divine identity of Jesus was clarified during the Arian and Nestorian controversies of the early church. In the fourth century, in attacking the Arian heresy, the Council of Nicaea (AD 325) declared that Jesus Christ is *homoousios* with the Father. Jesus Christ is not a temporal, mutable, imperfect creature, but 'true God of true God', as the Council's creed put it.

In the fifth century, the unity of Christ's person was further clarified: there was no human person in Jesus Christ alongside God the Logos. Nestorius was condemned at the Third Ecumenical Council (held in Ephesus in 431) because he undermined the unity of the person of Christ. Cyril, his main opponent, won the day by arguing that Jesus is personally identical with the Son of God, the second person of the Trinity. This view encapsulates a theological point of the utmost importance. Our saviour is not a mere man, assisted and enabled by God, but God himself.[4] Jesus Christ—whose name we bear, whom we worship, and for whom we are called to live and to die—is the incarnate Son of God. His humanity is fully united with his divinity in one person. His human birth, life and death are those of 'one of the Holy Trinity'.

This means that the human life of Jesus cannot be seen outside the context of the Son's relationship with the Father and the Spirit. Jesus' humanity shares in the life of the Trinity. The Father sent the Son to the world. The Son became man of the Holy Spirit and the Virgin Mary. At his baptism, the Spirit descended upon him and then led him to the wilderness to be tempted by the devil. The Son came to do the will of the Father. His death was the result of his submission to the Father's will. Eventually, God raised him from the dead.

It is impossible to understand Jesus and his sinlessness unless we know who he really is. And we cannot know this unless we also look at his relationships with the Father and the Spirit, which condition both his being and his acts.

The 'Nature' of Sin and the Humanity of Jesus

Sin must not be understood primarily in forensic terms, for instance as the transgression of divine law. It must be seen primarily in relational terms. Sin primarily consists in parting company with God. Likewise, salvation is the result of the re-establishment of this relationship.

Sin, therefore, implies a broken relationship with God. But this brokenness goes far deeper than its external manifestations in human action. Human sinfulness consists first of all in a deep ontological, existential and structural deformation and depravity of man's very being. It is this deep, existential and ontological captivity to sin that is subsequently expressed in sinful activity. Sinful activity, in turn, reinforces human depravity and alienation from God.

This understanding of sin had been quite typical of Christian thought until the rise of modernity. In modern times, the Socinians (who, interestingly, were notable for their anti-Trinitarianism) seem to have been the first to criticize the church's teaching on original sin as unsustainable and to reduce sin to sinful action. According to this new understanding, which came eventually to prevail in (secular) modernity, sin was identified with sinful acts that were products of man's free will. Therefore, a person should be characterized as virtuous or sinful exclusively on the basis of those acts that are products of his free will. No one is a sinner, unless he has freely committed sinful acts.[5]

Only such an understanding of sin makes it possible to attribute a fallen/sinful human nature to Christ and still claim that he was not a sinner by reason of not having committed any sinful acts. But, as we have seen, this view is seriously flawed. It overlooks the fact that we are sinners not only because we commit sinful acts, but also because we are ensnared in the sinful 'law of the flesh'—in the passions of pride, unfaith, self-love, avarice, concupiscence and lust, to mention but a few—which lead us to sin. It overlooks the fact that our alienation from God affects not only what we do but also what we are, and that salvation, which is coterminous with the re-establishment of our relationship with God, consists not only in changing our acts but also in changing ourselves. Sin and salvation affect not only the fruits of the tree, but also the tree itself!

The Double Failure of Nestorianism

Patristic and conciliar Christology proclaimed that Jesus Christ is hypostatically identical with God the Logos, who is 'one of the Holy Trinity'. His humanity shares in the life of the Trinity, because it is the humanity of God the Son. This sharing, which the Greek Fathers called 'deification' or *theosis*, is the corollary of the hypostatic unity between the divinity and the humanity of Christ. This unity was so deep that it profoundly affected Christ's humanity. It healed it and made it sinless and holy from the very moment of Jesus' conception. In Jesus Christ we see humanity redeemed; we see the real, authentic man, the image and likeness of God.

The Nestorians, however, thought differently. As we all know, they put forward a loose unity between God the Logos and his humanity. But what is less well known is that they also entertained the view that Christ bore a sinful human nature. So, Nestorius, for instance, argued that 'For this [cause] also he [Christ] took a nature which had sinned . . . he had all those things which appertain unto our nature, anger and concupiscence and thoughts, and although also they increased with the progress and increase of every age [in his life], he stood firm in thoughts of obedience.'[6]

Similar views were put forward by Theodore of Mopsuestia, who has been characterized as the spiritual father of Nestorianism, at least by the decisions of the Fifth Ecumenical Council (AD 553), which condemned him not only for dividing Christ but also for claiming that

> Christ was troubled by the passions of the soul and the desires of human flesh, was gradually separated from that which is inferior, and became better by his progress in good works and faultless through his way of life . . . and . . . became after the resurrection immutable in his thoughts and entirely without sin.[7]

For the council, Theodore's Christ was not the incarnate Son of God who came to the world as our redeemer, but a sinner, himself in need of redemption. The 'double failure' of Nestorianism—namely its claim that Christ was both loosely united with God and a sinner—must come as no surprise, simply because sinfulness is the result of separation from God and, therefore, is understandably part and parcel of Nestorian, divisive Christology.

A Pseudo-Chalcedonian Objection

Sometimes the objection is raised that the position that the human nature of Christ was sinless is at odds with Chalcedonian Christology. According to the logic of the objection, Chalcedon pointed to the fact that Christ should be as truly and fully human as we are, and this, so the objection goes, inevitably entails that he must have borne a sinful human nature as we all do.

This objection arises from a theologically valuable sensitivity to avoid any latent Christological docetism that would remove Christ from our human condition and thus run the danger of eliminating any relevance that his human life and death may have had for us. But the objection attempts to avoid this danger in the wrong way. In fact, there are three problems with it. First, it is historically mistaken. The Council of Chalcedon had nothing to do with justifying the view that Christ bore a sinful humanity. On the contrary, its definition makes it clear that Christ did *not* assume our sinfulness.

Second, the objection turns Christ into a sinner. As Oliver Crisp has justifiably argued, to say that Christ has a fallen nature means that he also bears original sin and is sinful, which is fatal to the argument.[8] Indeed, to turn Christ into a sinner is a cost that Christian theology cannot afford.

Third, the objection implies a false understanding of human nature. Sin is *not* a defining characteristic of human nature. If this were the case, only sinners would be real human beings—Adam before the fall, or the saints in the eschatological kingdom, would not be. If being a real man means being a sinner, then given the relational understanding of sin outlined above, alienation from God and authentic humanity would be coterminous. However, this is not a tenable theological position, but a worn-out claim of modernity.[9]

In fact, we would go so far as to reverse the above-mentioned claim and say that authentic humanity is humanity in God. Humanity cannot be thought of as something complete and self-contained prior to and independently of God—let alone against him. Unity with God *is* a defining characteristic of authentic humanity, without which the latter is not what it really is. This is why sin, which consists exactly in alienation from and in opposition to God, does not make us more but less human. Sin is a privation that distorts and minimizes our humanity.[10] Christ was fully and authentically human, not in spite of the fact that his humanity was sinless, but because of it. Christ was not a sinner. What he assumed, he sanctified and redeemed. He redeemed our nature, not our sinfulness. In him, *we* are justified, not our sin.

Jesus' Engagement with Our Sinfulness

Although his humanity is not sinful, Jesus is deeply involved in the predicament of our sinfulness. This claim will be developed in a fourfold manner.

First, Jesus' sinless nature was deeply affected by some of the consequences of the Fall. St John of Damascus articulated clearly a distinction between blameless (sinless) and blameworthy (sinful) consequences of the Fall. He argued that hunger, thirst and weariness, for example, are natural and blameless passions resulting from the Fall.[11] These do not turn their bearer into a sinner. The sinful passions, by contrast, do. Jesus would have been a real man even if he had assumed our nature without its post-lapsarian blameless passions. However, he assumed our blameless/sinless passions so that he might share fully in our tragedy and pain. He chose to be 'similar to us in everything, sin apart'.

Second, Jesus was born in a fallen and sinful world. He lived under the same conditions as we do. He was faced with the various forms of evil that dominate this world and with the pain and suffering that they impose upon their victims.

Third, Jesus was not an isolated individual. Although it is a mistake to say that he bore a universal human nature (in which case both his particularity and his sinlessness would be compromised), he still somehow took upon himself the sin of the world and thus saved us from it while remaining sinless in being and act.

Fourth, Jesus died. He underwent death, which is the result of sin, in spite of his being without sin. In all these ways Jesus was engaged with our sin; he shared deeply in the tragedy of our fallen lives, while remaining free from sin and by implication able to redeem us.

A False Argument for Jesus' Sinlessness: The Roman Catholic Doctrine of the Immaculate Conception

In his foreword to Thomas Weinandy's book *In the Likeness of Sinful Flesh*, Colin Gunton made the point that if the Roman doctrine of the Immaculate Conception is accepted, then one has to accept also the view that the humanity of Christ (taken of Mary) was of necessity sinless.[12]

Gunton was right in arguing that the doctrine of the Immaculate Conception leads to the sinlessness of Christ. But this is a doctrine that we should not and need not use to this end. We should not use it simply because it is mistaken. And we need not use it, because the sinlessness of Christ does not depend upon it. It will suffice for the defence of the sinlessness of Christ to argue with Gregory of Nazianzus that 'the unassumed is unhealed, but what is united with God is saved'. Our salvation is due to the unity of our humanity with God, and not to Mary's alleged Immaculate Conception.

The question of Christ's sinlessness, however, involves other parameters beyond those related to his humanity. One of these is related to his temptations. Very often, behind the view that the humanity of Christ was sinful, stands the assumption that this is a necessary condition for the uncompromised reality of his temptations. The following section will counter this assumption.

The Sinlessness of Jesus and His Temptations

Scripture makes it clear that Christ was tempted. However, if he had a sinless, non-fallen nature was it possible for him to be tempted? Or do we have to accept that he had a fallen nature, if we are to take his temptations seriously?

In attempting to answer this question, we need to nuance our discussion by distinguishing between temptations arising from within a person, and others coming from outside. Only the former presuppose that he who is tempted bears 'the law of the flesh' and thus 'is tempted by his own [sinful] desire', as James writes (Jas. 1.14). As long as one bears a sinless nature, one is only tempted by outside sources.[13] If, however, a temptation arises from within him, he will be immediately stained by sin, even if he does not succumb to the temptation.

What is of particular interest for our topic is that being tempted from outside does not compromise the reality of the temptation. Eve was tempted from outside (by the serpent, as the story has it) *before* the Fall, and fell as a result of succumbing to the temptation. Needless to say, the temptation would have been equally real if it had been rejected. Turning to Christ, we do not have to postulate that he bore a sinful nature in order to safeguard the reality of his temptations. Christ was tempted, not by any sinful desires of his own, but by the devil and by sinners (for instance, the Pharisees).

The fact that the temptations of Christ originated from outside him, however, does not mean that they were always present only in their external, objective form without being experienced subjectively. In some cases, there was a point of contact between the external origin of the temptation and Christ himself. For instance, in his first temptation in the wilderness, the devil appealed to Christ's hunger, whereas in Gethsemane his predicament was related to the natural desire for life and aversion to pain and death. These points of contact, however, did not link with sinful dispositions or desires in Jesus, but with human sinless desires, which lead to actual sin only if misused. In the examples just mentioned, hunger and natural love for life (and aversion to pain and death) were the two sinless desires of Jesus, which would have led to actual sin if they had been fulfilled independently of God's will and in opposition to it.

However, could this ever happen? Namely, could Christ ever sin? Is it the case that Christ could sin but eventually did not, or do we have to believe that Christ could not sin anyway? Which one of the two versions of Christ's sinlessness is theologically valid, the *non posse peccare* or the *posse non peccare*?

The *non posse peccare* and *posse non peccare* Dilemma

Jesus Christ is the Word of God incarnate. By definition God cannot sin , even in an incarnate state.[14] Given that God the Logos incarnate is the unique personal subject not only of his divine but also of his human acts, he could not sin. The possibility of Christ's sinning would exist only if there were in Christ a double (divine and human) personal agency. This, however, would split his personal unity by introducing a second, personal principle of willing and acting alongside the Logos. In other words, given that the Logos cannot sin, if Jesus could sin, then Jesus could will differently from and independent of the Logos, and could sin in opposition to God the Logos. The Nestorian flavour of this view is obvious.

Christ cannot do certain things because of the kind of person he is. However, a person is who he is because of his relationships. The fundamental relationships of Christ, who is 'one of the Trinity' in the flesh, are those with the Father and the Spirit. This relational identity of Christ also makes it impossible for his humanity to will and act in a manner that is independent of God and potentially sinful. Christ's human desires, decisions, acts of willing and actions were those of the incarnate Son, who is in constant and unbroken communion with the Father and the Spirit.

What has just been said is related to Christ's human moral perfection. The humanity of Christ was a holy humanity. Christ was the 'mature' and eschatological Adam, to recall Irenaeus. His humanity is the highest possible embodiment of holiness that has ever existed and will ever exist, because its unity with God the Logos and its relationship with the Father and the Spirit is the closest possible. His unwavering stability in the good is an indispensable characteristic of his moral perfection—the possibility of opting for evil is a sign of moral weakness, to say the least. However, in Christ there is no moral weakness whatsoever. Christ is free from both actual and potential sin.

But how can it be that Jesus' *non posse peccare* does not compromise the reality of his freedom? The first thing to say in response to this question is that Jesus possesses human freedom. The tradition has been very clear on this. Let us only recall the insistence of St Maximus the Confessor and the Sixth Ecumenical Council in the seventh century on the existence of a human self-determining will in Christ, an insistence that safeguarded and expanded Chalcedon's emphasis on the integrity of Jesus' humanity on the level of his human volition. The fact that Jesus could not sin does not presuppose a lack of a human will or its suppression by the divine will. Jesus' sinlessness is due to the fact that he freely submitted his human will to the divine will of the Father.[15]

The view that the human freedom of Jesus is compromised by the fact that he could not sin presupposes a mistaken understanding of freedom. According to this understanding, the possibility of sinning is a determining characteristic of freedom. But neither actual nor potential sin is a determining characteristic of freedom. If this were so, God, who cannot sin, would not be free. But if, by contrast, authentic human freedom is the kind of freedom that reflects God's freedom, a person who cannot sin is freer than a person who can.[16] Freedom even from potential sin is an eschatological gift already present in Jesus.[17]

Moreover, a proper understanding of Jesus' freedom must have as its starting point its relational character. Jesus' freedom was in no way the freedom of an independent human individual that stands opposite God, as modernity may have it. Nor is it conditioned upon its actual or potential opposition to divine freedom. Authentic human freedom is freedom in God, not against him. To say the opposite would imply a dualism which has engendered worn-out arguments for atheism. Christ's human freedom is conditioned by his loving relationship with God the Father and the Spirit.[18] This is not a negation but an affirmation and perfection of human freedom.

However, the view that Christ's freedom was conditioned by his being the incarnate Son of God and by his relationship with the Father and the Spirit does *not* suggest a deterministic understanding of Jesus' life. It is not freedom, or self-determination, or the possibility of choosing that is excluded from Christ but only the possibility of choosing evil. But as Paul Helm has argued, 'since in theory there may be more than one "sinless" choice in a given set of moral circumstances, we do not have to adopt a strict determinism in order to account for Christ's non posse peccare'.[19] And furthermore, as Jacques Dupuis has claimed, 'Jesus exercised genuine freedom of choice as to the course of action through which he would best fulfil his mission. It must be stressed that Jesus invested in such choices an extraordinary sense of initiative, invention, and responsibility. Nor was scope for such choices wanting'.[20]

Finally, the view that Jesus could not sin is deeply in conformity with the biblical narrative. The opposite view makes our salvation merely accidental. According to it, Christ may well have failed to redeem us, in which case he would have been defeated by sin and the devil. But this contradicts the whole thrust of the biblical narrative, in which God's promises and the prophecies point to the coming of the Messiah and the establishment of the eschatological kingdom.[21] If the *non posse peccare* is denied, the promises of God and the prophecies would be at best only potentially true overstatements and at worst just false. But this is not tenable.[22]

But what about Jesus' temptations? If we accept that Christ could not sin, can they be taken seriously?

The Impossibility of Christ's Sinning and the Reality of His Temptations

It is certain that we should compromise neither the sinlessness of Jesus nor the reality of his temptations. The only legitimate theological option available to us is to understand the temptations of Christ in a way that does *not* compromise his sinlessness. This means that we should exclude certain forms of temptations—temptations for instance that arise as a result of having sinned in the first place or temptations that have their origin in a sinful passion already present. However, a sinless person, even a sinless person that is not able to sin, can experience the severest of temptations. How can this be so?

The view that the possibility of sinning is a *sine qua non* for the reality of temptations is mistaken. People are often tempted to do things they are *not* capable of doing. Nevertheless, this does not necessarily diminish the intensity of their temptations. However, there is another reason why the reality and intensity of the temptation may have nothing to do with the possibility of succumbing to it. This is that the possibility of succumbing to a temptation does not depend (only) on its intensity (the more intense a temptation, the more likely one is to succumb to it) but also on the person tempted. So a person with a weak and sinful will may succumb to a very weak temptation; he may even sin without being tempted and, in fact, without 'reason'. On the other hand, a person whose will is conditioned by his relationship with God may well remain stable even in the face of the fiercest temptation. Coming now to Christ, the fact that he could not sin does not mean that he was not tempted or that he was not tempted severely enough. It simply means that he was the Son of God in the flesh, directing his sanctified human will towards the fulfilment of the will of the Father, with whom, as well as with the Spirit, he was in a continuous unbroken relationship.

Let us briefly see how this is exemplified in Jesus' life. Jesus was tempted to turn the stones into bread in the wilderness in order to satisfy his hunger. The fact that he did not, would not, and could not do it, was not due to the fact that his temptation was either unreal or weak (he had fasted for forty days after all!). The reason was that his will was conditioned by his relationship to the Father and the Father's will. As he himself said to his disciples after his discussion with the Samaritan woman, 'my food is to do the will of him who sent me and to finish his work' (John 4.43). Christ was so devoted to his mission to fulfil the will of the Father that any possibility of deviation had to be excluded, and any of his natural (sinless) desires had to be satisfied only in a way that would be compatible with the Father's will.[23]

If we move on to Christ's temptation in Gethsemane, we will discern the same pattern. The fact that Christ was determined to obey the will of the Father did not make either his fear less real or his agony less severe. Jesus' prayer in Gethsemane expressed the wish that things could take a different course, but only with the crucial proviso that God the Father would allow this to happen. It would be both textually and theologically arbitrary to conclude from his prayer to the Father that Jesus ever oscillated between obeying or disobeying him. Christ only asked whether the will of the Father for our redemption could be fulfilled in a way that would not require his passion, without this ever implying any possibility of his disobeying him.[24]

Epilogue

One of the severest temptations of theology, particularly in modern times, has been to take for granted the data of our own thought and experience and then attempt to adjust our understanding of God, Christ, man and the world to our own *Vorverständnis*. Indeed, if man is to be defined on the basis of our own experience, namely the experience of the Fall, sin, and separation from God, then 'we are bound to say that unfallen man or man restored by redemption is not properly speaking "man" but something of a super-man'.[25] The question of Christ's sinlessness will be more appropriately approached if we avoid constructing him in our image and after our likeness, and if we let him, the incarnate, beloved Son of the Father, be the exemplary prototype of our humanity and of our freedom.

Notes

1   I would like to thank the members of the Research Institute in Systematic Theology at King's College London, who heard an earlier version of this paper and made useful comments. I would like to thank in particular Dr Paul Metzger and the Revd. Professor Andrew Louth for reading an earlier draft of this paper and making helpful suggestions. I gratefully mention Professor Colin Gunton, with whom I repeatedly discussed aspects of its content, and who contributed so substantially to my theological education.

2   The only exception to this rule is Nestorianism, for which see later in the chapter. Kelly M. Kapic mentions also the eighth-century Spanish Adoptionists, but here again we have a divisive Christology. Attempts made by modern theologians to read into the Fathers of the church the view that Christ bore a sinful humanity are clearly mistaken. For such an attempt, see T. F. Torrance, *The Trinitarian Faith: The Evangelical Theology of the Ancient Catholic Church* (Edinburgh: T&T Clark, 1988). For treatments of the question of whether Jesus bore a fallen or non-fallen human nature, see Kelly M. Kapic, 'The Son's Assumption of a Human Nature: A Call for Clarity', *International Journal of Systematic Theology* 3 (2001), pp. 154–66, and Oliver Crisp, 'Did Christ have a *Fallen* Human Nature?', *International Journal of Systematic Theology* 6 (2004), pp. 270–88.

3   Dietrich Bonhoeffer, *Christology*, tr. John Bowden (London: Collins, 1966), p. 112 (emphasis mine). A detailed presentation of the theologians who espouse views similar to those of Irving, Barth and Bonhoeffer would not essentially contribute to the tackling of the central questions of this article and is therefore beyond its scope.

4   Although Jesus is not a human person, he does possess a human will, which he freely submitted to the Father's will.

5   For an informative treatment of the notion of sin and its development in modernity, see Wolfhart Pannenberg, *Systematic Theology*, II, tr. Geoffrey W. Bromiley (Edinburgh: T&T Clark, 1994), pp. 231–75.

6   Nestorius, *The Bazaar of Heracleides*, tr. and ed. G. R. Driver and Leonard Hodgson (Oxford: Oxford University Press, 1925), p. 63. There are some doubts regarding the authenticity of the first part of *Heracleides* (pp. 1–86), but the views expressed in our quotation are typically Nestorian.

7   See N. P. Tanner, *Decrees of the Ecumenical Councils*, I, *Nicea 1 to Lateran 5* (London: Sheed & Ward/Washington, DC: Georgetown University Press, 1990), p. 119. I have slightly modified Tanner's translation.

8   I have no time to go into more detail, so I point the reader to his article, 'Did Christ Have a *Fallen* Human Nature?'

9   Barth is wrong in claiming that by assuming a fallen (in the sense of sinful) humanity God established solidarity with us. This is erroneous, for the simple fact that sin is not relational but anti-relational. It cannot be used as a basis for solidarity and relationship, for it is precisely their perversion and destruction. For Barth's view, see

Karl Barth, *Church Dogmatics*, I/2, *The Doctrine of the Word of God*, ed. G. W. Bromiley and T. F. Torrance (Edinburgh: T&T Clark, 1956), p. 152.

[10] Therefore, to say that Christ bore a sinful humanity is *anti*-Chalcedonian in that it minimizes the humanity of Jesus.

[11] St John of Damascus, *Exposition of the Orthodox Faith* 2.12; PG 94, 1081b. It is noteworthy that for St John the sinful passions are *not* natural.

[12] Colin E. Gunton, 'Foreword', in Thomas Weinandy, *In the Likeness of Sinful Flesh: An Essay on the Humanity of Jesus* (Edinburgh: T&T Clark, 1993), pp. x–xi.

[13] St John of Damascus makes this point; see *Exposition of the Orthodox Faith* 2.12; PG 94, 1081b.

[14] Swinburne's argument that God would never put himself in a position in which he could sin is theologically sound. See Richard Swinburne, 'Could God Become Man?', in *The Philosophy in Christianity*, ed. Godfrey Vesey (Cambridge: Cambridge University Press, 1989), p. 67.

[15] For more on this, see my book *The Byzantine Christ: Person, Nature, and Will in St Maximus the Confessor* (Oxford: Oxford University Press, 2004).

[16] An understanding of freedom as something to which we are called and which is achieved through our being set free *from* sin (and not *for* sin) is undoubtedly biblical (for some relevant biblical references, see, for instance, John 8.34–6; 2 Cor. 3.17; Gal. 5.1, 13); in the last resort, to be set absolutely free from sin means to be set free even from the possibility to commit sin. Pannenberg mentions Augustine's view that 'the will that cannot sin at all is more free than the will that can either sin or not sin', *Systematic Theology*, II, p. 258 n. 287.

[17] Adam, being good but not yet perfect, did not enjoy this perfect state of freedom, which characterized only Christ.

[18] Colin E. Gunton, in *The Promise of Trinitarian Theology*, 2nd edn (Edinburgh: T&T Clark, 1997), p. xxvi, quotes from the British Council of Churches report on Trinitarian doctrine, which points out that obedience is not always 'a mere external relation', but can also be 'a hearing stemming from love': British Council of Churches, *The Forgotten Trinity*, I, *Report of the BCC Study Commission on Trinitarian Doctrine Today*, ed. Alistair Heron (London: British Council of Churches, 1989), p. 33.

[19] Quoted in T. A. Hart, 'Sinlessness and Moral Responsibility: A Problem in Christology', *Scottish Journal of Theology* 48 (1995), pp. 53–4.

[20] Jacques Dupuis, SJ, *Who Do You Say I Am? Introduction to Christology* (New York: Orbis Books, 1994), p. 133.

[21] It is noteworthy that, as Jaroslav Pelikan, for instance, has remarked, in Judaism 'the immutability of God was seen as the trustworthiness of his covenanted relation to his people in the concrete history of his judgement and mercy, rather than as a primarily ontological category': *The Christian Tradition: A History of the Development of Doctrine*, I, *The Emergence of the Catholic Tradition (100–600)* (Chicago: University of Chicago Press, 1975), p. 22. Doubtless, God's immutability, reliability and trustworthiness stand or fall with the consummation of the economy of our salvation in Jesus Christ.

[22] Actually, the impossibility of Christ's sinning must be seen not only in moral but also in epistemological terms. If Jesus Christ is *God* revealing to himself, the possibility of his revealing us a false picture of God must also be excluded.

[23] In saying this, I focus more on Christ's humanity, which implies a low Christology. However, at the same time we must stress again, from a high Christology, that this humanity was moved by God the Word for the fulfilment of our salvation, in a way

that neither compromised his human self-determination nor could ever have allowed for the slightest deviation. In Christ, there was a perfect communion and 'synergism' between the divine and the human that guaranteed both his freedom and his sinlessness.

24 Trevor Hart's suggestion ('Sinlessness and Moral Responsibility', pp. 53–4) that Jesus' temptations would be real only if he did not know that he could not sin is not helpful. Christ knew that he could not sin because he knew who he was; and yet, his temptations were real. It can even be said that the knowledge that there is no possibility of succumbing to a temptation can make temptations more, not less, severe; but I have no time at present to go into this in more detail.

25 John D. Zizioulas, 'Human Capacity and Human Incapacity: A Theological Exploration of Personhood', *Scottish Journal of Theology* 28 (1975), p. 401.

10

The Atonement

Georg Pfleiderer

The Atonement as the Essence of Christianity, and the Task of Trinitarian Theology (in Homage to Colin E. Gunton)

'Atonement' is, as its syllables indicate, the process of an unification of persons, (individuals or groups) who were separate from each other—separate mostly in an unfriendly sense. Therefore, 'atonement' (in Greek *katallage*) in this general and quite profane sense means turning enemies into friends. There are similar expressions in the semantic field with mostly stronger cultic ('religious') connotations, like 'reconciliation', 'propitiation' or 'salvation'; however, 'atonement', as it is attributed to the relationship between God and human beings and represent the whole semantic field, can be understood as the essence of Christianity.

The Bible identifies no comprehensive or clearly dominant concept for understanding 'atonement'. The actual plurality of notions and concepts, by which the New Testament continues the Old Testament, challenged later theologians and church leaders to find systematic concepts able to unify this variety of biblical understandings. However, if we survey the history of these theological attempts to develop a coherent theory of atonement which integrates the plurality of New Testament ideas, imageries and theological interpretations, we have to agree with Robert W. Jenson 'that no theory of atonement has ever been universally accepted. By now, this phenomenon is itself among the things that a proposed theory of atonement must explain.'[1] This phenomenon should be reflected in the systematic structure of such a theory.

Colin E. Gunton gives a fine example of such an integrative theory in his book *The Actuality of Atonement*.[2] This theory develops from the general epistemological consideration that the gap between biblical vocabularies—the religious, or sometimes even mythological imagery, metaphors and traditions that New Testament authors use to describe the atonement realized in and by Jesus Christ—and conceptual theological theories (as developed throughout the history of Christianity) is in fact not as deep as modern theologians usually assume. On the contrary, Gunton suggests that a metaphoric element grounds every theological doctrine. This metaphorical foundation is an—if not the—essential characteristic of the specific structure of theological knowledge.

But which metaphors should we choose to depict the work of atonement realized for us by God in Jesus Christ? Gunton concentrates on three key metaphors: victory, justice and sacrifice. Each of them is already present in the New Testament, but are just three among several others. The prominence of at least two of them results from their support of atonement theories which became influential in different periods of church history. Following a famous article by the Swedish theologian Gustav Aulén (published in 1931),[3] Gunton recalls that the metaphor of 'victory' was the key metaphor for a concept of atonement which had its peak of influence in the early centuries of Christian theology, especially in the East. 'Justice' can be understood as the key metaphor of the leading Western theory of atonement during the Middle Ages and even longer, as seen in the doctrine Anselm of Canterbury developed in his book *Cur Deus Homo* (written between 1093 and 1097).

With the metaphor of 'sacrifice', things become difficult; 'sacrifice' seems to be already implied through the other two, raising doubts about whether it is actually a metaphor on its own. Nevertheless, referring as it does to the phenomenaon of cult as the centre of (ancient) religion, the connotations of 'sacrifice' differ significantly from the military semantic field of 'victory' belongs to and also from the area of justice.

'Sacrifice' is connected with the area of culture for which the symbolic structure of acting, and therefore the linguistic figure of the metaphor, seems to be significantly more characteristic and important than for the others. The essence of a sacrifice is that it stands for something other than itself; the essence of sacrifice is a symbolic—but not less 'real'—representation. This might have been the precise reason why understanding the meaning and 'functioning' of sacrifice became difficult in modernity, as Gunton notes.[4]

How can one entity, especially how can one individual, 'really' represent others without replacing them? How can Jesus Christ die for us and our sins? This is indeed the most striking intellectual problem typical modern thinkers have always had with the Christian doctrine of atonement.[5] Therefore, quoting J. S. Whale, Gunton declares: 'In our modern world sacrifice has become a mere figure of speech', a 'dead metaphor.'.[6] In this precise and critical way, the metaphor of sacrifice is in Gunton's approach connected with the age of modernity.

Gunton's idea of framing the plurality of biblical and Christian concepts of atonement by a typology is in fact not a new proposal. Nineteenth-century theologians used to distinguish between objective and subjective theories of atonement. Gunton's typology stands in critical opposition to this distinction, as he is convinced that the fundamental interest of every doctrine of atonement must be to conceive it as both objective and subjective (even if many theories emphasize more the one or the other). Indeed, Gunton claims that the three metaphors he stresses refer to theories that have both aspects.

Does Gunton's approach bear more similarities to the oldest and most famous predecessor of such typologies, for example the doctrine of the three offices of Jesus Christ as it was outlined by theologians of the Reformation like Andreas Osiander and especially John Calvin? In the important *Catechism of Geneva* and in the different editions of his *Institutes of the Christian Religion*, concerning Jesus Christ, Calvin distinguished between the offices of the prophet, the king and the priest. He understood these three functions as the central elements of the work of the Messiah as he is described in the Old Testament.[7] Modern historical exegesis and theology has often argued that this typology finds insufficient support in New Testament theologies.[8] Nevertheless, it was taken up by such famous and dissimilar theologians as Friedrich Schleiermacher[9] and Karl Barth.[10] Gunton's approach can be understood as an interesting continuation and systematic variation of those remarkable theories of atonement, especially of the latter. Compared with Barth's concept, Gunton not only takes into account historical criticism (of the classical doctrine of the three offices), but also makes systematic use of a theory of metaphor and makes it a metatheoretical claim, as his typology refers to both the imagery of the New Testament and the history (of the theory) of theology.

Gunton's doctrine of atonement, in common with Barth's, holds that the threefold typology actually structures the theory of atonement as such and in its entirety. However, one of the structural differences between them is that in the *Church Dogmatics* Karl Barth finds a systematic explanation for the threefold typology. It is provided by the doctrine of the Trinity, which stands behind soteriology, but in connection with two Christological doctrines: the two natures of Christ and the two states of Christ. The result is a complex and artistic dialectical structure, which cannot be unfolded here.[11] In short, the soteriological aspect of Christ as a priest is (dialectically) related to the work of the Father (Christ as true God, *vere Deus*); the image of Christ as a king is related to the work of the Son (Christ as true human being, *vere homo*); the metaphor of Christ as the prophet is connected with the work of the Holy Spirit, namely with its function of announcing and mediating reconciliation towards us (Christ as the true witness).

Gunton's theory of atonement also makes links to the doctrine of the the Trinity. These links are however stressed to a lesser degree and are more contingent than in the *Church Dogmatics*. Gunton interprets the metaphor of victory, but in a way also the metaphor of justice, as related to the work of the divine Father in creation, namely to 'creation in general'.[12] The metaphor of sacrifice seems to be linked more closely to the divine Son, but also to the Holy Spirit, because this metaphor makes atonement understandable as a process by which creation is not simply restored but—as Irenaeus has already regarded it—completed towards a 'perfected creation'.[13] Gunton is obviously more hesitant than Barth was to unfold a theory of atonement in such a strict and elaborate Trinitarian way. This hesitancy probably has to do with his basic consideration that theology is founded on metaphors and not on logical concepts, and must therefore not be conceived as a strict system.[14] Nevertheless, on the one hand, a closer analysis of Gunton's argumentation would show that there are in fact certain conceptual ideas behind the selection and interpretation of the three metaphors.[15] On the other hand, there is the problem that a metaphorical typology, conceived in a completely non-conceptual way, seems to become an 'idea [which indeed] rather has a more poetic [or historic] than a dogmatic value'.[16]

Therefore, I would very much like to combine the fundamental insights of Gunton with some structural elements of Barth's systematic approach. That is, I propose to take up Gunton's typological use of metaphor, but unfold it in a way that allows it to link up consistently with the three aspects of the doctrine of the Trinity. In this respect, the doctrine of the Trinity can function as the grammatology of the key theological metaphors of atonement. In what follows, I will try to show how this approach yields not a merely formal and artificial framework, but rather a conception that can throw some analytical light on the understanding of these key metaphors. As such, it should be able to relate them to three fundamental questions every doctrine of atonement should be able to answer:

1. What does it mean to say that it was God and only God, God the creator, who could be the subject of atonement in the events of the death and resurrection of Jesus Christ?
2. What does it mean to say that the atonement in Jesus Christ is actually unique, 'objective', universal, and effective for all who let themselves participate in it?
3. What does it mean to say that atonement—although it is unique, objective, universal and effective—is still ongoing, particular, and very often not obviously effective?

Answering these three questions demonstrates how the doctrine of Trinity is an intellectual testimony to the essentially Christian experience that 'in Christ we encounter no one else but God, the real God and really God'.[17]

Towards a Theory of the Atonement from the Perspective of a Trinitarian Metaphorology

The Protological Perspective: Atonement as the Constitutional Act of an Order of Life—'Victory'

One strong notion of atonement already to be found in the New Testament in respect to the soteriological function of Jesus Christ is the picture that Jesus has power over the demons (Matt. 12.24, 27, 28; 17.18; Mark 1.34, 39; Luke 11.14; Jas 2.19. According to the religious ideas of antiquity, demons were transcendent powers—some good, some evil—exerting influence on human beings by guiding or even possessing them. In individuals, they were believed to cause illnesses. In a more general sense, demons could also be understood as various types of (transcendent) powers; political principalities, for example, could be interpreted as a result or even an incarnation of demonic power (Col. 1.16).

In the religious context of antiquity, which is in this respect similar in the Bible, a force which was able to threaten and even dominate the demons and the transcendent powers could be either divine or satanic, as Satan was believed to be the master of the demons (Matt. 12.24). According to the Gospels, the force or power in Jesus obviously was divine because it was combined with other manifestations of divine sovereignty, namely his close relationship with his divine Father and his forthcoming kingdom, as well as his powerful preaching, his healing of the blind and the lame, and his fellowship with the poor and the outsiders of society.

Frequently, when the Gospels depict Jesus expelling demons who were terrifying and torturing individuals, the coming of the kingdom of God and the atonement Jesus proclaimed and incorporated is revealed as something which is not merely peaceful; it is revealed as a powerful and therefore violent struggle against the potent forces which resist it (Matt. 10.34). In patristic theology, especially in the more popular theologies of the early centuries, this idea was taken up into a full-fledged conception of atonement. Either Christ's descent to hell was interpreted as his victorious fight against the underworld, or the incarnation and death of the immaculate Son of God was understood as an instrument of a divine trick on Satan, who swallowed the immaculate unlawfully and therefore had to set him free, as well as all his captors with him. Thus, in such conceptions, the atonement is understood as the impact and gift of the dramatic, and also as a victory of the essentially good God over the demonic powers of evil.

This model, which Aulén called the 'classic type of atonement',[18] is dualistic. In its logic there are absolutely no rules to which the two parties of the deadly warfare agree. There is, so to speak, no world-order behind this battle except the battle and the agreement to fight the battle itself. From the perspective of systematic theology, this dualistic character—and not so much its mythological background and 'setting'—is its chief flaw; it places God and Christ on one side of the conflict. Why is this a flaw? Because it results from a logical and a moral contradiction. The interior, logical or even formative contradiction is that the conception in fact presupposes a *just* world-order, namely one that makes God good and Satan evil, whereas during the conflict, the *just* world-order is actually suspended. Moreover, it is merely power, and not the interior, supremely moral quality of God, through which God overwhelms evil. This is the second contradiction. In this model, the good power defeats the evil force with its own weapons. However, this would mean that God accepts the rules of evil, which are war and not peace, hate and not love. These logical but also moral contradictions are particularly evident in the idea of a divine trick on the devil, which has always made the model most difficult to 'swallow' for the more analytically oriented and modern mind.

Nevertheless, these specific flaws and contradictions can also be understood as resulting from a fundamental strength of this conception. As such, as logical inconsistencies, they indicate that the atonement must indeed be understood as the effect of a divine power which transcends all rules, exactly for the reason that nothing but omnipotent divine power constitutes all rules; it produces and provides the ground for an order of life; it founds its structures, forms and rules of interaction; it makes life possible.

Here, the affinity of that conception to the Trinitarian aspect of God, the creator, becomes visible. Setting the grounds for an order in which life, peaceful life, is possible, is the first attribute and work of the Trinitarian God; as such, it is also the basic idea of atonement. Turned into an ethical perspective, one can say that the atonement provided in Jesus Christ, with its power of a new creation, overcomes 'structural evil' in all its potential forms and disguises—estrangement, self-estrangement, unjust structures in the political and social orders of societies—which seem beyond the reach of individual actions.

The Christological Perspective: the Atonement as the External and Contingent Order of Life—'Justice'

In the classic model of atonement, God proves his omnipotence by demonstrating his absolute sovereignty under the conditions of every system of social order, be that the order of peace and love, or of hate and war. If this analysis is true, then we have to admit that there is, in fact, a hidden order or at least a rule which guides God's sovereign action; it is the rule 'to pay like with like'. This is the idea of distributive justice. Atonement or reconciliation means nothing else but the installation, or the reinstallation, of this rule as the divine order of life. It is radically different from chumminess. This is the basic idea of Anselm of Canterbury. We can understand Anselm's theory of the atonement as an attempt to explain how distributive justice can logically be understood as the absolute, divine law of reality and life even though life seems constantly to contradict its validity.

On this basis and compared with the classic model, Anselm's theory of atonement has three fundamental advantages (1) It conceives sin and evil as the violation of the fundamental law of distributive justice and therefore in the same moment as a breaking of the relationship between human beings and God. (2) This includes the absolute fatality of sin: as sin breaks the rule of all (good) action of finite beings, no finite act is able to reinstate the rule.[19] (3) Therefore only God as the sovereign and guarantor of all order is able to reinstall the validity of distributive justice.

Nevertheless, Anselm's basic idea that *Deus-homo*,[20] the God-man and only the God-man, is able to 'pay' for the sins of the sinners—to offer satisfaction on behalf of sinful mankind and for their favour—has serious structural flaws. First, it actually replaces its initial understanding of sin as a breaking of the order of justice by the metaphorology of taking something away, stealing something (namely 'honour'). Secondly, sin is therefore not an absolute fatality anymore, but a relative loss. Third, for the same reason, with regard to the interior logic of the 'mechanism' of atonement, God becomes the object; he receives satisfaction as a gift provided to him by his Son (the God-man). Fourth, in reconciliation, the order of distributive justice therefore remains something external to human beings and their self-understanding. They are in the order of distributive justice by their participating in the species of human beings, but this participation is not the aspect of their life which needs reconciliation; rather, it is the one aspect that does not need reconciliation.

These structural flaws may be understood to follow from a replacement of metaphors which happens in Anselm's model without his noticing—a replacement of the legal metaphorology of justice (and social relationships) by a metaphorology of material property,[21] if not of finance.[22] In my opinion, this is indeed the case. But why does this replacement happen? I would like to suggest a 'strong' reason: it happens because in some manner there actually is a structural affinity between those two metaphorologies; they both refer to 'external' aspects of social relationships. But atonement/reconciliation will only happen if people are able to internalize the law. True reconciliation is not only to be conceived as the act of reinstalling the social order (of justice); it is also the act which makes individuals actually capable of acting rightly. Atonement only happens where people are able to internalize the law to act morally.

Nevertheless, the precise external character of law and justice concerning social relationships is also the strength, the grain of truth, of Anselm's model. First, it hints at the fact that a genuine change of interior attitudes and behaviour, which is the aim and result of true atonement, is not possible without, so to speak, input from 'outside'. It is a fundamental Christian conviction that sin is so deep and indeed burdensome that it cannot be overcome by a new way of thinking. This remains simply wishful thinking, if it does not refer to an 'external' reality as the condition of its possibility—the mere facticity of God in Jesus Christ understood as the actual overcoming of the sin and self-estrangement of humanity.

Second, the 'weight' of sin is its actual 'facticity'. It is in fact not simply a violation of a general rule of behaviour, but does real harm to real individuals (even myself). The change of attitudes so central to subjective atonement models cannot compensate for the damage that has happened in the past: it does not bring the victims to life again. There is an ontological, metaphysical deficiency in the (modern) stress on the essentially subjective and 'internal' (and moral) character of the atonement. The Christian tradition has referred to this deficiency by speaking of Jesus Christ as the eschatological judge. Thus, the 'rational' and universal order of distributive justice becomes transparent in virtue of the necessity that it is itself founded on the external, actual and contingent—but nevertheless universal—act of God's reconciliation in Jesus Christ. Therefore, 'justice' as a metaphor of atonement represents the Christological element of the Trinity.[23]

The Pneumatological Perspective: The Atonement as The Internal and Symbolic Order of Life—'Sacrifice'

While the metaphor of 'victory' refers to the 'vital' fundamental element of human life (which is the power of creation) and the metaphor of 'justice' refers to the rational and nevertheless contingent form of life as social life, the metaphor of 'sacrifice' stands for the internal principle and procedure of human life which is symbolic, cultural communication. The essence of all such communication is signification. We cannot communicate with one another or with God without using signs, symbols and metaphors. However, as a genuine, religious metaphor, 'sacrifice' does not simply affirm the symbolic and metaphorical character of human life but reflects it in a critical way. The essence of the sign is to be destroyed, deciphered, to release its meaning: 'unless a grain of wheat falls into the earth and dies, it remains but a single grain; but if it dies, it bears much fruit' (John 12.24). This is the first notion.

The second notion stemming from the metaphor of 'sacrifice' is that all cultural communication is partly based on the contingency of utterance and understanding. There is no guarantee that the other party understands what I want to say. That is contingent; it is a gift, that is, if communication occurs. It is exactly this contingency to which the metaphor of sacrifice refers: there is—spoken within the logic of the biblical metaphor—no causal relationship between the grain falling into the ground and its fruitfulness. We have to sow it—but we also have to let it grow. We have to expose ourselves to misunderstanding if we want to be understood. This is exactly the miracle of communication— the miracle of understanding each other despite the fact that we are different from one another. The miracle that we can develop individual perspectives and life-styles and still live in communicative relations with each other—this is, if it happens and wherever it happens, according to Christian beliefs the work of the Holy Spirit (cf. Acts 2). This is the third and final aspect of atonement—it is redemption.

In its reference to the semiotic structure of human life and reality, the metaphor of 'sacrifice' also reveals that all attempts to unfold and explain the atonement as the event on which human life as such is based appear to result in contradiction. This is not a flaw peculiar to the specific historical models being discussed here, nor to the theological interpretation of reality in general; it rather shows that all metaphors are indeed self-contradictory. The atonement understood as 'sacrifice' reflects the fact that all our intellectual theological interpretations are themselves metaphorical suggestions of the reality beyond them, which can only be experienced by their mediation. The Protestant theological tradition spoke of the *media salutis* (mediations of salvation—the Divine Word (the Scripture), the sacraments (baptism, Eucharist), and the church—by which the living and resurrected Jesus Christ becomes present to us.[24]

The Atonement, The Trinity and Human Life

Following Colin E. Gunton, we have taken three metaphors as key soteriological metaphors, representing three different models of atonement and three different periods in the history of theology. The analysis of these three theories of atonement shows that each of them connects its interpretation of reconciliation to a fundamental element of human life as communicative life: its vital ground, its rational external rules, and its internal semiotic structure. According to Christian belief, in all these dimensions human life is dependent upon salvation. According to Christian belief, atonement or reconciliation is actually provided for human life in all its dimensions. This is what a Trinitarian-structured doctrine of atonement seeks to elaborate.

If these observations and arguments are true, what follows from them for a present-day theology of the atonement? It follows that such a theology should try to balance these three elements equally. An equal balance seems to be attainable, if the theological understanding of atonement accounts for the systematically central character of the metaphor of sacrifice.[25] The Christian understanding of the metaphor of sacrifice starts with the acknowledgement that the sacrifice of the cross makes all human sacrifices—cultic and otherwise—unneccessary and redundant (cf.. Heb. 10.10–14). It has provided all cultural acts of signification with an unambiguous sense of meaning. Given Jesus Christ's personal sacrifice on the cross at Golgotha, all our cultural acts of significance express that we are set free to be human.

Notes

1. Robert W. Jenson, *Systematic Theology*, I, *The Triune God* (New York: Oxford University Press, 1997), p. 186.
2. Colin E. Gunton, *The Actuality of Atonement:. A Study of Metaphor, Rationality and the Christian Tradition* (London and New York: T&T Clark, 1988; repr. 2003).
3. Gustav G. Aulén, 'Die drei Haupttypen des christlichen Versöhnungsgedankens', *Zeitschrift für Systematische Theologie* 8 (1931), pp. 501–38.
4. Cf. Gunton, *The Actuality of Atonement*, pp. 115–20.
5. For example, Fausto Sozzini and the Socinians in the sixteenth and seventeenth centuries, Kant in the eighteenth century, and David Friedrich. Strauss in the nineteenth century; cf. G. Wenz, 'Geschichte der Versöhnungslehre', in *Der Evangelischen Theologie der Neuzeit*, 2 vols. (Munich: Chr. Kaiser Verlag, 1984, 1987).
6. Gunton, *The Actuality of Atonement*, p. 115.
7. Calvin's argument was that prophets, kings and priests were the (only) persons anointed with the holy oil: cf. *Institutes of the Christian Religion*, 1.2.15.
8. A precise critique and very specific reformulation of the doctrine was given by Albrecht Ritschl in his *Die Christliche Lehre von der Rechtfertigung und Versöhnung*, 2nd improved edn, III (Bonn: die positive Entwickelung der Lehre, 1883), pp. 386–403. Recently, Wolfhart Pannenberg has renewed the criticism of the doctrine of the three offices of Jesus Christ, arguing that 'the idea rather has a more poetic than a dogmatic value, as it can hardly be proved to be a necessary expression of the content of the meaning of the history of Jesus': *Systematische Theologie*, II (Göttingen: Vandenhoeck & Ruprecht, 1991), p. 493.
9. Cf. Friedrich Schleiermacher, *The Christian Faith*, paras 102–6.
10. Karl Barth, *Church Dogmatics*, IV/1–3.
11. See Eberhard Jüngel, 'Einführung in Leben und Werk Karl Barths', in *Ökumenische Theologie*, IX, *Barth-Studien* (Zurich and Cologne: Gütersloher Verlagshaus, 1982), pp. 22–60, esp. p. 55.
12. Gunton, *The Actuality of Atonement*, p. 149.
13. Gunton, *The Actuality of Atonement*, p. 154.
14. Although this rejection of theology as a (closed) system was also one of the fundamental convictions of Karl Barth, of his *Church Dogmatics* in general, and the doctrine of atonement as its core element in particular, it is in fact structured intensively by such a conceptual frame, which is indeed derived from the doctrine of the Trinity.
15. As I see it, this has to do with the question of natural (victory => power!) and ethical (justice!) order in general ('creation') and the question of its particular and historical realization (the atonement as a Christological and pneumatological process).
16. Pannenberg, *Systematische Theologie*, II, p. 493.
17. B. Oberdorfer, 'Man müsste sie erfinden. Die Trinitätslehre ist kein überflüssiges Dogma, sondern ein Fenster zum Himmel', *Zeitzeichen* 5:8 (Aug. 2004), p. 56 (my translation).
18. Aulén, 'Die drei Haupttypen', p. 537.
19. Anselm explains this structural asymmetry of good and evil human acts by the idea that all good acts human beings ever can do are as such demanded by God. Therefore,

it is impossible to recompense even one evil act by a multitude of good acts: 'Si me ipsum et quidquid possum, etiam quando non pecco, illi debeo ne peccem, nihil habeo quod pro peccato reddam' Anselm, *Cur Deus Homo* 20.

20   Anselm, *Cur Deus Homo* 6.

21   Cf. the famous description of the 'weight' of sin: 'Nondum considerasti quanti ponderis sit peccatum': Anselm, *Cur Deus Homo* 21.

22   This might reflect the rise of an economy of money as the beginning of early capitalism. The slide from the first to the second metaphorology might have happened because Anselm conceives social relationships also in the metaphorology of honour, which can be understood in a personal, but also in a quasi-material sense (to harm somebody's honour—to damage it).

23   The connection is therefore based on the observation that law – justice – always faces the problem of validity and acceptance. Despite its claim for rationality (natural law), its actual validity is based on external physical force. Every law is in fact positive law. This irreducible tension of its universal claim for validity and acceptance and its actual positive character is the link between the structure of justice and Christology.

24   Cf. H. Schmid, *Die Dogmatik der evangelisch-lutherischen Kirche dargestellt und aus den Quellen belegt*, ed. H. G. Pöhlmann, 9th edn (Gütersloh: Gütersloher Verlagshaus, 1979), pp. 319–93.

As mentioned above, I would indeed dare to assert that it is modern theology and soteriology in particular in which those aspects of atonement referred to by the metaphor of sacrifice become essential for the interpretation of reconciliation as such. The ordinary notion of the modern history of the atonement is that it is strongly infected by ethically oriented tendencies. Indeed, the Socinian criticism of the interior logic of sacrifice and representation leads in the thinking of Kant and many of his theological followers to an ethically oriented (and in this sense anthropological) concentration and reduction of the doctrine of the atonement. Nevertheless, it was this ethical concentration that also brought the idea of Jesus' free act of self-dedication, his consequent obedience, and therefore his *ethical* conduct of representation without replacement, into the focus of interpretation. As Luther, Hegel and Barth observed, divine self-alteration is the essential structure of atonement. For Albrecht Ritschl and Wilhelm Herrmann, and also for Rudolf Bultmann, Friedrich Gogarten and Dorothee Soelle, self-dedication, and in this sense representation, is the core of soteriology. These are all attempts to reformulate the idea of 'sacrifice' without falling into the trap of a simple replacement of human beings by Jesus Christ or the trap of making God an object of reconciliation.

25   The reason for the difference between this systematic perspective and the exegetical results is that a systematic interpretation can use 'sacrifice' as a metaphor.

11

The Personal Spirit and Personal Appropriation of the Truth

James M. Houston

I first met Colin Gunton, as a student of Hertford College, Oxford, in the early 1960s when I was teaching there in a different discipline. Colin confessed to me not long before his passing that he never felt trained effectively as a theologian. Perhaps this inner sense of inadequacy allowed the Holy Spirit personally to empower his studies, which have contributed remarkably to recent Trinitarian scholarship. He saw clearly that Western theology had often minimized the particular influence of the Holy Spirit, tending to make him less than fully personal. I agree with Gunton, and from my perspective, such minimizing of the Spirit surfaces in the Western doctrine of the *filioque* and the Reformation emphasis on Word over Spirit. Even more significant, perhaps, is how the contemporary identity with its idealism, personalism and individualism, and now reinforced by technical and economic pragmatism, stand in stark contrast to the early Christian identity depicted in the New Testament, in which so much attention is given to the Holy Spirit.

Then there is disenchantment and emotional burnout in Christian ministry today. Is this evidence of the lack of a personal experience of the Holy Spirit? Jacques Pohier, a former French Dominican priest, has written a moving confession of the 'decomposition' of his religious personality, as previously shaped by a Thomist theology to be 'priestly'. He has had to redefine his whole sense of 'being Christian'. Yet in his book, *God in Fragments*, he refers only once to the Holy Spirit: 'when it is a question of God, Jesus Christ and their Spirit',[1] implying that Pohier is not trinitarian, but binitarian in his theology. There is no sense of a personal experience of the Holy Spirit, for his former priestly personality was only shaped by his ecclesial community. Pohier illustrates poignantly the disenchantment of many Christian casualties within the institutional church and the radical changes now taking place.

Lastly, there are the popular, multiform expressions of African, South American and Korean Pentecostalism, where the Spirit appears to be blowing almost at gale force. These celebrate healing ministries and the power to overcome sorcery, and promise riches for the impoverished. But this apparently holistic, omnipresent appreciation of the Holy Spirit reflects little or no real understanding of the triune God of grace. Such spiritualistic approaches are vulnerable to the intrusion of all manner of spirits: African paganism, Brazilian Afro-Spiritism and Korean shamanism.

The aim of this paper is to trace some of this history and to show how the renaissance in Trinitarian theology offers hope for correcting the current imbalance in two ways: by emphasizing the personal nature of the Spirit, and by doing the same for its corollary, the personal appropriation of the truth. The implications are great, not only for our experience of the Spirit, but also for our view of acquiring wisdom, since the Spirit is the Spirit of truth. Responsible theological reflection on the person of the Holy Spirit is greatly needed today to counter the alienation of the human spirit in technical and institutional life, to discern abuses in the charismatic movement, as well as to foster doctrinal ecumenism between the West and the East. As Hilary of Poitiers stated: 'Concerning the Holy Spirit . . . we cannot remain silent because of those who do not know Him.'[2] Inevitably, this will always reopen the *filioque* debate, as illustrated by John Paul II's official stance since 1995.[3] Let us revisit this ancient debate.

The *Filioque* Controversy

Tertullian first used the text of John 16.14 (in reference to the Holy Spirit), 'He will take from what is mine', as Christ does from the Father, to express the communication of the divine substantiality; he expressed this with the Latin verb *procedere*.[4] Hilary of Poitiers expressed it more emphatically: 'The Spirit of truth proceeds from the Father; he is sent by the Son.'[5] He amplified this elsewhere, saying: 'If anyone thinks there is a difference between receiving from the Son [John 16.15], and *proceeding* [*procedere*] from the Father [John 15.26], it is certain that it is one and the same thing to receive from the Son and to receive from the Father.'[6] It is in this sense of communicating divinity through *procession* that Ambrose of Milan first formulated the *filioque*: 'The Holy Spirit when

He proceeds [*procedit*] from the Father and the Son, does not separate himself from the Father and the Son.'[7] Augustine of Hippo was more careful in distinguishing the Holy Spirit's procession from the Father as a form of communion from the Spirit's relation to the Son as one of abiding in the Son's incarnate life: 'The Holy Spirit proceeds from the Father as principle [*principaliter*] and, through the latter's timeless gift to the Son, from the Father and the Son in communion [*communiter*].'[8] Implicitly, Augustine recognized that the Holy Spirit is different by both procession and reception, and yet in communion he is the Spirit of the Father and of the Son. This was acceptable to Maximus the Confessor as an Eastern Father, who summed up the issue thus: 'For the procession they [i.e. the Romans] . . .showed that they themselves do not make the Son cause of the Spirit. They know indeed that the Father is the sole cause of the Son and of the Spirit, of one by generation and of the other by filiation [*ekporeusis*]'.[9] In view of the Western heritage's laudable efforts to guard against Arianism and its associated heresies through attention to the *filioque*, it is surprising to see a careful scholar like C. F. D. Moule state that the *filioque* doctrine is 'a lamentable dissension, constituting one of the most deplorable chapters in the history of hair-splitting theology'.[10]

It is true that the *filioque* was never part of an ecumenical creed, nor is there any direct or explicit biblical support for the dogma, although the Holy Spirit is both of the Father (John 15.26) and of the Son (Galatians 4.6). Christ reveals grace and truth, which the Holy Spirit communicates to the world (John 16.15), not the Spirit's eternal substance. With this in mind, the ecumenical formula is acceptable to all Christians today: 'the Holy Spirit proceeds from the Father and reposes in the Son'. And yet, while this ecumenical formulation expresses contemporary concerns, it does not account for the valid concerns of the religious context in which the *filioque* was formulated.

It should be remembered that the closeness of the relationships between the three Persons underlies the unity of the Trinity as *one God*. Such theological terms as 'proceeding' and 'begetting' are not human terms to be understood in their normal sense. So it should be as abhorrent to Christians as to Jews or Muslims to interpret the mystery of Almighty God in gender-based or tritheistic terms. Rather the term 'proceeding from' stresses the full deity of the Son, against the Arianism that continued in the West among the Teutonic tribes long after the issue was settled in the East by the Council of Constantinople in 381. It continues today to protect us against the vogue of numerous 'spiritualities' that are not Christ-centred, nor expressive of the deity of Christ, but which detach the Spirit from the Sonship of Jesus Christ. As Gerald Bray has claimed, if it is the work of the Holy Spirit to remake us in the image of Christ, adopted as the children of God, then the Holy Spirit must share in the hypostasis of the Son.[11] Lawrence Osborn has added succinctly: 'The *Filioque* clause is an invaluable reminder that the Holy Spirit is not an undefined divine creative force, but is characterized by his being the Spirit of Christ. It closes the door on both the excesses of certain parts of the charismatic movement as well as on the syncretism of much that passes for spirituality.'[12]

However, as Orthodox theologians fear, the *filioque* doctrine might lead believers both 'to *depersonalize* and to *subordinate* the Holy Spirit'.[13] Perhaps a greater fear should be that the West, still dominated by the Enlightenment, should downplay the role of the Holy Spirit in its culture of 'technology'. The Western Church has tended to institutionalize the doctrine of the Holy Spirit, awarding the Spirit more prominence in sacramental rites than in the lived faith of its members. In protest against the abstraction of 'god', Vladimir Lossky has affirmed that '*Ousia*, in the Trinity, is not an abstract idea of divinity, a rational essence binding three divine individuals, as humanity for example is common to three men.'[14] Rather, the principle of unity is personal. According to Kallistos Ware, 'the Spirit is a *person*. He is not just . . . an insentient force, but one of the three persons of the Trinity; and so, for all his seeming elusiveness, we can and do enter into a personal "I–Thou" relationship with him.' As the third member of the Holy Trinity, the Holy Spirit is *coequal* and *coeternal* with the other two; 'he is not merely a function dependent upon them nor an intermediary that they employ'.[15] The Spirit is truly personal.

Having spoken of the strengths and weaknesses of the *filioque* doctrine, let us now turn our attention to the Reformation emphasis on Word and Spirit. Whereas this section spoke to the personal nature of the Spirit, the next two sections will address primarily the personal appropriation of the truth.

Word and Spirit

While the Reformers protested against ritualism as a substitute for the Holy Spirit, the same tendency to subordinate the Spirit occurred with the new supremacy given to the Scriptures. The Reformed mediation of Word and Spirit renewed the prophetic utterances of the Old Testament prophets, giving priority to the doctrine of *creatio per*

Verbum as expressive of Word and Spirit in creation. It was further expressed in the promised blessings of Israel's messianic hope, in the prophets. For was it not the prophecy of Joel that the Spirit would come to all God's people, not just to the anointed king or priest? Joel writes, 'I will pour out my spirit on all flesh . . . Then everyone who calls on the name of the Lord shall be saved' (2.28, 31), a passage cited later by Peter at Pentecost (Acts 2.17–21) This became a favourite passage of the Puritans, who inherited the Renaissance reverence for the recovery of textual study of the classics, in conjunction with a new awareness of textuality created by the printing press. The Renaissance recognition of the individual consciousness became the further Reformation freedom of the exercise of individual conscience, in conjunction with the translation of the Bible into vernacular languages, a democratization they interpreted as anticipated by the prophets. John Calvin could thus argue:

> the highest proof of Scripture is uniformly taken from the character of him whose word it is. The prophets and apostles boast not in their own acuteness, or any qualities which will win credit to the speakers, nor do they dwell on reasons; but they appeal to the sacred name of God, in order that the whole world may be compelled to submission.[16]

It is appropriate for every thoughtful Christian, argues Calvin, that 'we maintain the sacred Word of God against gainsayers', yet it is only the Holy Spirit who will actually convert the heart of the unbeliever, not our clever reasoning. Elsewhere Calvin states further:

> Let it therefore be held as fixed, that those who are inwardly taught by the Holy Spirit, acquiesce implicitly in Scripture; that Scripture, carrying its own evidence along with it, deigns not to submit its proofs and arguments, but owes its full conviction with which we ought to receive it to the testimony of the Spirit.[17]

Just as God alone is the only fit witness of himself in the written Word, so also the Word does not come to be accepted in the human heart without being 'sealed by the inward testimony of the Spirit'. With his strong Trinitarian framework, Calvin thus focuses on God the Creator in book 1 of the *Institutes*, on Christ as our Mediator and Redeemer in book 2, and on the Church in book 4. So then, should book 3 not be about the Person of the Holy Spirit? Instead, it is a classic on the Christian life. Why? Because, states Calvin, this is 'the mode of obtaining the grace of Christ, the benefit it confers, and the effects resulting from it'. For the personal power and presence of the Holy Spirit is only evidenced in the faith produced in the Christian's new formation, 'in Christ'. So he concludes book 3 with the awareness that the Person of the Holy Spirit is 'personalized' in the life of the believer by the latter becoming more truly a worshipper, 'until God himself shall be all in all'.[18]

This Reformed teaching about the Holy Spirit led to the strong Calvinist tradition of godliness as being 'godly learning'. But later it was perverted, for the secular humanism of Petrus Ramus and his logical system of education profoundly influenced the presentation of systematic theology as well as the preaching style of many influential preachers.[19] Later still, the exaggerated abstraction of the philosophy of knowledge led to the demand for the autonomy of human reason, a concern that Pietist reformers like Spener spoke against. The radical reformer Carlstadt had protested that 'the outer Word', whether it was Scripture or a theological system about Scripture, was not so important as 'the inner Word', the assurance of the Holy Spirit's presence inwardly experienced in the believer.[20] Subsequent specialization has led to the split between theology and exegesis, both of which may have no relevance to Christian formation. So Hans Urs von Balthasar has issued the mild rebuke that the Protestant bias is towards 'the interpretation of the word' while the Roman Catholic or 'Marian' attitude is more towards 'the acceptance of the word'.[21] Without a proper unity of Word and Spirit, theological scholarship has eclipsed the Holy Spirit.[22]

Against this historical and contemporary backdrop, it is encouraging to witness the developing ecumenical concern to recover 'Word and Spirit', to elicit a more personal faith beyond the tendencies of nominalism in church liturgy and rites, and of the arid scholasticism of professional theologians. Since the Second Vatican Council, Catholic theologians such as Henri Cazelles have sought in the Scriptures a 'new, life-giving gift of God, a creative power . . . an historical witness to human life "in the Spirit", what we call "grace"'.[23] Exegesis has moved full circle from Aquinas's interpretation that the 'literal sense' of Scripture is what is God's Word, towards the Origenist recovery that the 'spiritual sense' is expressive of the Spirit's operation within the mind and heart of the reader. As John Breck argues, 'the "literal sense" is also a "spiritual sense", insofar as both the author's witness and the saving events to which He bears witness are both inspired and molded by the Holy Spirit'.[24] Georges Barrois in his book *The Face of Christ in the Old Testament* points out that scriptural typology is based upon the premiss that the events of Israel's history point forward as well as reflect back upon the motif of 'promise and fulfilment'. They are united in the double relationship of the Spirit's presence and role in salvation history and in the eschaton.[25] No doubt, typology has been wildly abused in the history of exegesis, and yet it is expressive also of openness to the Spirit of God to communicate his word within us and through us. Yet that 'openness' must be doctrinal, not simply the expression of human experience.

A further contribution to highlighting the Holy Spirit's presence in the Word is Klaus Berger's suggestive 'ecstatic reasoning'. Ecstasy and reason are integrated in the reader of the Bible, when Scripture is experienced as 'love, joy, peace', truly as the fruit of the Spirit, coming from without, to transform the inner life of the believer. As Berger puts it, 'The joy of which Paul speaks is calm, anxiety-free rationality that allows all that is necessary for righteousness to be done easily and without hindrance.'[26] Further to what has been said here, the next section will analyse alternative conceptions of knowledge—knowledge as abstraction and knowledge as participation.

Knowledge as Abstraction or Participation?

The renewal of Trinitarian theology in this generation has focused most attention on the diversity of actions undertaken by 'the economic Trinity' in the context of human salvation. For at the heart of the divine revelation is that God's life is shared with us in Jesus Christ, by his Spirit. This emphasis is reflected in Karl Rahner's famous dictum: 'The basic thesis which presents the Trinity as a mystery of salvation (in its reality and not merely as a doctrine) might be formulated as follows: The "economic" Trinity is the "immanent" Trinity and the "immanent" Trinity is the "economic" Trinity.'[27]

This Trinitarian renewal has generated a fierce debate in our generation between the two 'giants' of Catholic theology, Rahner and von Balthasar. Rahner claims that the Triune God is manifest by 'transcendent reason', implying that by the act of abstraction and self-transcendence the grace of revelation can be given us. He develops this thesis in his book *Spirit in the World*.[28] In response, von Balthasar insists that the fundamental cognitive moment is the apprehension of 'participation', which the whole philosophical tradition from Kant to Heidegger has ignored, in their obsession with the subjectivity of the thinker, and indeed, of making 'thinking' a substitute for reality itself. 'The autonomy of the thinker' has led to the disastrous loss of wonder and contemplative receptivity, of benefiting from a God-given, God-directed mode of 'knowing God' by his Spirit rather than by reason. Entering into such 'knowing' of the mystery of the Trinity is essentially participatory, like a drama in which we are actors, not spectators, of the truth.[29] The mystery of the ineffable God is 'aesthetic theology', meaning that God is more appropriately appreciated in his ineffable beauty than merely 'thought about.' For the mystery is most infinitely worshipful. Perhaps, argues von Balthasar, the single most significant consequence of the incarnation for us is the direct access we now have to God, because in Christ God has become man. This confidence of direct access is *parrhesia* (*pas* + *resis* = full liberty of speech), which is the significance of entering into prayer, as John 17 unfolds to the disciples, as the benefit of sharing in the triune life of God.[30] Thus, contemplation of the triune God of grace is more appropriate than conventional theological studies, involving a loving response of filial or indeed of bridal relationship to Christ *through the Spirit of God.*

This orientation conjoins the Western approach of 'hearing the Word' with the Eastern focus upon 'seeing the glory of God', rather than choosing between them. Both are needed. It is the Spirit of God that leads those who pray into an intimacy far deeper than any human relationship. For it is the intimacy between the Father and the Son. As the Son with the Father, or as Mary with the Word, the primary stance of the Christian is one of receptivity, of gratefully accepting 'being' as the foundational act of the creature before the Creator. Thus, the one who prays is receptive in thanksgiving, of whatever means God will use to conform us to the image of his Son by his Spirit. For it is especially by means of the Holy Spirit, as in Augustine's phrase *Donum Dei*, the Gift of God, or as von Balthasar puts it, the 'Handing-Over' of God, that the Father chooses us, calls us, and brings us to birth with his Son. Our glorifying God is the praise we bring him through our very existence. By glorifying God we reach 'the end of the world' since his glory transcends the furthest horizon of human existence, whereby we become possessed of God's love made visible by Christ's dying and rising, set free 'to live no longer for ourselves, but for him who died and rose for them' (2 Cor. 5.15). This is what von Balthasar calls 'the pneumatology of Christian existence', of the believer's need to be dispossessed of his own ego, *ex*-propriated, to *ap*-propriate the Saviour. This is the believer's new identity, of being handed over to the Triune God, since 'without me you can do nothing' (John 15.5). Because we are 'in Christ', Christ 'lives in us'. This then is where Christian speech becomes most appropriately *parrhesia*, the Spirit's boldness of divine love filling our being![31]

How Personal is the Spirit and the Appropriation of the Truth?

We will now seek to answer the question that has been with us from the beginning: How personal is the Spirit and the appropriation of the truth? The uniqueness of Christianity rests on the Trinitarian nature of God. The Triune God is a living—and lively—relationship of persons. The origins of Trinitarian faith do not lie in 'thinking', but in assimilating the historical experience of the personal character of God, whether as the God of Abraham, Isaac and Jacob, or indeed as the God and Father of our Lord Jesus Christ. True knowledge is cognoscent (Latin *cognosco*, *cum+gnosco*=know with, i.e. interpersonal in character), so the knowledge of God is only known through the presence of his indwelling Spirit, as the personal mode in which God gives himself to us. The prepositional features of the Greek *prosopon* and the Latin *persona* (*pros* 'towards', *per* 'through') already indicate relatedness, communicability, fruitfulness, even though their classical dramatic and legal biases fall short of true 'personhood'. As Augustine recognized that God's love is expressive of relationship, so too, the Christian is to receive love and live in relatedness. John Zizioulas has taken us forward to affirm with the Eastern Fathers that the unity of God lies in the communion of divine Persons, for 'Being is communion'. This Greek patristic concept of interpersonal personhood has now emerged as the dominant theme of contemporary Trinitarian theology. The challenge of this trend is now whether the theologian should move from human relations to the divine persons, a move that Catherine LaCugna, among others, has championed, or whether more critical distance must be given to the 'holiness of divine persons', as Alan Torrance has advocated.

The cultural alienation of modernity has forced us to take note of all the personalist efforts that stood opposed to Enlightenment idealism—from Hamann to Kierkegaard, Gabriel Marcel, Martin Buber, Emmanuel Mounier and John MacMurray. Attractive as they have all been, though, their efforts have inevitably failed since human personhood, not God's personhood, has been their primary concern. The same danger lies today in imposing an individualistic orientation upon the academic quest for 'personalness' in Trinitarian theology. A psychological model can be no substitute for the mystery of the Trinity. Selflessness is more than professional expertise likely to get closer to the person of the Holy Spirit. So when we ask, 'How personal is the Person of the Holy Spirit?', the answer can only be 'Much more than human minds can ever apprehend'. Otherwise, we will fall prey to modernity's intellectualistic and individualistic concerns, which replaced antiquity's more porous, interpersonal way of life with a more self-conscious individualistic orientation. The irony is that while we moderns may be able to appreciate personhood more intelligently we may be less adequately 'personal' than ever before!

Against this backdrop, we must remember that 'God is Spirit' (John 4.24). His attributes as 'Spirit' are both apophatic and kataphatic, mysterious and yet describable. Moreover, since spirituality is the content that belongs most of all to 'the person', argues Dumitru Staniloae, 'the person' is known to the extent that one reveals oneself to be understood by others.[32] So God's Spirit is as personal to us as we are willing and enabled to know him. For to 'know him' is to participate in union and communion with him, growing from a rational knowledge into the depths of being-with-him, 'as no one comprehends the thoughts of God except the Spirit of God' (1 Cor. 2.9–11). So the Eastern Fathers declare that full knowledge is the union between the one who knows and the one who is known, uniting knower and known in an eternal union. Dionysius the Areopagite speaks of those knowing God by unknowing, achieving in a union with God far more than can be known cognitively.[33] These have recognized that it is better to belong to God than to belong to one's self. Those who 'do not know God' have separated and closed themselves off from him. Conversely, the God who knows all things nonetheless finds himself incapable of 'knowing' those who are not willing to be 'known of God'. In judgement he says to them: 'I never knew you; depart from me, you evildoers' (Matt. 7.23). He does not force a person to love him, and therefore to 'know' him, for a 'godless man shall not come before him' (Job 13.16). How personal then is the Holy Spirit? As personal as we desire to know him, in self-abdication. Knowledge of God's Spirit involves opening ourselves to his transforming power to be conformed to the image of his Son. 'Through the Trinity,' Staniloae adds, 'the fully united divine persons, God fulfills the condition of perfect personal knowledge.'[34]

To partake of the knowledge of God also involves partaking of God's holiness. Since holiness pertains to God's transcendence as the 'Wholly Other', it reveals both the elevation of Creator over creature and God's condescension towards us. The holiness of God is not an impersonal mystery that reduces us to standing motionless in awe and fear; rather it is an attribute of a transcendent 'person', who engenders purification to make us more 'personal'. Cyril of Alexandria linked holiness closely to sacrifice, as indeed the Greek word *hieron* means both sacrifice and sacred. Jesus could state in prayer, 'For their sake I consecrate myself, that they also may be consecrated in truth' (John 17.19). One can only truly yield one's self to a person, and holiness comes from truly transcending oneself in total surrender to the absolute Person. This is what idolatry never can do, for it is surrender to an object that is the denial of the 'personal', an 'it'. But the power of such authentic surrender comes only from the Spirit of God's love, 'poured into our hearts by the Holy Spirit' (Rom. 5.5). Our lives then experience the infinitely personal character of the Holy Spirit as we are consecrated in self-renunciation to him, who is himself the Spirit of the Father and the Son. As Staniloae says:

> This surrender to absolute Person is a sanctifying self-sacrifice, for it is a transcending of self which goes beyond all that is relative . . . [H]e is consecrated and enters through that Person into a fully unlimited condition of complete freedom. He is consecrated because he forgets himself and is raised beyond himself in his own genuinely free communication with absolute Person . . . [T]he person realizes his own self in the most authentic manner, holiness.[35]

Thus, we are called to be 'saints', wholly set apart, anointed of his Spirit, to 'be holy even as he is holy' (Lev. 19.2). This spiritual life is communicable, in purity, sensibility and simplicity. Transparency is what communicates, for as Symeon the New Theologian observed, it is the light of holiness that brings transparency. Then the fruit of the Spirit is manifest to be 'love, joy, peace', radiating not only through the soul, but the body also. Moral courage then also thrives in the 'holy boldness' or *parrhesia* to which we have already referred. Yet it is not disruptive of relations, but rather gives freedom to others, so that it engenders peace: 'Strive for peace with all men, for the holiness without which no one will see the Lord' (Heb. 12.14). For in the divine Persons, there is no 'distancing', only reciprocal communion and loving fellowship. So the apostle urges, 'Do not put out the Spirit's fire', having previously enjoined us, 'always try to be kind to one another' (1 Thess. 5.15, 19). Each person of the Holy Trinity reveals himself in a distinctive way in the world, yet manifesting perfect unity with the other persons to reveal infinite love, which the Fathers could only describe as *perichoresis*. For the consciousness of the One is in the Other, and both united in the Third in endless communion. Such 'integration' is another name for 'infinite simplicity', where each 'I' discloses the other 'I' in endless self-giving to the Other.

How then can we conclude? It is sin, the sin of individualism, which so besets us today, with the breakdown of societal values in conjunction with the building up of technocratic values, to make us incredulous toward and blind to the 'personalness' of the Person of the Holy Spirit. And the hazards of professional scholarship and the institutionalism of the churches only intensify individualism. Sanctity needs therefore to be recovered in theological scholarship. And holiness is the test of true personhood, of life poured out sacrificially for the sake of divine love. Without the third Person, we would not experience the love between the Father and the Son, nor would we be recipients of the personal life of God. In our individualism, we would merely oscillate between a modalistic understanding of God, which knows of no fundamental distinction between the Persons of the Godhead, and a pantheistic understanding, which knows of no ultimate distinction between God and humanity. It is the person of the Holy Spirit that reveals the mystery of the Trinity to us, and by participation in the Spirit enables us to make true confession with Athanasius: 'Apart from the Spirit we are strange and distant from God, and by participation of the Spirit we are knit into the Godhead; so that our being in the Father is not ours, but is the Spirit's which is in us and abides in us, while by the true confession we preserve it in us.'[36]

Notes

1   Jacques Pohier, *God in Fragments* (London: SCM Press, 1985), p. 11.
2   Hilary of Poitiers, *On the Trinity* 2.29, in *The Fathers of the Church*, tr. Stephen McKenna (Washington, DC: Catholic University of America Press, 1968), p. 58.
3   Metropolitan Daniel Ciobotea, *Confessing the Truth in Love* (Iasi, Romania: Trinitas, 2001), p. 102.
4   Tertullian, *Against Praxeas* 25, in Ante-Nicene Christian Library, III ed. James Donaldson and Alexander Roberts (Edinburgh: T&T Clark, 1867), p. 621.
5   Hilary of Poitiers, *On the Trinity* 8, 26; p. 295.
6   Hilary of Poitiers, *On the Trinity* 8, 19; p. 289. Emphasis in original.
7   Ambrose, *Of the Holy Spirit* 2.5, in *Nicene and Post-Nicene Fathers* (NPNF), ed. Revd E. de Romestin and Revd H. T. F. Duckworth (repr. Grand Rapids: Eerdmans, 1979), p. 120.
8   Augustine, *On the Trinity* 15.4, in *Augustine: The Trinity*, ed. John E. Rotelle, the Works of Saint Augustine, pt 1, vol. V (Brooklyn, NY: New City Press, 1991), p. 417.
9   Maximus the Confessor, 'Letter to Marin of Cyprus'; quoted in Aidan Nichols, OP, *Byzantine Gospel* (Edinburgh: T&T Clark, 1993), p. 76.
10   C. F. D. Moule, *The Holy Spirit* (London: Mowbrays, 1978), p. 47.
11   Gerald Bray, 'The *Filioque* Clause in History and Theology', *Tyndale Bulletin* 34 (1983), p. 71.
12   Lawrence Osborn, 'The Holy Spirit in the Trinity', in *The Holy Spirit*, ed. Susan Harris (A theological conference held at the University of King's College, Halifax, Nova Scotia, May 31–June 3, 1992, Charlottestown, P.E.I.), pp. 8–9.
13   Bishop Kallistos Ware, *The Orthodox Way* (Crestwood, NY: St Vladimir's Seminary Press, 1999), pp. 91–2, italics in original.

[14] Vladimir Lossky, *Orthodox Theology: An Introduction* (Crestwood, NY: St. Vladimir's Seminary Press, 1978), p. 45.

[15] Ware, *The Orthodox Way*, pp. 91–2.

[16] John Calvin, *Institutes of the Christian Religion*, 1.7.4 (Mac Dill AFB, Fl.: MacDonald Publishing Company, n.d.), pp. 28–9.

[17] Calvin, *Institutes of the Christian Religion*, p. 5

[18] Calvin, *Institutes of the Christian Religion*, 3.25.12, p. 537.

[19] James M. Houston, 'Knowing God: The Transmission of Reformation Theology', in *Doing Theology for the People of God: Studies in Honor of J. I. Packer*, ed. Donald Lewis and Alistair McGrath (Downers' Grove, Ill.: Inter-Varsity Press, 1996), p. 229.

[20] Quoted in Gary D. Badcock, *Light of Truth and Fire of Love* (Grand Rapids: Eerdmans, 1997), p. 93.

[21] Hans Urs von Balthasar, *On Prayer*, 2nd edn, tr. A.V. Littledale (London: SPCK, 1973).

[22] Rowan Williams comes dangerously close to disrupting the unity of Word and Spirit, by arguing that our longer human history has assimilated previous canonical readings of the text, which have to be read 'diachronically' yet again by us through our experiences. He speculates that even within the New Testament there are 'rival bids for definition', not unity. So we are left to assume it is the subjectivity of 'our community' that translates the meaning of Scripture, not the Holy Spirit. This is precisely what Calvin attacked—that the church community had usurped the role of the Holy Spirit as interpreter of Scripture. See his *On Christian Theology* (Oxford: Blackwell, 2000), pp. 53–9.

[23] Henri Cazelles, quoted in John Breck, *The Power of the Word in the Worshiping Church* (Crestwood, NY: St Vladimir's Seminary Press, 1986), p. 36.

[24] Breck, *The Power of the Word in the Worshiping Church*, p. 38.

[25] George Barrois, *The Face of Christ in the Old Testament* (Crestwood, NY: St Vladimir's Press, 1974), pp. 43–4.

[26] Klaus Berger, *Identity and Experience in the New Testament*, tr. Charles Muenchow (Minneapolis: Fortress Press, 2003), p. 131.

[27] Karl Rahner, *The Trinity*, tr. Joseph Donceel (London: Burns & Oates, 1970), pp. 21–2.

[28] Karl Rahner, *Spirit in the World*, 2nd edn (London: SCM Press, 1968).

[29] See Vincent Holzer, *Le Dieu Trinité dans l'histoire: le différend théologique Balthasar–Rahner* (Paris: Cerf, 1995) for an exhaustive contrast between the two theologians.

[30] For further discussion, see von Balthasar, *On Prayer*.

[31] Aidan Nichols, OP, *The Word Has Been Abroad: A Guide through Balthasar's Aesthetics* (Washington, DC: Catholic University of America Press, 1998), pp. 244–5.

[32] Dumitru Staniloae, *The Experience of God* (Brookline, Mass.: Holy Cross Orthodox Press, 1994), p. 198.

[33] Pseudo-Dionysius, *On the Divine Names* 7, 872a, in *Pseudo-Dionysius the Areopagite: The Complete Works*, tr. Colin Luibheid (Mahwah, NY: Paulist Press, 1987), pp. 109–10.

[34] Staniloae, *The Experience of God*, p. 246.

[35] Staniloae, *The Experience of God*, p. 231.

[36] Athanasius, *Against the Arians*, in *NPNF*, 2nd series, IV, ed. James Donaldson and Alexander Roberts (repr. Grand Rapids: Eerdmans, 1980), pp. 406–7.

12

The Trinity and the Church[1]

Miroslav Volf

Today, the idea that the church as a community should take its shape from the communion within the Holy Trinity enjoys the status of an almost self-evident proposition. Yet, it is surprising that hardly anyone has carefully examined just how they correspond or where this analogy reaches its limits. As a result, discussions of correspondences between the church and the Trinity often say nothing more than the platitude that unity cannot exist without multiplicity nor multiplicity without unity,[2] or they demand of church members the completely selfless love of God.[3] The former is so vague that no one cares to dispute it, and the latter so divine that no one can live it. In short, we simply have no detailed examination of the correspondences between the Trinity and the church, and the framework of the present chapter is too limited for such a task. My goal here is only to sketch out the Trinitarian foundation of a non-individualistic Protestant ecclesiology within the framework of a critical dialogue with the writings of Joseph Ratzinger and John Zizioulas. We begin by reflecting on the possibilities and limitations of correspondences between the church and the Trinity.

Correspondences and Their Limits

'The mystery of the triunity can be found only in the deity itself, not in the creature', says Erik Peterson at the end of his influential essay 'Monotheismus als politisches Problem'. This *theological principle* not only 'breaks in a fundamental fashion with every sort of "political theology"',[4] but also dooms from the outset every attempt to think about the church in terms of the Trinity. The unity of creatures simply can never correspond to the mysterious unity of the Triune Creator.[5] Peterson does go on to add that faith in the Trinity not only politically fulfils the negative function of depriving worldly monarchs of the chance to legitimate themselves theologically by denying the existence of a heavenly monarch, it also emphasizes positively that Christians should pursue political engagement 'under the presupposition of faith in the triune God'.[6] Yet, any serious implementation of this *socioethical principle* relativizes precisely the above-mentioned theological principle; that is, although the Triune God cannot be used to bestow legitimacy on any political power there are still creaturely correspondences, however imperfect, to this mystery of triunity. Otherwise, even when Christians take political action under the presupposition of Trinitarian faith, their actions are reduced to purely, sterile criticism.

Peterson's ambivalence about the relationship between the Trinity and created reality is grounded in the character of the relationship itself. On one hand, God's triune nature remains a mystery that we can only worship but not imitate. On the other hand, both the entire history of God with the world and the worship of God as the answer to this history aim precisely at the indwelling of the triune God in the world. Any reflection on the connection between the Trinity and the church must take into account both God's uniqueness and the world's purpose in becoming the dwelling place of the triune God.

Correspondences

The idea that the Trinity is the highest reality has important consequences for the fundamental question of *the relationship between the one and the many*, a question that, since Parmenides, has been part and parcel of philosophical discussion in the West and for which significant parallels can be found in various other cultures and world religions. According to a schematic presentation by Odo Marquard, such discussion sets two traditions in opposition. The tradition of universalizing philosophies brings to bear 'the precedence of the one before the many. . . . Wherever multiplicity rules, we have an unfortunate situation that must be remedied; it must be universalized, totalized, globalized, egalicized, emancipated, revolutionized.' By contrast, the tradition of pluralizing philosophies brings to bear 'the precedence of the many over the one'. According to Marquard, the rule of unity—such as of one science as well as of one political party—is 'an unfortunate situation that must be remedied; it must be detotalized, decentralized, differentiated, pluralized, traditionalized, regionalized, individualized'.[7]

To think consistently in Trinitarian terms means to escape this dichotomy between universalization and pluralization. If the Triune

God is *unum multiplex in se ipso* (as per John Scotus Erigena), if unity and multiplicity are equiprimal in him, then God is the ground of both unity and multiplicity. Indeed, only the notion of unity in multiplicity can claim to correspond to God.[8] Since God is the one God, reality does not, as Aristotle's metaphor suggests, disintegrate into individual scenes like a bad play.[9] Yet, since the one God is a communion of the divine persons, the world drama does not degenerate into a boring monologue. Trinitarian thinking suggests that, in a successful world drama, unity and multiplicity must enjoy a complementary relationship.

Even these brief, abstract considerations about the one and the many show us that the way we think about God is decisive not only for our ecclesiology but for the entirety of Christian thought. Of course, very different emphases are still possible within the various Trinitarian positions that argue against the pre-eminence of either the one or the many. For this reason, both those more inclined toward pluralization (political theologians, liberation theologians, feminist theologians, and theologians of religion) and those more inclined toward universalization (traditional Orthodox and Catholic theologians) can consider themselves bound to *Trinitarian* thinking. In theological discussion itself, however, it is not so much the pre-eminent significance of the doctrine of the Trinity, with its denial of the dominance of the one or the many, that ends up being the bone of contention for theological and especially ecclesiological thinking. Rather, people disagree about the concrete manifestation of the Trinitarian doctrine and the ecclesiological and social implications that we can and should draw from it.

At the same time, we must be careful not to *overestimate* the influence Trinitarian thinking has had on political and ecclesial realities. Throughout history, the church has managed to interpret such connections in widely divergent ways. The bishops of the fifth century, for example, apparently sensed no contradiction between an affirmation of Trinitarian faith and the near-sacralization of the emperor.[10] By contrast, John Smyth, who apparently advocated modalism, cannot be accused of clericalism.[11] This is why we should not expect too much of any rethinking of the doctrine of the Trinity, however necessary it might be. The conceptualization process does not simply proceed in a straight line from above (the Trinity) to below (the church and society), shaping social reality.[12] Ecclesial and social reality, on the one hand, and Trinitarian models, on the other, are mutually determinative, just as ecclesial and social models and Trinitarian models are mutually determinative. Conceiving of the church in correspondence to the Trinity does not mean much more than thinking with theological consistency, all the while hoping that reality will not prove to be too recalcitrant. And of course, our ideas about the Trinity and what it tells us about social relations should be shaped primarily by the scriptural narratives of the Triune God.

But the correspondences between Trinitarian and ecclesial communion do not derive just from the desire to understand the relationship between the one and the many. In substance, the connection is grounded in Christian baptism. Through baptism 'in the name of the Father, of the Son, and of the Holy Spirit', the Spirit of God leads believers simultaneously into both Trinitarian and ecclesial communion. For this reason, churches do not emerge from baptism as images of the Triune God that have been fashioned by human beings but as concrete experiences, rendered possible by the Spirit, that anticipate the one communion of the Triune God with God's glorified people (1 John 1.3–4; Revelation 21–2). From this perspective, it is understandable why insight into the Trinitarian character of the church evolved in parallel with the growing consciousness of God's triune nature (1 Cor. 12.4–6; 2 Cor. 13.13; Eph. 4.4–6), a consciousness grounded in the activity of the Father, the Son and the Holy Spirit in salvation history and evidenced in New Testament triadic formulae. If Christian initiation is a Trinitarian event, then the church must speak of the Trinity as its determining reality.

Because churches, in the power of the Holy Spirit, already form a communion with the Triune God, ecclesial correspondence to the Trinity can become an object of hope and therefore a goal for humans. The parallels between Trinitarian and ecclesial relationships are not simply formal. They are also ontological because they are soteriologically grounded.[13] Jesus' high-priestly prayer, that his disciples might become one—'As you, Father, are in me and I am in you, may they also be in us' (John 17.21)—presupposes communion with the Triune God, mediated through faith and baptism, and aims at its eschatological consummation.[14] The church's ongoing communion with the Triune God, directed toward this consummation, implies that the correspondences between the Trinity and the church are not purely formal and that they involve more than any particular relationship between the one and the many. The relationships among the many in the church must reflect the mutual *love* of the divine persons.

The New Testament witness concerning the relevance of the Trinity to the church has shaped the ecclesiological traditions of both the East and the West. Thus, for example, the most important teacher in the early Greek church, Origen, writes that the church is full of the Holy

Trinity.[15] Similarly, Cyprian, who decisively influenced the ecclesiology of the West, views the church as *de unitate Patris, et Filii, et Spiritus Sancti, plebs adunata*.[16] The notion of the *imago Dei* influenced both ecclesiological traditions, and both of them developed differently, in ways commensurate with their different understandings of the Trinity.[17] Still, it seems that only in the past century have theologians undertaken a more sustained, conscious reflection on the Trinitarian dimension of the church. The topic was treated first in the theology of the Eastern church,[18] especially with regard to the ecclesiological consequences of the *filioque*,[19] but was quickly picked up in other Christian traditions as well[20] and made its way into various ecclesiastical and ecumenical documents.[21]

Predictably, the idea of a correspondence between the church and the Trinity has remained largely alien to the Free Church tradition.[22] If someone understands the church as a covenant among people who make themselves into a church, as John Smyth suggests, then that person cannot understand the church in analogy to the Trinity. Were the divine persons to unite into a fellowship—as the common Free Church ecclesial model has it—the result would be tritheism, rather than a Trinity. For Smyth, the theological grounding of the church is not Trinitarian but *Christological*. The church is 'the kingdom of Christ'; 'the regenerate sit together with Christ Jesus in heavenly places'. In communion with Christ, every Christian is a king, just as every Christian is also a priest and a prophet.[23] If personal faith plays a decisive role in salvation, then this soteriological focus exclusively on Christ can, strictly speaking, ground only the salvation of the individual but not the church community. Each person stands directly under the dominion of Christ; what they will be as a community remains unclear, emerging rather simply from that which each is to be in and for himself or herself.

My intention here is to make a contribution to the Trinitarian reshaping of Free Church ecclesiology. The understanding of faith as our being simultaneously incorporated into both Trinitarian and ecclesial communion is the cornerstone of a Trinitarian understanding of the church, since only by understanding the initiation process—baptism—itself in triune terms, and understanding the church as more than just a fellowship based on human initiative, can we arrive at the notion that Christian fellowship should reflect the Trinitarian unity of God. Here I will try to show how those assembled in the name of Christ, even if they number only three, can be an eikon ('image') of the Trinity.

Although this suggestion may seem radical, it is not new. Tertullian, albeit in his Montanist period, had already brought together the ecclesial and Trinitarian 'three':

> For the Church is itself, properly and principally, the Spirit Himself, in whom there is a Trinity of one divinity, Father, Son, and Holy Spirit. He unites in one congregation that Church which the Lord said consists of three persons. And so, from that time on, any number of persons at all, joined in this faith, has been recognized as the Church by Him who founded and consecrated it.[24]

Tertullian's allusion to Matt. 18.20 is unmistakable. It is precisely as the congregation assembling in the name of Christ that the church is an image of the Trinity.[25] I will develop Tertullian's idea in dialogue with the Catholic and Orthodox traditions. To this end, I will relate John 17.21 ('As you, Father, are in me and I am in you, may they also be in us') to the following ideas: (*a*) the ecclesiality of the church, building on Matt. 18.20 ('where two or three are gathered in my name, I am there among them'); (*b*) the mediation of faith, building on Gal. 2.20 ('I live, but it is no longer I who live, but it is Christ who lives in me'); and (*c*) the structure of the church, using 1 Cor. 14.26 ('when you come together, each one has a hymn, a lesson, a revelation . . .').

Although any consideration of the relationship between the Trinity and the church presupposes a complete doctrine of the Trinity, such comprehensiveness is not possible here. Instead, I will use a significantly modified version of the social model of Trinitarian relations, particularly as proposed by Jürgen Moltmann (though also by Wolfhart Pannenberg), developing those aspects that help illuminate correspondences between the Trinity and the church. But first, several preliminary methodological remarks are in order concerning the mediations necessary for understanding the church in relation to the Trinity. Here I will briefly clarify the limits of the church's ability to image the Trinity and then examine the actual correspondences between the Trinity and the church.

The Limits of Analogy

Although concepts about the Trinity can undeniably be converted into concepts about the church, it is equally undeniable that this process of conversion has its limits, unless we want to reduce theology to anthropology or, in reverse, to elevate anthropology to theology. Our notions of the Triune God are not the same as the Triune God, even if God is accessible to us only through these notions. A given doctrine of the

Trinity is a model that comes to us from salvation history and is formulated by analogy to our cultural experience,[26] a model we use to approach the mystery of the Triune God, not to comprehend God completely, but to worship God as the unfathomable One and to imitate God in our own, creaturely way. Trinitarian models bring God to expression in the same way all language about God does, namely, as God who is revealed anthropomorphically but who always remains hidden *'in the light of his own being'*[27] because God dwells 'in unapproachable light' (1 Tim. 6.16). As Peterson has emphasized, the *mystery* of triunity is indeed found only in the deity itself.

It does not follow from this, however, that, as Immanuel Kant believed, 'absolutely *nothing can be acquired for practical life* from the doctrine of the Trinity'.[28] Strictly speaking, we do not have a concept of a God in several persons.[29] Rather, we have models (the *doctrine* of the Trinity) with which we try to circumscribe the Triune God, and these *can* be translated into 'practical life' because they describe God through the categories of our own lives, be they psychological or social. Through our relationships with others, we give expression to the relationships among the divine persons. That we genuinely are describing God, rather than just a piece of the world, derives from the fact that God's self-revelation breaks through in this world. The *this-worldly character* of God's self-revelation makes it possible to convert Trinitarian ideas into ecclesiological ideas.

The Trinitarian models are not simply projections of ideal social models. Just as Trinitarian models speak about the Triune God as distinct from humans, we must also distinguish models of the Triune God from those of the church. The words 'person' and 'communion' in ecclesiology cannot be identical with the same in the doctrine of the Trinity. They can only be understood as *analogous*. If the *doctrine* of the Trinity represents an initial mediation between the self-revelatory Triune God and the church, then we also need this second mediation between any given doctrine of the Trinity and ecclesiology. Because God is accessible to *us* in our own thoughts about God, the absence of this second mediation risks deifying the church or stripping God of the divine nature.

The necessity of these two mediations is based in the creaturely nature of human beings. Humans are creations of the Triune God and can correspond to God only in a *creaturely* fashion. But we need a third mediation, too, grounded in the difference between the historical and the eschatological aspects of being Christian. The correspondence of ecclesial to Trinitarian communion is always lived on the path between baptism, which places human beings into salvific communion with the Triune God, and the eschatological new creation in which this communion is completed. Here the connection between the church and the Trinity acquires an inner dynamic, moving between the historical minimum and the eschatological maximum. For *a sojourning* church, only a dynamic, unfolding understanding of its correspondence to the Trinity can be meaningful and effective. If the church remains in a static, minimal correspondence to the Trinity, it misses the possibilities God gives it along with giving it its very being. If, by contrast, the church reaches for a static, maximum correspondence, it risks failing its historical reality, and, if it claims to realize this maximum, its self-understanding turns into ideology. None of these three cases would do justice to the idea of the church as a sojourning people of God. The ecclesiologically relevant question is how the church is to correspond to the Trinity *within history*.

Accordingly, the methodological decision to understand the correspondence of the church to the Trinity not merely 'from above' finds a firmer grounding, in addition to the formal one already mentioned. Although the life and structure of the church should correspond to the divine communion—through which the church is constituted and toward which it lives—we also need to consider the conditions under which it lives on this side of God's new creation in order to know *how* the church should reflect the divine communion during its day-to-day sojourn toward eschatological consummation. If to these historical limits we also add the creaturely restriction—limitations on the parallels between the Trinity and human communities—it follows that those parallels can be developed only *after* we gain clarity on the anthropological, soteriological and ecclesiological issues involved (even though, at the same time, anthropology, soteriology and ecclesiology must be developed in the light of Trinitarian doctrine).

Trinitarian Persons and the Church

Although we cannot separate the Trinitarian persons and relations, we still need to distinguish between them. Hence, I will examine first the correspondences between, on the one hand, the character of the different Trinitarian persons—their relationality and their mutual interpenetration—and, on the other, that of ecclesial persons and local churches. Then I will look at what the processions and structure of the divine relations tells us about structuring our ecclesial relations.

Relational Personhood

Ratzinger's definition of Trinitarian personhood as *pure* relationality—*persona est relatio*—has two important consequences. First, the persons become so transparent that it is difficult to distinguish them from the one underlying divine substance.[30] As a result, the one substance gains the upper hand over the three persons, and the three persons risk becoming redundant. If behind the actions of each divine person there is no 'I', then the three are superfluous in the economy of salvation, and 'the Triune God's relationship to us is . . . unitary', as Catherine LaCugna correctly maintains with regard to Augustine's doctrine of the Trinity.[31] Second, the persons seem to dissolve into relations: the Father becomes fatherhood; the Son, sonship; and the Spirit, procession. Understood in this way, these persons are not only superfluous but also incapable of action. Pure relations—the act of begetting, the activity of being begotten, and that of procession—can no more act in salvation history than they can be petitioned in prayer or praised in worship.

To do justice to the salvation history from which knowledge of the Trinity is actually acquired, we need to conceive of the Trinitarian persons *as subjects*. God's external works are not to be attributed to the one undifferentiated divine essence but rather proceed from the divine persons. In other words, personhood cannot be seen as pure relation, any more than relation can be seen merely as a manifestation of personhood. Rather, person and relation simultaneously emerge and mutually presuppose one another. This is one of the basic insights of Moltmann's doctrine of the Trinity: 'Here there are no persons without relations; but there are no relations without persons either. Person and relation are complementary.'[32] The divine persons are constituted through *generatio* and *spiratio* as subjects who, though different, are mutually related from the outset and are inconceivable apart from these relations. Furthermore, they manifest their own personhood and affirm that of other persons through their mutual acts of giving and receiving.[33]

Seeing Trinitarian persons and relations as complementary makes it possible to conceive ecclesial personhood in correspondence to Trinitarian personhood. Here I will address only the relationality of the divine and ecclesial persons, addressing their subjectivity in the context of the structure of Trinitarian and ecclesial relations.[34] Like the divine persons, ecclesial persons cannot live in isolation from one another; Christians are constituted as believing persons through their relations with other Christians, and they manifest and affirm their own ecclesial personhood in mutual giving and receiving (see Phil. 4.15). Within the context of the complementary nature of person and relationship, the structure of our lives can indeed be described accurately with Ratzinger's notion of 'being from and toward', though this 'being' is now no longer 'pure [and] unreserved'.[35] Christians live from and toward others.

Although the relationships of ecclesial and Trinitarian persons correspond to each other, a distinction does remain between the two. I am not referring to the fact that humans remain persons even if they live in isolation from one another, whereas the Trinitarian persons are inconceivable without the most intimate of communion. Humans can live *as humans* in isolation from, or even in hatred toward, one another (though in reality, they always become human beings through others and remain related to others even in hatred or indifference). This derives from their being created through *God's relationship to them* by means of their relationships with those around them, rather than through *their relationship* either to God or to those around them. *As Christians*, however, people cannot live apart from fellowship with other Christians. Salvation has an indispensable ecclesial structure, and in this sense, relations between Trinitarian and ecclesial persons do correspond.

Yet the difference between the two remains. It consists, first, in the fact that human beings, though determined by one another, are not communion, as the Trinity is, but rather must always be *held together* by an implicit or explicit covenant. Because of the creaturely nature of humanity, ecclesial communion must always be also a communion of the will, even if people's ecclesial being and ecclesial will are mutually determinative.

Second, ecclesial communion this side of God's new creation can correspond only in a broken way to the perfect mutual love of the Trinitarian persons. The church's fellowship is always in transition between the historical minimum and the eschatological maximum of its correspondence to Trinitarian love. The minimum consists in being from others and being together with others, for only a *communion* of persons can correspond to the Trinity. The maximum consists in perfect being toward others in the love in which persons give of themselves to one another and thereby affirm one another and themselves.

Ratzinger defines relations between local churches in analogy to the pure relationality of the Trinity. Only when churches have given up all 'holding onto one's own' can the 'coalescence into unity' come about.[36] However, such a union, emerging from *pure* relationality, results in the dissolution of the respective individual identities of the various local churches. If we begin with the complementary nature of person and relation in the Trinity, then ecclesial persons and ecclesial communities alike appear as distinct and yet mutually related entities, affirming one another in mutual giving and receiving (see Rom. 15.26–7; 2 Cor. 8.14).

But do local churches necessarily act from and toward each other in the way the divine persons do? I think not. Nor is Ratzinger able to apply this structure of communality consistently to the relations among local churches. Although a loving alliance is indeed desirable among local churches, it is *not an absolute condition* of ecclesiality, unless we choose to understand love objectively, as Ratzinger does, following Augustine, as 'standing in' the Eucharistic communion. That choice results, however, in an elimination of the aspect of love involving 'being toward others'. Ratzinger himself uses the word 'love' equivocally. In a Trinitarian and maximal-ecclesiological sense, he uses it to refer to the from/toward structure; in a minimal-ecclesiological sense, however, it refers to the from/with structure. This reflects the position of Catholic tradition, which asserts that only being from others and being together with others, but not being toward others, is indispensable for ecclesiality. The sojourning church corresponds to the Trinity only in part.

The question arises, however, whether being with others is indispensable for the *minimum* of correspondence between Trinity and church. It is true that a local church, even as a fellowship of mutual giving and receiving, could not correspond to the Trinity if it intentionally separated itself from other churches and did not seek communion with them. If a church is open to other churches, however, it already corresponds partially to the Triune God, just as by seeking communion with other churches, it corresponds to the eschatological gathering of the entire people of God in communion with the Triune God and, in so doing, actually is a church in the first place. Hence, the minimum of interecclesial correspondence to the Trinity seems to consist not in being with all others but in being from others and *seeking* to be toward all others.

Perichoretic Personhood

In their mutual giving and receiving, the Trinitarian persons are not only interdependent but also *mutually interpenetrating*, something to which the Johannine Jesus repeatedly refers: 'so that you may know and understand that the Father is in me and I am in the Father' (John

10.38; cf. 14.10–11; 17.21). This mutually internal abiding and inter-penetration of the Trinitarian persons, which, since Pseudo-Cyril, has been called perichoresis,[37] determines the character both of the divine persons and of their unity.

Perichoresis refers to the reciprocal *interpenetration* of the Trinitarian persons.[38] In every divine person as a subject, the other persons also indwell; all mutually permeate one another, though in so doing, they do not cease to be distinct. In fact, the distinctions between them presuppose *that* very interiority, since persons who have dissolved into one another cannot exist in one another. Perichoresis is, as Prestige says, 'co-inherence in one another without any coalescence or commixture'.[39] This is why both of these statements can be made: 'Father and Son are in one another', and 'Christians are in *them*' ('in *us*'—plural!: John 17.21). Being in one another does not abolish Trinitarian plurality; yet, despite the abiding distinction among the persons, their subjectivities do overlap. Each divine person acts as a subject, and at the same time the others act as subjects in each person, which is why the Johannine Jesus can utter paradoxically, He eme didache ouk estin eme ('My teaching is not mine': John 7.16). This statement takes on its full theological weight only if we do not try to resolve the tension between 'mine' and 'not mine' on one side or the other but instead emphasize both equally. Within personal interiority, what is mine is simultaneously not mine without ceasing to be mine, just as the reverse is also true.

From the interpenetration of the divine persons, there emerges what I call their *catholicity*: 'The Father is in me and I am in him' (John 10.38) implies that 'whoever has seen me has seen the Father' (John 14.9–10). The one divine person is not only itself but also carries within itself the other divine persons,[40] and only in this indwelling of the others within it is it the person it really is. The Son is Son only insofar as the Father and the Spirit indwell him; without this interiority of the Father and the Spirit, there would be no Son. The same applies to the Father and to the Spirit. In a certain sense, each divine person is in its own way the other persons, which is why rather than ceasing to be unique, in its very uniqueness it is a completely *catholic* divine person.

This reciprocal interpenetration of the divine persons determines the character of their unity. The notion of perichoresis offers the possibility of overcoming the alternatives *unio personae/unitas substantiae*.[41] The unity of the Triune God is grounded neither in the numerically identical substance nor in the accidental intentions of the persons but rather in their *mutually interior being*. As Moltmann puts it, 'By the power of their eternal love, the divine persons exist so intimately with, for, and in one another that they themselves constitute themselves in their unique, incomparable and complete union.'[42] The unity of the divine essence is the obverse of the interpenetration and catholicity of the divine persons.

In a strict sense, human beings have no perfect equivalent to the interpenetration of the divine persons.[43] Another human self cannot be within me as the subject of action. People are always external to one another *as subjects*. Someone might at most adduce the experience of complete mutual love as proof to the contrary; yet despite all the so-called selflessness of love, it is not the beloved Thou who is the subject of love but rather the loving self itself. A self in this sense, one that through love has become selfless, is indeed a self that can embrace or enter empathetically into the other, but it is not a self that, as a distinct self, can indwell or be indwelled by that other. The indwelt of other persons is an exclusive prerogative of God.

But the divine persons indwell human beings in a different way than they do one another. This is evident already in the fact that their interpenetration is strictly reciprocal, which is not the case between God and humans. To be sure, it is not only the Spirit and, together with the Spirit, the Son and the Father who are in human beings; humans are also in the Spirit (see Rom. 8.9).[44] They are not, however, indwelling the Spirit as subject; otherwise, they would also be the agents of the Spirit's actions just as the Spirit is the agent of theirs; the Spirit, after all, 'blows where it chooses' (John 3.8a). If people were interior to the Spirit in the same way the Spirit is to them, the conclusion 'the wind blows where it chooses . . . . So it is with everyone who is born of the Spirit' (John 3.8) would be reversible. But it is not. This indwelling is one-sided. The Spirit indwells human persons, whereas by contrast, humans indwell *the life-giving ambience of the Spirit*, but not the Spirit itself.

At the ecclesial level (and at the creaturely level in the broader sense), only *the interpenetration of personal characteristics* can correspond to the interpenetration of the divine persons. In our daily personal encounters, what the other person is flows consciously or unconsciously into what I am. The reverse is also true. In this mutual giving and receiving, we give to others not only something apart from ourselves but also a piece of ourselves, something of what we have made of ourselves in communion with others. And from others we take not only what they give but also a piece of who they have become. Each person gives of himself or herself to others, and each person uniquely takes others into himself or herself. This process of mutually internalizing each other's personal characteristics occurs in the church as the Holy Spirit indwells Christians. The Spirit opens them to one another and allows them to become *catholic persons*, each in his or her uniqueness. It is here that they, in a creaturely way, correspond to the catholicity of the divine persons. This catholicity of Christians, however, cannot be limited ecclesially. A catholic person internalizes, at least minimally, not only that person's Christian siblings and friends but also his or her *entire world* of the Creator as well as of every creature. Every person is catholic insofar as that person reflects, in a unique and differentiated way, the entire, complex creaturely reality in which the person lives.

Mutual giving and receiving presupposes a connection of some sort, however rudimentary. If I am utterly isolated from others, I can neither give nor receive anything from them. This is why the communion of persons precedes their catholicity, just as the interiority of persons precedes their full unity. But because human persons cannot be internal to one another as subjects, their unity cannot be conceived in a strictly perichoretic fashion, as is often suggested.[45] Does this not make the local church, in a way different from that of the Trinity, merely a union of Christians? Is it not precisely the correspondence between the unity of the church and the unity of the Triune God that requires the mutual indwelling of human persons, and does not the New Testament also conceive unity by way of the mutual indwelling of persons? Thus in John 17.21, Jesus requests 'that they may all be one, *as* you, Father, are in me and I am in you'. Yet, already for *theological* reasons, this 'as' (*kathos*) may be interpreted in the sense not of identity but rather of similarity.[46]

In that case, however, human perichoretic unity does not necessarily follow from divine perichoretic unity; we must ask what the similarity between divine and human unity consists in. This theological consideration is confirmed exegetically insofar as the statement 'as you, Father, are in me and I am in you' is continued not by 'may they also be *in one another*' but by 'may they also be *in us*'. Human beings can be in the Triune God only insofar as the Son is in them (John 17.23; 14.20); and if the Son is in them, then so is the love with which the Father loves the Son (John 17.26). But because the Son indwells human beings through the Spirit, *the unity of the church is grounded in the indwelling of the Spirit*—and, with the Spirit, in the indwelling of the other divine persons—*in Christians*. The Holy Spirit is the 'one person *in* many persons'.[47] It is not the mutual perichoresis of human beings but the indwelling of the Spirit common to everyone that makes the church into a communion which corresponds to the Trinity, a communion in which personhood and sociality are equiprimal. Just as God constitutes human beings through their relationships with each other, so the Holy Spirit indwelling them constitutes them through ecclesial relationships as a communion of persons. As such, they correspond to the unity of the Triune God, and as such, they are instantiations of *the one* church.

If human beings cannot indwell one another, then churches as fellowships of human beings can indwell one another even less. For this reason, then, the divine perichoresis cannot serve as a model of *inter*-ecclesial unity. Nor are churches subjects that the Holy Spirit might indwell apart from the Spirit's indwelling the hearts of their members. Hence, in the Holy Spirit, churches relate to one another not so much as collective subjects but as the *people* of whom they consist, be they laity or clergy. In modern societies, this takes place in direct personal encounters as well as through mediating institutions and mechanisms of interaction.

Nevertheless, the perichoresis of the divine persons does possess inter-ecclesial relevance. Here, the correspondence between the Trinity and the church builds on the *catholicity* of the divine persons. Like individuals, entire communities have their specific identifying characteristics, acquired either through the cultural context of which they are part or the exceptional personalities active among them. And they pass these characteristics on to other churches. By opening up to one another both diachronically and synchronically, local churches enrich one another, becoming increasingly catholic. In this way, they also increasingly correspond to the catholicity of the Triune God, who has already constituted them as catholic churches, because they *are* anticipations of the eschatological gathering of the entire people of God.

The Structure of Trinitarian and Ecclesial Relations

The relationships among the divine persons and their personal interpenetration logically presuppose the generation of the Son and the procession of the Spirit, since only persons who already are can be said to relate to and exist in one another. In discussions of the Trinity, the structure of Trinitarian relations has been consistently determined by the notions of generation and procession. Here I will examine in what sense generation and procession structure Trinitarian relations, asking which particular aspects of the Trinity ought to be reflected in ecclesial structures.

As I have tried to show, although Ratzinger conceives of relations within the church in a Trinitarian fashion, he sees church structure monistically. The paradox is all too apparent. Because the persons are pure relations, God can act externally only as the one undifferentiated divine being that is, as *one* 'person'. Acting externally, this one divine nature corresponds to the one church that, together with Christ, constitutes one subject and thus becomes capable. Hence, for both the Trinity and the church, the 'one' is structurally decisive: the one divine nature, the one Christ, the one pope, and the one bishop. This in turn corresponds to the filioquistic linear doctrine of the Trinity; the Spirit is the third who proceeds from the Son and who, within the economy of salvation, cannot determine the Son. This is why, though the Spirit can indeed vivify the structures of the church, it can hardly determine their form.

The hierarchical structure of the church derives from the systemic dominance of the one and from the priority of the whole. Because only the one can ensure the unity of the totality, the pope must rank above the bishop, just as the bishop must rank above the congregation. Although their power, like the divine pure relationality, is theoretically always vicarious (it is Christ who acts through them), it is always played out as personal power enshrined in church law, at least on this side of the final consummation. If we conceive of the relationships among ecclesial persons in analogy to the Trinity, the many within the church body necessarily remain defencelessly subject to this personal power of the one. Personal rights cannot be derived from this understanding of persons as pure relation, which erroneously presupposes realized eschatology and is unable to do justice structurally to the abuse of power. Because persons understood in this way are also embedded in a monistic hierarchical structure of relations, the understanding of person as pure relation can easily degenerate into repressive ideology.

John Zizioulas conceives of the structure of ecclesial relations in a consistently Trinitarian fashion. He does so on the basis of a non-filioquistic Trinitarian theology that gives primacy to the person of the Father. The relations between the one and the many are reciprocal. Just as the Father constitutes the Son and the Spirit and is simultaneously conditioned by them, Christ constitutes the church and is simultaneously conditioned by it in the Spirit, as the bishop as the image of Christ constitutes the ecclesial community and is conditioned by that community as a pneumatic entity.

For Zizioulas, however, this reciprocal relation between the one and the many is asymmetrical. The Father constitutes the Son and the Spirit, while the Son and the Spirit only *condition* the Father; Christ constitutes the church, while the church only *conditions* Christ. Accordingly, the bishop constitutes the church but is only *conditioned by* the church. The monarchy of the Father and the subordination of the Son and the Spirit ('a kind of subordination', Zizioulas writes[48]) are reflected in the dominion of Christ over the church as well as in the hierarchical relations within the church itself. Like the Trinitarian person, the ecclesial person is inconceivable without hierarchy.[49] The function of the order of lay people is exclusively responsorial; they follow the bishop, who is acting *in persona Christi*, and speak the liturgical amen. Moreover, Zizioulas understands the *order* of lay people as an undifferentiated unity; all lay people have the same liturgical function. Lay people are thus placed into a hierarchically structured polarity of the one and the many in which they not only remain subordinated as a whole but are also virtually insignificant as individuals.

If we begin with the Trinitarian model I have suggested, the structure of ecclesial unity cannot be conceived by way of the one, be it the pope, the patriarch or the bishop. Every ecclesial unity held together by a mon-archy—by a 'one-(man?) rule'—is monistic and thus also un-Trinitarian. Reflecting on the fact that no *one* human being can correspond to the Trinitarian relational network, Heribert Mühlen has concluded that ecclesiastical *office is* to be exercised collegially, even the office of the pope![50] This is a step in the right direction. Such a 'trinitarianization' of office would correspond to the collegial exercise of office in the early church (Phil. 1.1; 1 Thess. 5.12; Rom. 12.8). Yet this step alone would not suffice, for the correspondence between the structures of the Trinity and the church would still be conceived ecclesiologically in an overly hierarchical fashion. Although this would break the dominance of the one, the dichotomy between the now 'trinitarianized' office and the congregation that says amen would still remain. This is unavoidable if we distinguish in principle rather than in function between universal and particular priesthood. The order of priests then corresponds to the Triune God and acts in God's name over against the congregation.

Thinking about church structure in a consistently Trinitarian way means seeing not only the clerical roles but also *the entire local church itself*—lay and ordained—in terms of the Trinity. The high-priestly prayer of Jesus brings all who believe in him into correspondence with the unity of the Triune God (John 17.20; cf. 1 John 1.3). Paul, too, seems to be arguing from a Trinitarian perspective when he admonishes the Corinthian congregation to unite (1 Cor. 12.4-6; cf. Eph. 4.3-6).

The various gifts, services and activities of all Christians correspond to the divine multiplicity. Just as the one deity exists as the Father, Son and Spirit, so do these different divine persons distribute different gifts to *all* Christians. That these gifts are distributed for the benefit of *all*, however (1 Cor. 12.7), corresponds to the divine unity; *the same* Spirit, *the same* Lord, and *the same* God (the Father) are active in all these different gifts.[51] The reciprocity among Trinitarian persons finds its correspondence in an image of the church in which *all* members serve one another with their specific gifts of the Spirit, imitating the Lord through the power of the Father. Like the divine persons, they all stand in a position of mutual giving and receiving.[52]

At the Trinitarian level, unity does not presuppose the unifying one but is constituted through perfect love, which is the very nature of God and through which the divine persons exist in one another. By contrast, ecclesial (as well as every other creaturely) unity is inconceivable without the one, though when this one is part of the ecclesial communion itself, this very fact puts it in tension with the structure of Trinitarian relations. It is no accident that the New Testament attests to no particular charisma of unity, though, for example, people with episcopal charisma are to work especially on behalf of unity, based on their specific role.[53] Not until the letters of Ignatius does the preservation of unity become a specific task of the bishop. Here, the synedrios tou episkopou ('council of the bishop') corresponds to the henotes theou ('unity of God').[54] The bishop is thereby in a position to preside within the church eis topon theou ('in the place of God') and thus to ensure its unity.[55] But the New Testament itself does not yet witness to this understanding. There, the unity of the church seems to come about through the indwelling of the *one Spirit*—and with it, of the entire holy triunity—in *every person*.[56] Accordingly, as with the Trinity, *every* person as a bearer of the Spirit participates in creating unity. This is also commensurate with the New Testament admonitions to foster unity, which are in fact directed to all the members of the congregation (1 Cor. 1.10–17; Eph. 4.3).

If Trinitarian persons are not identical with relations, then we can also conceive of the *rights* of ecclesial persons in correspondence to the Trinity. It would, of course, be utterly inappropriate to ascribe rights to the divine persons solely to justify ascribing them to ecclesial persons as well. 'Rights legitimate the social practice of claiming goods on moral grounds', writes Nicholas Wolterstorff correctly.[57] However, for the divine persons, such a 'practice of claiming goods' is inconceivable since they live in perfect love; they dwell in one another as persons and mutually *give everything* to one another. Hence, they can have no formal rights that might legitimate this 'practice of claiming goods'— and that might be asserted through corresponding sanctions. These rights presuppose the possibility of persons being abused, and they are meaningless without this possibility. With regard to the divine persons, however, this presupposition is impossible.

Understanding the divine persons as interdependent and mutually indwelling centres of action corresponds to understanding ecclesial persons as interdependent and catholic subjects. As such, they are bearers of the inalienable rights that protect them from abuse, not only for their own sake—the equivalent of an individualistic understanding of human rights—but also because of their communion with others and with God.[58] People in the church *can* have these rights because as individuals they are to correspond to the relations of the divine persons. But they *must* have these rights if they are to live in correspondence to the divine persons, because they are living on this side of God's new creation. The rights of all the members of the church, lay and ordained, are based in the correspondence between *the sojourning church* and the Trinity.

Personal rights, of course, cannot replace mutual love between persons. Rather, properly understood, rights go hand in hand with such love; they protect against the abuse of persons and are an expression of love before consummation. Because they are also grounded in the Trinity, they simultaneously point toward their own suspension in God's new creation, a creation in which human beings in communion with the Triune God will reflect perfect divine love.

Notes

1　This essay is an abridged and edited version of the chapter 'Trinity and Church' in *After Our Likeness: The Church as the Image of the Trinity* (Grand Rapids: Eerdmans, 1998). The reader is encouraged to look there for a fuller treatment of this theme.

2　Bruno Forte, *Trinität als Geschichte: Der lebendige Gott—Gott der lebenden*, tr. J. Richter (Mainz: Grünewald, 1989), p. 200.

3　Joseph Cardinal Ratzinger, *Auf Christus Schauen: Einübung in Glaub, Hoffnung, Liebe* (Freiburg: Herder, 1989), p. 142.

4　Erik Peterson, 'Der Monotheismus als politisches Problem', in *Theologische Traktate* (Munich: Kösel, 1951), p. 105.

5　Peterson, 'Der Monotheismus als politisches Problem', p. 104.

6　Peterson, 'Der Monotheismus als politisches Problem', p. 47 (prefatory remark).

7　Odo Marquard, 'Einheit und Vielheit: Statt einer Einführung in das Kongressthema', in *Einheit und Vielheit: XIV. Deutscher Kongress für Philosophie, Giessen*, ed. Odo Marquard (Hamburg: Meiner, 1990), p. 2.

8   Walter Kern, 'Einheit-in-Mannigfaltigkeit: Fragmentarische Überlegungen zur Metaphysik des Geistes', in *Gott in Welt: Festschrift Karl Rahner*, ed. H. Vorgrimler (Freiburg: Herder, 1964), 1.207–39.

9   According to Aristotle, the universe, like any well-organized community, must have only one *arche*, since multiple rule is anarchy: 'The rule of many is not good; let one be the ruler'; in this context, Aristotle cites the *Iliad* for support: Aristotle, *Metaphysics* 1076a, tr. Hippocrates G. Apostle (Bloomington, Ind.: Indiana University Press, 1966).

10 Alois Grillmeier, 'Auriga mundi: Zum Reichskirchenbild der Briefe des sog. Codex Encyclicus (458)', *Mit ihm und ihm: Christologische Forschungen und Perspektiven* (Freiburg: Herder, 1975), pp. 386–419.

11 John Smyth, *The Works of John Smyth*, ed. W. T. Whitley (Cambridge: Cambridge University Press, 1915), p. 733. See also Yves Congar's remarks concerning the ecclesiological significance of the *filioque* in *I Believe in the Holy Spirit*, 3 vols (New York: Seabury Press, 1983).

12 According to John Zizioulas, ecclesial experience decisively shaped the development of the patristic doctrine of the Trinity: *Being as Communion: Studies in Personhood and the Church* (Crestwood, NY: St. Vladimir's Seminary Press, 1985).

13 Alistair MacFadyen has come to a similar conclusion; in his view, the Trinity is not merely a social model but 'a consequence of God's redemptive and creative relationship with us' ('The Trinity and Human Individuality', *Theology* 95 (1992), pp. 10–18).

14 Ernst Käsemann, *Jesu letzer Wille nach Johannes 17* (Tübingen: Mohr-Siebeck, 1966).

15 *ho de en te Ekklesia tugchanon te pepleromene tes hagias Triados*: Origen, *Selecta in Psalmos*; PG 12, 1265b.

16 Cyprian, *Liber de Oratione Dominica* 23, PL 4, 553.

17 Hermenegild Biedermann, 'Gotteslehre und Kirchenverständnis: Zugang der ortho-doxen und der katholischen Theologie', *Theologisch-praktische Quartalschrift* 129 (1981), pp.131–42.

18 Grigorios Larentzakis, 'Trinitarisches Kirchenverständnis', in *Trinitä: Aktuelle Perspektiven der Theologie*, ed. W. Breuning (Freiburg: Herder, 1984), pp. 73–96.

19 Congar, *I Believe in the Holy Spirit*, p. 271.

20 For the Catholic tradition, see Heribert Mühlen, *Una mystica persona*, 3rd edn (Munich: Schöningh, 1968); for the Protestant tradition, see Jürgen Moltmann, *The Trinity and the Kingdom: The Doctrine of God* (New York: Harper & Row, 1981), pp. 200–2.

21 For example, see the documents of the Second Vatican Council (*Lumen gentium*, 2–4; *Unitatis redintegratio*, 2); in this regard, see Walter Kasper, 'Kirche als Communio: Überlegunen ßur ekklesiologischen Leitidee des ßweien Vatikanischen Konßils', in *Die bleibende Bedeutung des ßweiten Vatikanischen Konßils*, ed. F. Cardinal König, Schriften der Katholischen Akademie in Bayern 123 (Düsseldorf: Patmos, 1986), pp. 62–84 .

22 For an exception, see the most recent document (1989) of the Catholic–Pentecostal dialogue, 'Perspectives on Koinonia: Final Report of the International Roman Catholic/Pentecostal Dialogue (1985–89)', *Pneuma* 12 (1990/IV)', p. 29.

23 Smyth, *Works*, pp. 274, 740.

24 Tertullian, *De pudicitia* 21 in *Ante-Nicene Christian Library*, III, ed. James Donaldson and Alexander Roberts (Edinburgh: T&T Clark, 1897), p. 119.

[25] Joseph Cardinal Ratzinger, *Volk und Haus Gottes in Augustins Lehre von der Kirche*, Münchener theologische Studien 2/7 (Munich: Zink, 1954).

[26] Concerning the doctrine of the Trinity as a model, see Catherine Mowry LaCugna and Kilian McDonnell, 'Returning from "The Far Country": Theses for a Contemporary Trinitarian Theology', *Scottish Journal of Theology* 41 (1988), pp. 191–215.

[27] Eberhard Jüngel, *Gott als Geheimnis der Welt: Zur Begründung der Theologie des Gekreuzigten im Streit zwischen Theismus und Atheismus*, 3rd edn (Tübingen: Mohr-Siebeck, 1978), p. 500, italics in original.

[28] Immanuel Kant, 'Der Streit der Fakultäten', in *Werke in sechs Bänden*, ed. W. Weischedel (Darmstadt: Wissenschaftliche Buchgesellschaft, 1964), p. 50, italics in original.

[29] Kant, 'Der Streit der Fakultäten', p. 50.

[30] See Colin E. Gunton, *The Promise of Trinitarian Theology* (Edinburgh: T&T Clark, 1991) for his analysis of Augustine's doctrine of the Trinity.

[31] Catherine Mowry LaCugna, *God For Us: The Trinity and the Christian Faith* (San Francisco: Harper & Row, 1991).

[32] See Moltmann, *The Trinity and the Kingdom*, p. 172.

[33] See pp. 169–70.

[34] See pp. 167–71.

[35] Joseph Cardinal Ratzinger, *Introduction to Christianity* (London: Burns & Oates, 1969).

[36] Ratzinger, *Introduction to Christianity*, p. 135.

[37] G. L. Prestige, *God in Patristic Thought* (London: SPCK, 1956), p. 298.

[38] Dumitru Staniloae, 'Trinitarian Relations and the Life of the Church', in *Theology and the Church*, tr. Robert Barringer (Crestwood, NY: St Vladimir's Seminary Press, 1980).

[39] Prestige, *God in Patristic Thought*, p. 298.

[40] Similarly Dumitru Staniloae, *Orthodoxe Dogmatik* 12/15 (Einsiedeln: Benziger, 1984).

[41] See Hilary of Poitiers, *De trinitate* 4.42: *Unum sunt, non unione personae se substantiae unitate*; PL 10, 128.

[42] Jürgen Moltmann, 'Die einladende Einheit des dreieinigen Gottes', in *In der Geschichte des dreieinigen Gottes: Beiträge zur trinitarischen Theologie* (Munich: Kaiser, 1991), p. 124.

[43] Contra Verna Harrison, 'Perichoresis in the Greek Fathers', *St Vladimir's Quarterly* 35 (1991), pp. 53–65.

[44] Concerning the presence of the Son in human beings and of human beings in the Son, see John 6.56; 14.20.

[45] As the parallel in 1 Chron. 12.39 suggests, the proverbial expression 'one heart and soul' (Acts 4.32) is not to be interpreted in the sense of an interiority of persons, even though 'heart' does refer to the personal centre of a human being.

[46] Rudolf Bultmann, *The Gospel of John: A Commentary* (Philadelphia: Westminster Press, 1971).

[47] Mühlen, *Una mystica persona*, p. 197.

[48] Zizioulas, *Being as Communion*, p. 89.

[49] John D. Zizioulas, 'Die pneumatologische Dimension der Kirche', *Internationale Katholische Zeitschrift 'Communio'* 2 (1973), p. 141.

[50] He speaks of the 'trinitarianization' of the pope, adding, however, that this 'does not *necessarily* mean that the latter must consist in establishment of a triumvirate':

Heribert Mühlen, *Entsakralisierung: Ein epochales Schlagwort in seiner Bedeutung für die Zukunft der christlichen Kirchen* (Paderborn: Schöningh, 1971), p. 257.

51 This theological interpretation of 1 Cor. 12.4–6 is plausible only in light of two presuppositions, namely, (1) that 'Spirit', 'Lord' and 'God' are not simply different names of the one person but references to different persons and (2) that 'gifts of grace', 'services' and 'activities' describe different dimensions of the same reality—the charismata.

52 See, in this regard, Donald Gelpi, *Pentecostalism: A Theological Viewpoint* (New York: Paulist Press, 1971).

53 Christian Link, Ulrich Luz and Lukas Vischer, 'Unterwegs zur Einheit', in *Sie aber hielten Fest an der Gemeinschaft* (Zurich: Benziger, 1988).

54 Ignatius, *Philadelphians* 8.1.

55 Ignatius, *Magnesians* 6.1.

56 It is perhaps not without significance that in both 1 Cor. 12.4–6 and Eph. 4.3–6, texts admonishing readers to foster unity, the sequence in the triadic formulae is not 'God (Father)–Lord–Spirit', but rather 'Spirit–Lord–God (Father)'.

57 Nicholas Wolterstorff, 'Christianity and Social Justice', *Christian Scholar's Review* 16 (1987), p. 212.

58 Paul Ramsey has defined these rights as 'whatever it is necessary for me to have in order to be with and for fellow man': *Christian Ethics and the Sit-In* (New York: Abingdon, 1961).

13

The Eucharist and the Mind of Christ: Some Trinitarian Implications of T. F. Torrance's Sacramental Theology

Paul D. Molnar

Colin Gunton criticized Augustinian theology for its tendency toward modalism and an impoverished view of the Holy Spirit, which tended to undervalue both the humanity of Jesus and ours. He also believed that the failure to see the connection between the doctrine of the Trinity and the community sanctioned inappropriate views of the church that either identified the true church with the clergy or some invisible reality to be realized in the future. Emphasis on the Holy Spirit, together with a properly conceived Christology, Gunton believed, would lead to a more appropriate view of the church as a community of believers united in and through the Trinitarian God acting to perfect creation here and now in the power of the Holy Spirit.[1] Such a view would avoid a falsely authoritarian view of the church and sacraments, while seeing both as expressions of what the Trinitarian God is doing in history prior to the second coming.

Deeply appreciative yet critical of T. F. Torrance's Trinitarian theology, Gunton stressed that 'there are resources in Torrance's work which are waiting to be developed' that could help overcome these difficulties. Especially important to Gunton was Torrance's paper 'The Mind of Christ in Worship: The Problem of Apollinarianism in the Liturgy',[2] which we shall explore here to see how some of Gunton's concerns might be addressed and how and why Torrance agreed and disagreed with Barth in order to offer a properly Trinitarian view of the Eucharist.

Emphasizing Christ's high-priestly function in worship, T. F. Torrance opposes separating the immanent and economic Trinity and all forms of dualism and Apollinarianism. Underestimating Christ's high-priestly function leads to a Pelagian or dualistic view of the sacraments. If Christ is not seen as having died for all people 'irrespective of their response', then the unconditional and costly nature of God's grace is missed:

> We need to learn . . . that salvation by grace alone is so radical that we have to rely upon Christ Jesus entirely in everything . . . Because he came as man to take our place, in and through his humanity our humanity is radically transformed, and we become truly human and really free to believe, love and serve him.[3]

This theme structures Torrance's understanding of the Lord's Supper by obviating Pelagian conceptions of atonement and priesthood.[4]

Both the *homoousion* and Torrance's frequent assertion that what God is toward us in Christ and the Holy Spirit (in the economy) he is eternally and antecedently in himself, means the Lord's Supper must be seen as grounded in and participating in the eternal communion of Father, Son and Holy Spirit. This is an unshakeable ontological and epistemological foundation for understanding the sacrament. With his Chalcedonian view of Christology, Torrance avoids both Nestorianism and Eutychianism (Apollinarianism) and elaborates a view of the Eucharist that does justice not only to Christ's humanity and ours, but actually shows how the elements in the Lord's Supper are neither identical with nor separable from the risen and ascended Lord who makes himself present through the Spirit as the main celebrant of the Lord's Supper. These are the positive features of Torrance's theology alluded to by Colin Gunton.

Torrance's Criticism of Barth

For Torrance, as for Calvin and Barth, there is an intrinsic unity between baptism and the Lord's Supper because the former signifies our justification through Christ's atonement and the latter signifies our renewal in Christ between the time of his ascension and second coming: baptism and the Lord's Supper are anchored in Christ himself as the one who actively gives meaning to them through the activity of the Holy Spirit.[5] While Torrance does not believe Barth actually fell into Gnostic dualism, he did criticize Barth's sharp distinction between Spirit baptism and water baptism, claiming it led him 'back into a mode of thought which he himself had sharply rejected in earlier volumes [of the *Church Dogmatics*]'.[6] Torrance disavowed 'an intermediate realm of supernatural grace between God and man',[7] which falsely encouraged the idea that grace is a spiritual healing medicine poured into humanity, so that God could not directly interact with humanity in his Word and Spirit; this opened the door to a 'hidden deism' which still affects the way baptism is seen today, with the idea that sacraments contain grace and are 'instruments for "conferring or causing grace" in the recipients'.[8]

Torrance believed that there are two possible reactions to the idea that baptism contains or causes grace: first, 'a return to a sacramental dualism . . . in which the meaning . . . is found not in a direct act of God but in an ethical act on the part of man made by way of response to what God has already done on his behalf', and second, 'an even stronger unity between water-baptism and Spirit-baptism objectively determined by the saving act of God in the incarnate Son and by his direct act now through the Spirit'.[9] Torrance takes the second option, which sees God directly acting within the economy and thus interacting with us in space and time, and thinks Barth chose the former alternative, which was inconsistent with his dynamic Trinitarian theology and with his view of the incarnation and God's actions in creation and redemption.

Torrance suggests, as did Alasdair Heron,[10] that because Barth saw Christ as the only sacrament, he separated our ethical behaviour from God's direct actions so that the sacrament was seen as our *response* to what God has done in Christ rather than as the inclusion of our response in his ongoing objective priestly mediation of us to God. Torrance is not minimizing the salvation accomplished in the incarnate Son, nor is he suggesting that salvation is not by grace alone. He agrees with Barth that Christ is uniquely the one who is *mysterion* in such a way that he is the 'matter', which alone gives meaning to the church's action in the Lord's Supper.[11] But, unlike Barth, he is saying that the sacramental action of the church realizes Christ's once-for-all atoning action by a direct new act through the Spirit uniting us to Christ's humanity and thus to the Father. Gunton rightly wanted to stress this thinking in calling attention to the importance of the Holy Spirit for a proper view of divine and human freedom in Christ. Proper emphasis on the Holy Spirit eschews Nestorian and Apollinarian views of the Eucharist.

Torrance helps us to see both the historical and theological factors at work in Christology and worship in a way that gives due weight to Christ's humanity and thus to ours:

> The mystery of the Eucharist is to be understood in terms of our participation through the Spirit in what the whole Jesus Christ, the incarnate, crucified, risen and ascended Son, is in himself, in respect both of his activity from the Father towards mankind and of his activity from mankind towards the Father.[12]

God has acted mightily on our behalf as saviour and has restored human being 'to proper sonship in the image of God'. Reconciliation must 'be translated into terms of human life and activity. Hence the Son of God came not simply to act *in* man but *as man*.'[13]

Apollinarianism in the Liturgy

Torrance emphasized the place of the mind of Christ in mediating our worship of the Father.[14] If we neglect the mind of Jesus in its oneness with the mind of the Father, then the whole nature of worship changes and Apollinarianism in the liturgy arises. Worship and prayer are bound up with our conception of justification. Seeing justification merely as 'a non-imputation of sin in which we believe' suggests we are justified 'by *our* faith'; but justification should mean our 'feeding upon Christ, a participation in his human righteousness, so that to be justified by faith is to be justified in him in whom we believe, not by an act of our faith as such'. Rather than relying on our prayers and thus on ourselves, we rely on Christ's *vicarious* prayer, which included his word and deed in his self-offering to the Father. 'Vicarious' should not imply that Jesus did not fully experience our human limitations but that he did so by way of condescension, without compromising his unique Sonship, for our benefit. Thus to pray in Christ's name is to pray the 'Our Father'; 'it is the *Abba Father* of Christ himself which cries in us through the Spirit of the Father'.[15]

Early liturgies directed Eucharistic prayers through Christ the one Mediator to the Father so that we pray not only *in* and *through* Christ but *with* Christ.[16] Later liturgies, especially from the Middle Ages, directed these same prayers mainly *to* Christ, especially after the Arian crisis; this suppressed Christ's human mediation and led to a type of liturgical Monophysitism, namely, Apollinarianism, which is particularly insidious because it replaces Jesus' human mind with the divine mind of the Logos.

By allowing Christ's humanity its proper role in mediating worship, Torrance grounds our worship in the incarnation and overcomes the dualism he criticizes in Barth. Proper worship takes place *through Christ*. Apollinarianism eliminates Jesus' full humanity and supposes that because the divine mind is changeless and sinless, it replaces Jesus' human mind in order to save us. This robs Jesus of the full range of human experiences—incapacity, humiliation, suffering, temptation and death—and destroys Jesus' mediation *from the human side* towards God. It also undercuts the fact that Christ is *homoousios* with us.

Thus Apollinarianism cannot speak of a God who has 'come all the way to us'; Jesus' death is simply his own and not 'our death made his own by the vicarious action of the Son of God become man'.[17] This creates a chasm between God and us in Christ so that our worship cannot 'take place *in Christ* either'. Apollinarianism cannot see that our sinful human nature is healed by Christ's assumption of it; it *separates* our worship from the redemption of our human mind and soul in their estrangement from God; and it makes Christ's body only an instrument for salvation by considering salvation a direct action of God that bypasses our human intellectual constitution. Apollinarianism prevents a genuine relationship between God and the human soul, mind and will so that 'worship cannot be thought of as taking place *with* Christ'.[18]

Torrance relies on Athanasius and Cyril of Alexandria as a corrective. Cyril emphasized that 'what has not been taken up, has not been saved'.[19] Thus God *as* man lives within the limitations of our humanity in order to heal us without limiting himself in his nature as the Son who cannot be circumscribed by time and space: 'in Christ God did not come into man but became man, while remaining God, he lives as man, acting both divinely and humanly'.[20] Jesus lived an 'economic and vicarious ignorance ("for our sakes") by way of voluntary restraint of his divine knowledge throughout a life of *continuous kenosis*'[21] and so refused to violate its creaturely limitations. By opposing Apollinarianism, Cyril stressed that Christ's vicarious work in the likeness of our sinful flesh involved his priestly self-offering in obedience to the Father as the incarnate Word on our behalf.

Because this emphasis is missing in a number of contemporary theologies which stress that God must be able to suffer because love of another necessarily means need and suffering, they fail to see that God's freedom is not determined *by* suffering but embraces it in order to remove it as a final threat to us. Torrance understood the issue: any Apollinarian implication that Jesus' rational soul or human mind was replaced by the divine soul or mind means that God did not really become one with us in our human condition. Neither could there be Nestorian separation of the Son's divinity from the priestly office of his humanity, which would compromise the vicarious nature of what he did humanly for us 'in his economic condescension'. Apollinarian elimination and Nestorian separation imply the inconceivability of 'an immutable and impassible Deity becoming one with human beings in their contingency and passion'.[22] For Torrance, God remains impassible; his deity is not diminished in his vicarious human obedience in our place. But he experiences our suffering and pain because he healed our humanity from within human experience and history in the person of the Mediator:[23] 'It was not the *death* of Jesus that constituted atonement, but Jesus Christ the Son of God offering Himself in sacrifice for us. Everything depends on *who* He was, for the significance of His acts in life and death depends on the nature of His Person.'[24]

After Pentecost, Christ is the High Priest who presides through the Spirit in all liturgical acts: 'while he is offered by us in prayer to the Father, in reality it is he who offers us to the Father in the identity of himself as Offerer and Offering'.[25] Whenever Christ's vicarious representation is not properly emphasized, his mediation is restricted to his saving work on our behalf and Jesus is only seen as the meeting place of divinity and humanity; rather Christ prays with us and we pray with him. As Jesus' human priesthood became obscured, attention was focused on what the priest offers and on the bread and wine being turned into Jesus' own body and blood. Focus on Jesus' human priestly mediation was replaced with emphasis on the Holy Spirit coming upon the oblations and enabling people to offer the same offering which the only-begotten Son had offered to the Father.[26]

For Torrance, however, the *anamnesis* is not just something *we* do in *remembrance* of Christ's historical self-offering on the cross. Rather it

is something we do in and through the real presence of the whole Christ . . . so that the bread which we break and the cup of blessing which we bless are communion (*koinonia*) in the body and blood of Christ and the eucharistic offering of Christ to the Father which we make through him is communion (*koinonia*) in his own sacrificial self-offering to God the Father.[27]

Consequently we bring about neither the unity between ourselves and Christ, nor his real presence. Only the Holy Spirit makes effective all that he has done and still does for us.[28]

Real Presence

Christ's *real presence* is the 'whole Christ, not just the presence of his body and blood, nor just the presence of his Spirit or Mind, but the presence of the actual Jesus Christ . . . as Gift and Giver'.[29] Important consequences follow. First, Christ's real presence is his personal and creative presence among us, his 'self-giving to us'; we have no 'ecclesiastical, liturgical or intellectual' control over it. This same presence confronted the disciples on the road to Emmaus and in the upper room at Jerusalem, even though it now meets us in the form of the Eucharist as appointed by Jesus himself. Second, the whole Christ is present 'in the fullness of his deity and in the fullness of his humanity, crucified and risen . . . Jesus Christ clothed with his Gospel and clothed with the power of his Spirit, who cannot be separated from what he did or taught'.[30] Third, 'he creatively effects what he declares . . . "This is my body broken for you", "This is my blood shed for many for the remission of sins"'.[31] Fourth, the Eucharist

is the dominically appointed place . . . where we meet with Christ and have communion with him in his real presence, as he is the one place appointed by God within our space-time existence where heaven and earth, eternity and time, God and man fully meet and are for ever united, and the only place where God and man are reconciled.[32]

We are 'gathered up through communion with Christ into the living presence of God in the eternal communion of the Holy Trinity'. Hence the real presence 'is objectively grounded in *the presence of God to himself*, and as such is the profoundest and most intensive kind of presence there could ever be.' Fifth, we cannot construe Christ's real presence in the Eucharist 'in terms of anything we can analyze naturally in this world', but, because Christ is really present, there are indeed 'spatial and temporal ingredients in a proper understanding of the real presence'.[33]

Dualism and Phenomenalism

Serious problems have arisen in the Western understanding of the incarnation and real Eucharistic presence; they take different forms in Catholic and Protestant thought and are traceable to Platonic dualism and Aristotelian phenomenalism.

If attention is directed '*at* the Eucharist itself rather than *from* or *through* the Eucharist to its real ground in the paschal mystery of Christ', it is phenomenalized 'as something enshrining a hidden meaning or mystery in itself'.[34] This shift resulted when theology moved from a Christocentric to an anthropocentric starting point.[35] The Neoplatonic distinction between the real and the transient worlds 'laid the foundation for a dualist understanding of the relation between God and the world' and also of the sacraments by inhibiting 'a serious consideration of a real *becoming* of the intelligible in the sensible, or of the eternal in the contingent'.[36] Following Augustine 'sacraments came to be defined as outward and visible signs of inward and invisible grace'.[37] This led to a symbolic understanding of the sacraments, which threatened to lead to 'a merely spiritual interpretation of the real presence'.[38] But by assimilating grace to causality, this tendency was restrained by what Torrance calls an 'instrumentalist notion of sacramental grace'.

Catholic understanding of the real presence, interpreted in terms of *transubstantiation,* restricted Christ's real presence, 'defined in this phenomenalist, physico-causal way'. But this points to 'some docetic error in Christology', namely, 'to a transubstantiation of the human nature of Christ, leaving only a *species* to remain'.[39] With the causal connection between grace and the experience of the participants came the *ex opere operato,* which inevitably depersonalized real presence, and implied that the priest was 'given the power to do what Christ does, in *re-enacting his sacrifice'.*[40] This led to the ideas that Christ as the victim in the Eucharist is effected by the liturgy and that *'something is done to Christ* in the Eucharist'.[41] Eucharistic sacrifice seen as 'a cultic repetition of the immolation or propitiatory sacrifice of Christ is not far off'.[42]

The Receptacle/Container Notion of Space

These developments were also influenced by 'the receptacle or container concept of space' taken from Aristotle, which eventually led Latin theology to view God's presence mainly in a *spatial* manner *apart from time.* But, as Torrance notes, 'the relation between God and space is not itself a spatial relation';[43] God stands in a 'creative, not a spatial or a temporal relation' to the world. Neither heaven nor the incarnation 'contain' or limit God. Nicene theology developed a relational notion of space to stress that God was actually present in space and time in the incarnation (that is the sense of the 'he came down from heaven').[44]

Two problems follow. First, space was 'oriented to a centre of absolute rest in the earth and in the unmoved mover behind it'; space and time were detached from action and there followed a diminished emphasis in Latin theology on the 'dynamic interaction between God and historical existence and in eschatological perspective of the Eucharist'.[45] The eschatological perspective is extremely important; it keeps us focused on the resurrection 'as the enduring reality in the heart of the Church'.[46] Second, this concept of space involved 'interdependence and inseparability of the container and what it contains, which was essentially quantitative and volumetric'.[47] This gave rise to static and rigid concepts and led to 'highly artificial explanations as to how the body and blood of Christ are really present through the bread and wine'.[48] Medieval and Tridentine theology could hardly have avoided expressing Christ's real presence in these terms, which once served a positive function for the church but now only perform a disservice by focusing attention on 'the *corpus Christi* in the Eucharist as something in itself, rather than on the personal presence of Jesus Christ in his reality as crucified but risen and glorified Lord'.[49]

The Reformers focused on the Last Supper dynamically in its historical context, not as a 'timeless rite'. They 'identified grace with the *self*-giving of God in Christ, that is, with Christ himself', not a 'supernatural something in which believers participate more and more through the ministration of the Church'. They sought to

> interpret the Eucharist out of itself with reference to *who* is really present and to the communion he grants us to have with him in his body and blood through the creative operation of his Spirit . . . without attempting to explain *how* this actually takes place in terms of the kind of causal-spatial connections with which we operate in any natural philosophy . . .[50]

Tridentine concepts of 'really and substantially contains' and 'transubstantiation' never confronted the disagreement 'with the inner heart of catholic dogma as to the paschal mystery of Christ' and never got beyond the obsolete Aristotelian concepts to listen 'to the original datum of revelation with a view to a more faithful interpretation in the living continuity of the Church's life'.[51] Protestantism never quite overcame the dualism within its own Augustinian infrastructure, that is, the understanding of sacraments as visible or outward signs of invisible or inward grace and the shift toward inwardness and immediacy, which led to pietism, and a view of real presence in a spiritual and symbolic sense.

Whenever the Eucharist is understood in the context of dualism and whenever these problems are addressed without attacking that basic dualistic epistemology and ontology, then problems of the kind that have afflicted Western Christianity will remain unresolved. Gnosticism, Arianism, Monophysitism and Nestorianism refused to acknowledge that the eternal Son of God was directly active in our creaturely world of time and space in the history of Jesus Christ. Regarding the sacraments, dualism led people to focus on the Eucharistic rite itself 'with a serious loss in objective depth in the paschal mystery of Christ and a foreshortening of its meaning'.[52] Whenever the Eucharist is set within an Augustinian dualistic framework, its meaning tends to be found either in the rite itself and its performance or in the inward and moral experience of the participants, for then the Eucharist is regarded either as a holy mystery in itself enshrining and guaranteeing the divine mystery of the Church in the host, or as the appointed ordinance which occasions and stimulates deeper spiritual consciousness and awareness in believers.[53]

Conclusions

What can be learned from Torrance's emphasis on Christ's high priestly mediation and his rejection of dualistic epistemology and ontology in understanding the Eucharist in a Trinitarian way? First, God gives himself to us in Jesus Christ; the Gift is identical with the Giver. If our understanding of God's relation with the world is 'damaged' because of a dualistic perspective, then we will assume that God has not actually given himself within created time and space 'but only something of himself through a created mediation'.[54] A dualistic perspective actually divides the Gift from the Giver. The Catholic tendency focuses on the Gift in its concern for real presence, thought of 'as inhering in the Eucharist as such'.[55] The Protestant tendency focuses on ourselves as receivers over against the Giver. Torrance insists, against both of these tendencies, that because the Gift is identical with the Giver, God is immediately present in his own being and life through Jesus Christ; this self-giving 'takes place *in the Holy Spirit* who is not just an emanation from God but the immediate presence and activity of God in his own divine Being, the Spirit of the Father and the Son . . . this is a real presence of Christ to us'.[56]

Second, with respect to Eucharistic sacrifice, the Offerer is identical with the Offering: what 'the Incarnate Son offers to the Father on our behalf is his own human life which he took from us and assumed into unity with his divine life, his *self*-offering through the eternal Spirit of the Father'. Because the historical offering of his body on the cross is inherently one with himself as the Offerer, it is a once-and-for-all event which remains eternally valid. Understood dualistically, the Offerer and Offering are not finally one; 'neither is his offering once and for all nor is it completely and sufficiently vicarious'.[57] He becomes only a created intermediary and the offering is seen as a merely human offering so that no real mediation between God and creatures has taken place. Torrance insists that if Christ's human priesthood is seen within a Nestorian or Apollinarian framework 'then it becomes only a representative and no longer a vicarious priesthood, for it is no longer unique but only an exemplary form of our own';[58] thus it is no longer uniquely substitutionary.

This directs us to rely on ourselves 'to effect our own "Pelagian" mediation with God by being our own priests and by offering to him our own sacrifices'. Even if this is done 'for Christ's sake' and motivated by him, since it is not done '*with him*, and *in him* we have no access *through him* into the immediate presence of God'. If, however, 'Jesus Christ is himself both Priest and Victim, Offerer and Offering' who has effected atoning reconciliation and so for ever 'unites God and man in his one Person and *as such* coinheres with the Father and the Holy Spirit in the eternal Trinity, then, we participate in his self-consecration and self-offering to the Father and thus appear with him and in him and through him before the Majesty of God in worship, praise and adoration with no other sacrifice than the sacrifice of Christ Jesus our Mediator and High Priest'.

When the Church worships, praises and adores the Father through Jesus Christ, it is the self-offering and self-consecration of Jesus Christ 'in our nature ascending to the Father from the Church in which he dwells through the Spirit;' 'it is Christ himself who worships, praises and adores the Father in and through his members'[59] shaping their prayers and conforming them in their communion in his body and blood.

T. F. Torrance's achievement here is immense. By focusing on '*God as Man* rather than upon God in Man', Torrance embraces a high Christology which concentrates on the humanity of the incarnate Son of God and a view of Eucharistic worship and life 'in which the primacy is given to the priestly mediation of Jesus Christ':

> It is in fact the eternal life of the incarnate Son in us that ascends to the Father in our worship and prayer through, with and in him, in the unity of the Holy Spirit. While they are our worship and prayer, in as much as we freely and fully participate in the Sonship of Christ and in the whole course of his filial obedience to the Father, they are derived from and rooted in a source beyond themselves, in the economic conde-scension and ascension of the Son of God. The movement of worship and prayer . . . is essentially correlative to the movement of the divine love and grace, from the Father, through the Son and in the Spirit.[60]

This leads to a more unified soteriology which views incarnation and atonement as a single continuous movement of God's redeeming love which accentuates Jesus Christ's '*God-manward* and his *man-Godward* activity'. Focusing on Jesus' vicarious humanity emphasizes that Christ has put himself in our place, experiencing our alienated human condition and healing it. Eucharistic *anamnesis* is no mere recollection of what Christ has done for us once for all, but a memorial which 'according to his command' and 'through the Spirit is filled with the presence of Christ in the indivisible unity of all his vicarious work and his glorified Person'.[61]

We are grateful to Colin Gunton for directing us to Torrance's opposition to Apollinarianism in worship—to see both the church and the Eucharist in a more properly Trinitarian way that does justice not only to the humanity of the Word, but to our humanity as we are united to Christ and through him to the Father through the power of the Holy Spirit. Following Torrance's Eucharistic theology could help theologians better understand Christ's real presence and avoid dualism and phenomenalism. Stressing the direct interaction between the community and the risen Lord between the time of his ascension and second coming would prevent an authoritarian view of the church and sacraments, as Gunton himself wished to do.

Notes

[1]   See Colin E. Gunton, 'The Church on Earth: The Roots of Community', in *On Being the Church: Essays on the Christian Community*, ed. Colin E. Gunton and Daniel W. Hardy (Edinburgh: T&T Clark, 1989), pp. 48–80.

[2]   Colin Gunton, 'Being and Person: T. F. Torrance's Doctrine of God', in *The Promise of Trinitarian Theology: Theologians in Dialogue with T. F. Torrance*, ed. Elmer M. Colyer (Lanham, Md.: Rowman & Littlefield, 2001), p. 132.

[3]   Thomas F. Torrance, *Preaching Christ Today: The Gospel and Scientific Thinking* (Grand Rapids: Eerdmans, 1994), p. 37.

[4]   See Thomas F. Torrance, 'Toward a Doctrine of the Lord's Supper', in *Conflict and Agreement in the Church: The Ministry and the Sacraments of the Gospel*, II (Eugene, Ore. and Pasadena: Wipf & Stock, 1996), p. 137, and Thomas F. Torrance, 'The Mind of Christ in Worship: The Problem of Apollinarianism in the Liturgy', in *Theology in Reconciliation: Essays towards Evangelical and Catholic Unity in East and West* (London: Geoffrey Chapman, 1975), p. 172.

[5]   Torrance, 'The Mind of Christ in Worship', pp. 146–8.

[6]   Thomas F. Torrance, *Karl Barth: Biblical and Evangelical Theologian* (Edinburgh: T&T Clark, 1990), p. 134.

[7]   Thomas F. Torrance, 'The One Baptism Common to Christ and his Church', in *Theology in Reconciliation*, p. 99.

[8]   Torrance, 'The One Baptism', p. 98. 'Grace comes from beyond the self . . . As power acting on men it is not impersonal, but intensely personal . . . The real content of the word [*charis*] is still the person of Jesus Christ': Thomas F. Torrance, *The Doctrine of Grace in the Apostolic Fathers* (Pasadena and Eugene, Ore.: Wipf & Stock, 1996), p. 32.

[9]   Torrance, 'The One Baptism', p. 99.

[10] Alasdair I. C. Heron, *Table and Tradition: Toward an Ecumenical Understanding of the Eucharist* (Philadelphia: Westminster Press, 1983), pp. 156–7; see also Paul D. Molnar, *Karl Barth and the Theology of the Lord's Supper: A Systematic Investigation* (New York: Peter Lang, 1996), pp. 191–2, 299–303.

[11] T. F. Torrance, 'Eschatology and the Eucharist', in *Conflict and Agreement in the Church*, II, p. 178, and Torrance, 'Toward a Doctrine of the Lord's Supper', p. 142.

12 Torrance, 'The Paschal Mystery of Christ and the Eucharist', in *Theology in Reconciliation*, p. 117; and Torrance, 'Toward a Doctrine of the Lord's Supper', pp. 142–3.

13 Torrance, 'The Paschal Mystery of Christ and the Eucharist', p. 117. All italics in quotations from Torrance's work are in the original. By sharing our human being and life Christ consecrated 'himself for us that we might be consecrated through him, offering himself in holy obedience and atoning sacrifice to God for us that we, through sharing in his self-offering, may offer to God through him a holiness from the side of man answering his own'.

14 Torrance, 'The Mind of Christ in Worship', pp. 139–40.

15 Torrance, 'The Mind of Christ in Worship', p. 141. See also 'Toward a Doctrine of the Lord's Supper', p. 147.

16 Torrance, 'The Mind of Christ in Worship', pp. 17, 178.

17 Torrance, 'The Mind of Christ in Worship', p. 148.

18 Torrance, 'The Mind of Christ in Worship', p. 150.

19 Torrance, 'The Mind of Christ in Worship', p. 167.

20 Torrance, 'The Mind of Christ in Worship', p. 165.

21 Torrance, 'The Mind of Christ in Worship', p. 166.

22 Torrance, 'The Mind of Christ in Worship', p. 202.

23 Thomas F. Torrance, *The Trinitarian Faith* (Edinburgh: T&T Clark, 1988), p. 185.

24 T. F. Torrance, *God and Rationality* (London: Oxford University Press, 1971), p. 64.

25 Torrance, 'The Mind of Christ in Worship', p. 184.

26 Torrance, 'The Mind of Christ in Worship', pp. 194–5.

27 Torrance, 'The Paschal Mystery of Christ and the Eucharist', p. 119.

28 Torrance, 'Eschatology and the Eucharist', pp. 175–8.

29 Torrance, 'The Paschal Mystery of Christ and the Eucharist', p. 119.

30 Torrance, 'The Paschal Mystery of Christ and the Eucharist', p. 120.

31 Torrance, 'The Paschal Mystery of Christ and the Eucharist', p. 120.

32 Torrance, 'The Paschal Mystery of Christ and the Eucharist', p. 121.

33 Torrance, 'The Paschal Mystery of Christ and the Eucharist', p. 121.

34 Torrance, 'The Paschal Mystery of Christ and the Eucharist', p. 122.

35 Thomas F. Torrance, 'The Deposit of Faith', *Scottish Journal of Theology* 36 (1983), pp. 1–28.

36 Thomas F. Torrance, 'The Roman Doctrine of Grace from the Point of View of Reformed Theology', in *Theology in Reconstruction* (London: SCM Press, 1965), p. 175.

37 Torrance, 'The Paschal Mystery of Christ and the Eucharist', p. 122.

38 Torrance, 'The Paschal Mystery of Christ and the Eucharist', p. 123.

39 Torrance, 'The Roman Doctrine of Grace', p. 184. See also 'Eschatology and the Eucharist', p. 188. For Torrance, after Christ's resurrection and ascension, his true humanity excludes any 'docetic phantasm'. Thus bread and wine are not just 'species' but instruments of Christ's real presence ontologically uniting himself with his church.

40 Torrance, 'The Paschal Mystery of Christ and the Eucharist', p. 124.

41 Torrance, 'The Paschal Mystery of Christ and the Eucharist', p. 124.

42 Torrance, 'The Paschal Mystery of Christ and the Eucharist', p. 124.

43 Thomas F. Torrance, *Space, Time and Incarnation* (London: Oxford University Press, 1978), p. 2.

44 Torrance, *Space, Time and Incarnation*, pp. 2–3; see also chs 1 and 2.

45 Torrance, 'The Paschal Mystery of Christ and the Eucharist', pp. 124–5.

46 Torrance, 'Eschatology and the Eucharist', p. 174.

47 Torrance, 'The Paschal Mystery of Christ and the Eucharist', p. 125. See also *Space, Time and Incarnation*, p. 26.

48 Torrance, 'The Paschal Mystery of Christ and the Eucharist', p. 125. See also *Space, Time and Incarnation*, pp. 27–8.

49 Torrance, 'The Paschal Mystery of Christ and the Eucharist', p. 125. See also 'Eschatology and the Eucharist', p. 185.

50 Torrance, 'The Paschal Mystery of Christ and the Eucharist', pp. 126–7; see also Torrance, 'Eucharist and Eschatology', p. 186 and Torrance, *The Christian Doctrine of God: One Being Three Persons* (Edinburgh: T&T Clark, 1996), p. 193.

51 Torrance, 'The Paschal Mystery of Christ and the Eucharist', p. 127.

52 Torrance, 'The Paschal Mystery of Christ and the Eucharist', p. 130.

53 Torrance, 'The Paschal Mystery of Christ and the Eucharist', p. 131.

54 Torrance, 'The Paschal Mystery of Christ and the Eucharist', p. 131.

55 Torrance, 'The Paschal Mystery of Christ and the Eucharist', p. 132.

56 Torrance, 'The Paschal Mystery of Christ and the Eucharist', p. 132.

57 Torrance, 'The Paschal Mystery of Christ and the Eucharist', p. 133.

58 Torrance, 'The Paschal Mystery of Christ and the Eucharist', p. 133.

59 Torrance, 'The Paschal Mystery of Christ and the Eucharist', p. 134.

60 Torrance, 'The Mind of Christ', p. 212.

61 Torrance, 'The Paschal Mystery of Christ and the Eucharist', p. 136.

14

Trajectories of a Trinitarian Eschatology

Kelly M. Kapic

Introduction

One outworking of the recent renaissance of Trinitarian theology is a strong understanding—as the structure of this volume is meant to embody—that the recognition of God as triune must not simply be reduced to one 'chapter' among many. It is rather, a truth that informs all reflections on God, his people, and his world. Comparable conclusions about the proper place of eschatology are also being reached—although it seems to have begun more in biblical studies than dogmatics. No longer can one simply view eschatology as the final chapter in one's systematics, but rather the *eschatos* must guide one's entire theological structure.[1] Thus, as theologians have spoken of a renaissance in Trinitarian theology, we can also acknowledge a resurgence of eschatological thinking in the twentieth century.[2] By this I mean far more than the phenomenon of the best-selling *Left Behind* series, although one might argue that the two are not unrelated. My task here is not to retell the history of these renewals, but rather to explore two seminal themes that should inform our reflection. By examining the ideas of (1) *the unity of divine movement* and (2) *the eschatological man*, I aim to point out directions for developing a biblical and Trinitarian eschatology. The thoughts developed in this chapter are deeply influenced by Colin Gunton, a man who indelibly shaped my understanding of what it means to live before the face of God.

The Unity of Divine Movement

Is God United in His Purpose?

God creates in divine freedom, and in this gracious act he commits himself to his creation. In the light of the Fall, this leads us to a critical pastoral and theological question: *How are the Father, Son, and Holy Spirit united in the eschatological movement of reconciliation?* It continues to be a common problem that many of the flock imagine an angry Father who must constantly be convinced by the gentle Son to put up with his sinful people. In other words, believers are often convinced of Jesus' love for them, but less so of the Father's, and they consistently depersonalize the Spirit. This problem can be worsened if one too rigidly distinguishes the persons as Creator, Redeemer and Sanctifier, without at the same time stressing *perichoresis* (their mutual indwelling). Another symptom of the same disease is the tendency to downplay the radical nature of sin and view the Holy Spirit more like a weak breeze than the eschatologically intrusive breath of God who awakens the dead. One way to combat such misunderstandings is to develop a deliberately Trinitarian eschatology, narrating the full movement of God as Father, Son and Holy Spirit, from creation to consummation, from sending to ascending.

The question of unity in divine movement also provokes debates about universalism—will all, in the end, be redeemed? These debates are often fierce, and they can become hopelessly anthropocentric rather than theocentric. When eschatological conversation is self-consciously Trinitarian, however, we see that these are questions about the character of God. I have become convinced that all great theologians (e.g. John Owen and Karl Barth) must wrestle with universalism, not because they are more empathetic than others, but because the issue arises from their wrestling with the attributes of God and the cross of Christ.

One common problem in addressing universalism is the subtle temptation to pit the persons of the Trinity against one another. Can the Son want the salvation of the world if a reluctant Father does not? Does the Father love the world and send the Son to die for it if the Holy Spirit quickens only a few? How shall we conceive of the Triune God's love, commitment and judgement toward this world? However one conceives of the judgement (e.g. eternal, torment, cessation of being, etc.), as long as one believes that there can be the impossible possibility that some could reject Christ, then there appears to be a Trinitarian dilemma. What we must avoid is dividing up the Triune God by treating one of the persons as a maverick. These are some of the great paradoxes of Holy Scripture, and we must faithfully maintain the tensions found there, believing that God will be all in all (1 Cor. 15.28). Whether one ends up a universalist or not, this eschatological conversation must remain a *Trinitarian* discussion, otherwise we lose the heart of the issue.

Our hope is God himself, and therefore our eschatology is first and foremost about theology, not anthropology.[3] Herman Ridderbos argued this against Rudolf Bultmann, asserting that the Apostle Paul's eschatology was not *sub specie hominis*, but *sub specie Dei*, where 'past, present, and future occur . . . under the viewpoint of that God who is the Creator of heaven and earth and who conducts all things to their consummation'.[4] Our eschatological vision must be guided by the unity of divine movement in history, where the living God makes himself known by his actions, demonstrating that he has not abandoned his fallen creation, but rather works in, through, and over it as the Sovereign Lord.

Gregory of Nyssa and Augustine: Unity in Movement

When one of the Cappadocian fathers, Gregory of Nyssa, argues for the unity of God, he examines the eschatological activity of God in redemption, describing the divine operations and the harmony of divine purpose and direction.[5] The Father does nothing by himself, nor does the Son act apart from the Spirit,

> but every activity which pervades [*sic*] from God to creation and is named according to our manifold designs starts off from the Father, proceeds through the Son, and is completed by the Holy Spirit. On account of this, *the name of activity is not divided into the multitude of those who are active. The action of each in any regard is not divided and peculiar.* But whatever of the *anticipated things* would happen, whether for our providence or to the administration of the whole and to its constitution, *it happens through the three*, the things which do happen are *not* three distinct things.[6]

While acknowledging the proper distinctions among the divine persons, Gregory avoids statements that would separate them. As he points out, God gives us life, but that does not mean we receive 'three lives', but the 'same life' comes to us, 'activated by the Holy Spirit, prepared by the Son, and produced by the Father's will'.[7]

Another example Gregory gives of the divine order also has eschatological overtones—the judgement of God. He notes that Scripture claims both that God 'judges the whole earth' (cf. Gen. 8.25; Rom. 8.6) and that 'the Father judges no one' (John 5.22). Do these statements mean that 'Scripture wars with itself'? No, for God judges through the unity of divine movement, whereby the wisdom and power of God the Son judges the earth, perfecting 'all power in the Holy Spirit who judges'.[8] Gregory's comments emphasize the divine harmony of purpose, whereby Father, Son and Holy Spirit work the work not only of creation, but of re-creation and consummation.

Consequently, Gregory theologically frames salvation in terms of the Triune God, since 'the unity of activity prevents a plural counting'.[9] These warnings apply to those who might see different eras as belonging to the different persons of the Trinity (e.g. Joachim of Fiore, *c.* 1132–1202).[10] Gregory makes it clear that the Son does not reject those who believe, nor can salvation occur outside of the Spirit: 'No postponement occurs, or is thought of, in the movement of divine will from the Father through the Son to the Spirit.'[11] For eschatological concerns this is radically important, for although we tend to think in a linear fashion, the Triune God, from his infinite freedom, wills and acts, dynamically working salvation in time. The divine persons, Father, Son and Holy Spirit, all display divine love and judgement, and in this there is no division, but united purpose. In other words, the God of the beginning is the same as the God of the end, and thus we must avoid pitting protology against eschatology.

Although often portrayed as competing parties, the Cappadocians and Augustine agree that the movement of God comes from the Father through the Son and by the Spirit, that the relations of the three persons display divine unity from 'beginning' to 'end'.[12] Augustine's emphasis on God's unity is often stated as *opera trinitatis ad extra sunt indivisa* (the external works of the Trinity are undivided). But this summary can mislead if we use it to compromise Trinitarian distinctions. In his classic *De Trinitate*, Augustine himself claims that 'just as the Father and Son and Holy Spirit are inseparable [*inseparabilis*], so do they work inseparably'.[13] This claim is found in the midst of a defence of divine unity in movement and important biblical distinctions. Thus, the 'same three' were not all born by the virgin, nor did all die under Pontius Pilate, nor did they all rise from the grave. Neither did Jesus come down as the dove at the baptism, nor come as flame on the day of Pentecost, nor 'was it this same three that spoke from heaven, You are my Son'.[14] This helps us understand how Augustine can conclude, 'I say with confidence (though in fear I say it), that the Trinity is in a manner separable', noting the orthodox claim that the Father is not the Son, and the Son is not the Father, and the Holy Spirit is neither. He then demonstrates their 'inseparability' in terms of divine relations and action—what we are calling the unity of divine movement: 'this ineffable Divinity, abiding ever in itself, making all things new, creating, creating anew, sending, recalling, judging, delivering, this Trinity, I say, we know to be at once ineffable and inseparable'.[15] So, God is 'ineffable', but also known by his actions—not only creation, but also eschatologically through re-creation and ultimate deliverance. Augustine creatively holds together the incomprehensibility and true knowability of God. Thus, the actions of Father, Son and Spirit are the holy God's actions, and in his actions he is known and worshipped.

Gregory and Augustine are at one in their basic vision of the united will and action of the Triune God. The revelation of God is the revelation of Father, Son and Holy Spirit. This speaks to the purpose and plan of God whereby, through the Son and Spirit, the Father brings about the eschatological work of reconciliation and ultimate consummation. The direction and end are as determinative as the beginning. The movement of biblical narrative maintains the distinctions of the persons without losing the unity of God.

The Movement of God and Revelation

Although Karl Rahner's dictum is more often repeated than understood, there is general agreement about the impulse behind the idea that 'the economic Trinity is the immanent Trinity and the immanent Trinity is the economic Trinity': it reminds us that God has truly revealed himself in history. We need not collapse the distinctions between the ontological and the economic Trinity to state this. Rather than being embarrassed by the correspondence of the Triune God's self-revelation with the progress of that revelation, we might see a glory in this progression. The progressive nature of revelation and redemption reflects the way that humanity must now confront the anticipated consummation. For Abraham, Isaac, Paul and John, this is the living God who confronts and delivers them, a God who can be trusted for the future even in the midst of the turbulent present (cf. Hebrews 11).

Another Cappadocian father, Gregory of Nazianzus, in his poem 'De Spiritu Sancto', examines God's progressive revelation:

Who shows a fire's whole glow
to still-dim eyes, or gorges them with light insatiable?
It's better if, bit by bit, you bring on the fiery glowings,
lest you even hurt some way the springs of a sweeter light.
For, as of old the scriptures displayed the whole deity

of the royal Father, and Christ's great fame began to dawn,
disclosed to men of little understanding,
so also, later when the Son's shone more distinctly,
the brightness of the Spirit's deity glowed.[16]

Gregory elsewhere ties the progressive character of revelation to the triune nature of God in a covenantal structure.[17] This revelatory progression testifies both to human finitude and the patience of God.[18] God is not *becoming* triune, but he patiently reveals himself: he is not an evolving deity, but a God who is other than his creation, progressively making himself known.

Observations about revelation challenge us to maintain a dialectic between the teleological and eschatological: from the movement of time as past, present, and future, to the in-breaking of the future into the present, drawing us to the eternal and providing a taste of that which is to come. Our view of eternity and time must maintain this dynamic, for without it we lose the biblical tension between the (so-called) now and the not yet. Only a Trinitarian eschatology, presupposing the goodness of creation and the radical chaos of the Fall, can faithfully account for the divine electing love of the Father and the condescension of the Son and Spirit. God is not only the creator of time but its redeemer, and this redemption manifests our great eschatological hope.

The Eternal God Takes Time

The Athanasian Creed's dictum *ut unum Deum in Trinitate, et Trinitatem in Unitate veneremur* (for one God in Trinity and the Trinity in Unity we revere) guides our understanding of God and history, of time and eternity. Thus far we have been sketching the importance of divine unity in movement, wherein God reveals himself and demonstrates his plan of re-creation, which occurs by the Father, through the Son, in the Holy Spirit. Now we explore what it means to say that the eternal God has 'entered in' and that in this way he makes the consummation not only possible, but secure (cf. Matt. 1.23; 28.20).

Karl Barth argues that divine 'unity is in movement', but not at the expense of the eternality of the persons or 'their special relations to one another'.[19] The eternal and free God is other than his creation, so that 'God's essence cannot in any sense be burdened by an eternal partnership with the creature'. Nevertheless, our view of eternity must start, not in the abstract, but with the relationship between God and his creation, and with the relationship between 'eternity and time', which Barth believes is centred on the incarnate Christ.[20] This resonates with Gregory of Nazianzus' argument that the 'transcendent' Son of God became incarnate, and as such 'He remained what he was; what he was not, he assumed', namely a human nature.[21] Similarly, Barth argues that the Son did not cease to be eternal, but rather 'in its very power as eternity, eternity became time'.[22] Barth here emphasizes the eschatological healing of a fallen creation, which can only come through an earthly incarnation:

> In *Jesus Christ* it comes about that God takes time to Himself, that He Himself, the eternal One, becomes temporal, that He is present for us in the form of our own existence and our own world, not simply embracing our time and ruling it, but submitting Himself to it, and permitting created time to become and be the form of his eternity.[23]

Barth attempts to avoid diminishing God here; rather he argues just the opposite (whether he succeeds is, nevertheless, debatable). It is here that God displays his full power over the creation in becoming 'one with it without detriment to itself'.[24]

Barth's basic admonition is surely correct: *how* God has revealed himself *in Jesus Christ* should rule our reflections, rather than allowing our reflections about God to be ruled by our intuitions. There is a growing temptation in contemporary theology to collapse the Creator/creature distinction. Our post-Hegel world often posits a God in process who *requires* this world in order to be fully God, a view which I find objectionable.[25] It is a telling sign that pan(en)theism is no longer a troubling word in contemporary theology (cf. e.g., Clayton and Moltmann). Barth's proposal in the displayed quotation above would fail if he did not maintain the Creator/creature distinction: but Barth himself always safeguards this very distinction, even if his poetic language might taken differently. Though perhaps not achieving analytic precision, it may be that Barth's ambiguous statements about God, time and the incarnation should be considered a benefit, rather than a detriment.

One should not pit the eternality of God against the reality of the incarnation, according to Barth, but rather, one should see that 'true eternity has the power to take time to itself, this time, the time of the Word and Son of God'. Through the incarnation God 'masters time' and in this way 'He re-creates it and heals its wounds, the fleetingness of the present, and the separation of past and the future from one another and from the present.'[26] The key to Barth's observation is that God is not alien and distant, but presents *himself*, and thus we recognize that the 'power exercised in Jesus Christ consists in His triune being'.[27] Barth's insistence here on maintaining the economic and immanent Trinity, without sacrificing either, demonstrates his Christological method, which guards against being controlled by a foreign metaphysic.

Gunton also cautions against allowing a 'metaphysic of being' to predetermine how one understands the attributes of God.[28] The devastating result of that move is that it can become impossible 'to attribute to God forms of action without which the gospel ceases to be the gospel'.[29] Certain metaphysics deny that the eternal God can assume the temporal to himself in his incarnate Son. They produce similar problems for the assumption of a true human nature by the Son, and with the continuing humanity of the risen Christ—a doctrine essential to the church throughout the ages. Unless one allows that the eternal God has assumed the temporal in some fashion, then one will be tempted to compromise the doctrine of the ascension, which will weaken the eschatological doctrine of the continuing work of the Mediator.

A Trinitarian eschatological vision of communion with God, however, will see the birth, life, death, resurrection, ascension and return of the Christ *as the very point of eschatology*—the distinctly Christian hope in God. This eschatological hope is driven not by abstract reflections about time, nor by doomsday cultural observations, but by looking to the person and work of the Saviour, who was, is, and is to come. At the centre of our eschatological vision we must find the incarnate Christ, in whom we find the full self-revelation of God, and in this way we move from the panoramic to the particular; in other words, Jesus is the ultimate case study of our Trinitarian eschatology.

The Eschatological Man

Method: Christology as the Guide for Eschatology

Herman Bavinck claimed that eschatology 'is rooted in Christology and is itself Christology, the teaching of the final, complete triumph of Christ and his kingdom over all his enemies'.[30] For him, the revelation of God in Christ demonstrated the reality of the great cosmic battle in which the Father and Son by the Spirit war against Satan and evil. Similarly, Gunton posits that 'Christology provides the necessary control of eschatology . . . because Christ is the one in whom the end and its anticipations, the embracing of time by God's eternity, become real and therefore conceivable.'[31] Ingolf Dalferth likewise concludes that, rightly understood, eschatological reflection has but one subject, 'Jesus Christ, his life and message, cross and resurrection, and the soteriological implications of all this for our human existence and the whole of creation'.[32] These theologians echo Pauline theology, which anchors eschatological reflection in God's full revelation in his Son. Christ is not simply a past reality that shapes our present, but rather by the Spirit he is the person who brings the future into the present. God transforms the world in his reconciliation, a movement that does not escape judgement, but is actualized through it. To use the biblical language, Christ is 'the assurance of things hoped for' (Heb. 11.1)— God has been, is and will be faithful, as testified to and embodied in Jesus Christ, who has won the victory which is being fully realized by the power of the Spirit.

The Coming of the Kingdom

This essay has already noted the inseparable relationship between creation and consummation, exemplified in the New Testament language of the Kingdom of God. As is now well known, over the past century and a half there have been persistent questions about Jesus' eschatological vision. Some (e.g. Dodd) have argued that Jesus maintained a 'realized eschatology' in which all things were completed in him, while others (e.g. von Harnack, Borg, Crossan) depict Jesus in a completely non-eschatological fashion. The growing consensus (e.g. Ridderbos, Wright, Sanders), however, is that the New Testament contains an eschatological tension between the *now* and the *not yet* in which Jesus ushers in the Kingdom of God, anticipating its fullness to come.[33]

Jesus does not simply attest to some otherworldly kingdom, but he himself is, as Carl Braaten noted, the *autobasileia*—'the kingdom himself'.[34] In this way, Jesus did not point to some other future, but to himself as the future. This Christological orientation of eschatological reflection resonates with Pauline theology. Herman Ridderbos argues that Paul's proclamation 'is nothing other than the explication of the eschatological redemptive event that commenced with the advent of Christ and in his death and resurrection came to a provisional climax. All of Paul's preaching finds its starting point and motive in this eschatological orientation.'[35] This is why, argues H. D. Wendland, 'Paul's "eschatology" is "Christ-eschatology"', and the interdependence of these two is woven throughout Paul's preaching.[36] God's redemptive work in Christ is eschatological, maintaining both the realized and the yet-to-be-realized, which again points to the importance of the unity of divine movement. There are no cosmic surprises or lapses of purpose: rather, we discover in the revelation of God in Christ the radical nature and extent of redemptive action, for here the Son of God by the power of the Spirit assumes our true human nature. Jesus the Messiah lives, dies and rises again, and in so doing he brings a new aeon.

The Final Adam

Paul envisions in the risen Christ a window into the purpose and direction of God, a taste of heaven. In 1 Corinthians 15 Paul argues that the future resurrection of believers and the realized resurrection of Christ are interconnected, the latter securing the former. In contrast with the Pharisees' understanding, which anticipated only a general resurrection of the righteous, Paul seems to articulate a 'two-stage resurrection because, against all expectations, the Messiah has been raised in advance of everyone else'.[37] N. T. Wright argues that because of the confidence Paul finds in the risen Christ, he wants the Corinthians to 'think eschatologically'. Using Jewish apocalyptic categories Paul speaks

> not of an 'imminent expectation' of the end of the world, but of the way in which the future has already burst into the present, so that the present time is characterized by a mixture of fulfillment and expectation, of 'now' and 'not yet', pointing towards a future in which what happened at the first Easter will be implemented fully and the true God will be all in all.[38]

In 1 Corinthians 15, Paul uses several important images that further this point. First, he uses the language of first-fruits (*aparche*) for the risen Christ, building on the Septuagint's use of *aparche* for certain offerings to God. Richard Gaffin notes that these sacrifices were considered representative of a greater harvest:

> 'Firstfruits' does not simply have a temporal force. It does bring into view the initial portion of the harvest, but only as it is part of the whole ... 'Firstfruits' expresses the notion of organic connection and unity, the inseparability of the initial quantity from the whole.[39]

These sacrifices carry significance beyond their own particularity. Gaffin argues that the resurrection of Christ is not important simply because it is first, but because it organically connects the two resurrections: 'His resurrection is not simply a guarantee; it is a pledge in the sense that it is the actual beginning of the general event', and in a very real sense for Paul, these are not two different events, but 'two episodes of the same event'.[40] So the resurrection of Christ shapes the Christian eschatological hope, for it grounds our vision of the Triune God's intentions for his people.

A second essential image in 1 Corinthians 15 is the comparison of Adam and Christ, which Paul also uses elsewhere (cf. Rom. 5.12–21). After pointing out that the first Adam brought death to all, Paul then argues that in Christ 'all shall be made alive' (1 Cor. 15.22). Again in v. 45, he speaks not of Adam and *Christ*, but of the first man Adam and the *last or final Adam*. As Wright contends, Paul is not simply saying that there have been numerous Adams, with the Messiah just happening to be the last one.[41] Rather, Jesus is the *eschatos Adam*, the eschatological man, the one in whom creation is renewed, who by the Spirit brings the eschatological order, and who leaves no other to be expected.

Thus, when Paul speaks of the 'natural' as first and then the 'spiritual' (esp. 1 Cor. 15.44, 46; cf. v. 50), he is not devaluing the physical in contrast to the non-physical. Such a reading loses Paul's 'Christ-eschatology' in a sea of Platonic abstraction. The Apostle is talking about two aeons, two realities which cover all of history:[42] 'As the era of the first Adam, the psychical order is the preeschatological aeon, the incomplete, transitory, and provisional world-age. As the era of the last Adam, the pneumatic order is the eschatological aeon, the complete, definitive, and final world-age.'[43] Similarly, Wright argues that Paul is asking the Corinthians to imagine a redeemed body free of decay, permanent, and not transient. It is not the physical body that is bad—for it is a good God who created a good world—but the rebellion, the decay, and the last enemy, death.[44]

Paul does not contrast physical life with non-physical life, since he is here clearly speaking of a bodily resurrection.[45] Rather, life in rebellion against God is contrasted with life in the Spirit of God. The only way to move from the former to the latter is by the power of the risen Christ, who is the 'life-giving spirit' (1 Cor. 15.45). In Paul's mind, the great 'eschatological gift' is the Holy Spirit, the Spirit of Christ (cf. Rom. 8.9–12), who 'is the guarantee of our inheritance until we acquire possession of it' (Eph. 1.14).[46] Here our Christology and pneumatology come together. Gordon Fee captures this point: 'just as Christ put a human face on God, as it were, so also has he put a human face on the Spirit', and the Spirit 'is thus the very personal presence of Christ with and within us during our present between-the-times existence'.[47]

The good news that Paul proclaims so clearly in 1 Corinthians 15 is that 'Jesus has pioneered the way into the long-awaited future, the new age which the creator has planned'.[48] Only in light of this promise can we understand Paul taunting death, asking where its sting is (1 Cor. 15.54–5). He stares at death not with a naive smile but with tears and rage, defiantly confronting death and proclaiming, *in the midst of the sting and pain*, 'You have been beaten, you have been overcome, sin has been conquered and thus death will not keep us down. Christ is risen, he is risen indeed!' It is here that our eschatological hope shines, for in the face of the risen Christ the believer sees the redemption of God, who has conquered the chaos by entering in and overcoming it. This is no distant deity, but the compassionate God who seeks the lost and turns their tears into singing.

Jesus is the eschatological man, the hope of the world, and in him we see a true eschatological vision of reality. The Revelation to John captures this well: 'Grace to you and peace from him who is and who was and who is to come, and from the seven spirits who are before his throne, and from Jesus Christ, the faithful witness, the firstborn of the dead, and the ruler of kings on earth' (Rev. 1.4b, ESV). We have seen the 'favourable time', we are living in the last days (Heb. 1.1–3), which began with the Christ event, and we are told that 'now is the day of salvation' (2 Cor. 6.2). 'Today' we hear the voice of God, who calls us not to harden our hearts, but *to enter into* 'God's rest' (Heb. 4.7–14). Just as God found the first creation good and complete, so now he rests in the finished work of his risen Son, our great high priest.

Conclusion

The theme of unity in divine movement is a classic method for describing the Trinitarian dynamic of divine action. Here we apply it to eschatology. Father, Son and Spirit are unified not only in creation, but in re-creation and consummation, and this recognition guards us against both positing maverick divine persons and inappropriately erasing distinctions. God has made himself known in the full self-revelation of his Son, the eschatological man, who brought the Kingdom of God into the present, embodying a new aeon in himself out of the old, sinful, chaotic, perishable aeon of the fallen Adam. The risen Christ sends forth his Spirit into the world, manifesting the Kingdom, re-creating and reorienting, applying the love of the Father and the grace of the Son, bringing about a new order of fellowship and hope.

Notes

1   Early on, Geerhardus Vos concluded that 'to unfold the Apostle's eschatology means
    to set forth his theology as a whole': *The Pauline Eschatology* (Grand Rapids:
    Eerdmans, 1930, repr., 1952), p. 11.

2   See Ted Peters, *God as Trinity* (Louisville: Westminster John Knox Press, 1993);
    Christoph Schwöbel, 'Last Things First? The Century of Eschatology in Retrospect',
    in *The Future as God's Gift*, ed. Marcel Sarot and David Fergusson (Edinburgh: T&T
    Clark, 2000), pp. 217–41; John Thompson, *Modern Trinitarian Perspectives* (New
    York: Oxford University Press, 1994), esp. pp. 20–43.

3   Wolfhart Pannenberg, 'The Task of Christian Eschatology', in *The Last Things*, ed.
    Carl E. Braaten and Robert W. Jenson (Grand Rapids: Eerdmans, 2002), p. 5.

4   Herman N. Ridderbos, *Paul* (Grand Rapids: Eerdmans, 1975), p. 50; cf. p. 89.

5   Gregory of Nyssa, 'To Ablabius', in *The Trinitarian Controversy*, ed. William G.
    Rusch (Philadelphia: Fortress Press, 1980), pp. 149–61; also translated in *Nicene and
    Post-Nicene Fathers*, 2nd series, V, ed. Philip Schaff and Henry Wace (repr. Peabody,
    Mass.: Henrickson, 1994), pp. 331–6.

6   Gregory of Nyssa, 'To Ablabius', p. 155; emphasis mine.

7   Gregory of Nyssa, 'To Ablabius', p. 155.

8   Gregory of Nyssa, 'To Ablabius', p. 156.

9   Gregory concludes: 'No activity is divided to the *hypostases*, completed individually
    by each and set apart without being viewed together': 'To Ablabius', pp. 156–7.

10 See Robert C. Doyle, *Eschatology and the Shape of Christian Belief* (Carlisle:
    Paternoster, 1999), pp. 148–53; Jürgen Moltmann, 'Christian Hope—Messianic or
    Transcendent? A Theological Conversation with Joachim of Fiore and Thomas
    Aquinas', in *History and the Triune God* (New York: Crossroad, 1992), pp. 91–109.

11 Gregory of Nyssa, 'To Ablabius', p. 157.

12 Cf., Anthony Meredith, *The Cappadocians* (Crestwood: St Vladimir's Seminary
    Press, 1995), p. 110.

13 Augustine, *On The Trinity* 1.2.7, in *Augustine: The Trinity*, ed. John E. Rotelle
    (Brooklyn, NY: New City Press, 1991), p. 70.

14 Augustine, *On The Trinity* 1.2.7; pp. 69–70.

15 Augustine, *Sermon* 2, §2, in *Nicene and Post-Nicene Fathers*, 1st series, VI, ed.
    Philip Schaff (repr. Peabody, Mass.: Hendrickson, 1995), p. 259.

16 Gregory of Nazianzus, Poem 1.1.3, 'De Spiritu Sancto', ll. 20–8, PG 37, 408–15, in
    Gregory of Nazianzus, *On God and Man*, trans. Peter Gilbert (Crestwood, NY: St
    Vladimir's Seminary Press, 2001), p. 44.

17 See Gregory of Nazianzus, *Orations* 31.26, in Gregory of Nazianzus, *On God and
    Christ*, tr. Frederick Williams and Lionel R. Wickham (Crestwood, NY: St Vladimir's
    Seminary Press, 2002), p. 137.

18 Gregory of Nazianzus, *Orations* 31.27; p. 138.

19 Karl Barth, *Church Dogmatics*, II/1, *The Doctrine of God*, ed. Geoffrey W. Bromiley
    and T. F. Torrance (Edinburgh: T&T Clark, 1957), p. 615.

20 Barth, *Church Dogmatics*, II/1, p. 616.

21 Gregory of Nazianzus, *Orations* 29.19; p. 86.

22 Barth, *Church Dogmatics*, II/1, p. 616.

23 Barth, *Church Dogmatics*, II/1, p. 616, emphasis mine.

24 Barth, *Church Dogmatics* II/1, p. 616.

25 Cf. Thompson's critical note that for Moltmann, God 'is not truly God without his

history with humanity and creation and his suffering on the cross': *Modern Trinitarian Perspectives*, p. 34.

[26] Barth, *Church Dogmatics* II/1, p. 617.

[27] Barth, *Church Dogmatics* II/1, p. 618.

[28] For a more sympathetic understanding of a substance metaphysics, see William P. Alston, 'Substance and the Trinity', in *The Trinity*, ed. Stephen T. Davis, Daniel Kendall and Gerald O'Collins (Oxford: Oxford University Press, 1999), pp. 179–201.

[29] Colin E. Gunton, *Act and Being: Towards a Theology of the Divine Attributes* (Grand Rapids: Eerdmans, 2003), p. 23.

[30] Herman Bavinck, *The Last Things*, ed. John Bolt (Grand Rapids: Baker Books, 1996), p. 122.

[31] Colin E. Gunton, 'Dogmatic Theses on Eschatology', in Sarot and Fergusson (eds), *The Future as God's Gift*, p. 143.

[32] Ingolf U. Dalferth, 'The Eschatological Roots of the Doctrine of the Trinity', in *Trinitarian Theology Today*, ed. Christoph Schwöbel (Edinburgh: T&T Clark, 1995), p. 159.

[33] See Dalferth, 'The Eschatological Roots of the Doctrine of the Trinity', pp. 147–70; Arland J. Hultgren, 'Eschatology in the New Testament: The Current Debate', in Braaten and Jenson (eds) *The Last Things*, pp. 67–89; Herman Ridderbos, *The Coming of the Kingdom* (Philadelphia: Presbyterian & Reformed Publishing, 1962); E. P. Sanders, *The Historical Figure of Jesus* (London: Allen Lane, 1993), esp. pp. 169–248; Ben Witherington, *The Jesus Quest*, 2nd edn (Downers Grove, Ill.: Inter-Varsity Press, 1997); N. T. Wright, *Jesus and the Victory of God* (Minneapolis: Fortress Press, 1996), pp. 3–124.

[34] Carl E. Braaten, 'The Recovery of Apocalyptic Imagination', in Braaten and Jenson (eds), *The Last Things*, (2002), p. 20.

[35] Ridderbos, *Paul*, p. 32; cf. p. 39.

[36] Heinz Dietrich Wendland, *Geschichtsanschauung und Geschichtsbewusstsein im Neuen Testament* (Göttingen: Vandenhoeck & Ruprecht, 1938), p. 26; cited in Ridderbos, *Paul*, p. 49.

[37] N. T. Wright, *The Resurrection of the Son of God* (Minneapolis: Fortress Press, 2003), p. 360.

[38] N. T. Wright, *The Resurrection of the Son of God*, p. 333.

[39] Richard B. Gaffin, *Resurrection and Redemption*, 2nd edn (Phillipsburg, NJ: Presbyterian & Reformed Publishing, 1987), p. 34.

[40] Gaffin, *Resurrection and Redemption*, p. 35.

[41] Wright, *The Resurrection of the Son of God*, p. 341.

[42] Cf. Ridderbos, *Paul*, p. 66.

[43] Gaffin, *Resurrection and Redemption*, p. 83.

[44] See esp. Wright, *The Resurrection of the Son of God*, pp. 346–7.

[45] Wright makes this point throughout *The Resurrection of the Son of God*, e.g. 'When Paul said "resurrection", he meant "bodily resurrection"', p. 314.

[46] Cf. Ridderbos, *Paul*, p. 87.

[47] Gordon D. Fee, 'Paul and the Trinity: The Experience of Christ and the Spirit for Paul's Understanding of God', in Davis *et al.* (eds), *The Trinity*, pp. 66–7.

[48] Wright, *The Resurrection of the Son of God*, p. 355.

15

Revelation and Natural Rights: Notes on Colin E. Gunton's Theology of Nature

Esther D. Reed

Our topic is the problem of 'the natural' in Protestant theology and ethics, and Colin Gunton's response to it. The problem concerns how to conceive of 'nature' and 'the natural' without suggesting a free-standing theology that is independent of knowledge of God revealed in Jesus Christ. In this chapter I show that Gunton's work takes significant steps toward a theology of 'the natural' which is fully integrated with revealed theology. I begin with his perception of the problem, as developed with reference to the writings of Karl Barth, before comparing his approach with that of Dietrich Bonhoeffer. I also explore some implications of Gunton's work for an ethic of natural rights.

Gunton's *A Brief Theology of Revelation: The 1993 Warfield Lectures* exposes fundamental weaknesses in modern theologies, most notably the tendency to overemphasize the immediacy of revelation rather than its mediacy in nature, Scripture, tradition, etc.[1] It opens by identifying a problem in the structure of Karl Barth's theology:

> The overemployment of the category [of revelation] arose in the course of a proper reaction to [its] neglect, particularly in Barth's attempts to overcome the epistemo-logical challenges presented to him by his predecessors and to allow the God of Jesus Christ to come to rational expression on his own terms. But it was, I believe, an overemployment, and resulted in an imbalance in the systematic structure of Barth's theology, as well as in those that were influenced by him.[2]

Gunton presents the problem with reference to Hegel's phenomenology of consciousness, where 'immediacy' requires 'mediation' for its growth or development. For Hegel, there was a deep connection between the concept of mediation and idealist notions of history as the process wherein humans become ever more rational. Modern theologies countered this, says Gunton, by emphasizing the immediacy rather than the mediacy of revelation. His book explores the implications of this overemployment of the epistemological category of revelation for theologies of nature, Scripture and tradition. The pervasive influence of Hegel's philosophy of mediation is uncovered and readers are alerted to its colouring of, for example, Rudolph Bultmann's theology of existential immediacy, Wolfhart Pannenberg's theology of the resurrection, George Lindbeck's critique of the cognitive propositional conception of theology, and more besides. The book concludes by expounding the doctrine of revelation as a function of the doctrine of salvation and dependent upon an adequate pneumatology.

Revelation and a Theology of Nature

In this essay, I focus on lecture 3, entitled 'No Other Foundation? Revelation and the Theology of Nature', and I apply the rationale that Gunton develops to questions about natural rights within a theology of general revelation. Gunton wrote relatively little in the areas of Christian ethics and moral reasoning, yet the conceptual framework that he develops bears directly upon a present-day issue concerning the theology of natural rights, especially when we construe the issue that he raises as follows: what is the relation between a self-contained conception of natural law that is independent of God and one that is derived from the revealed will of God and an account of divine providence? Alternatively stated: what are the differences between teleological and eschatological reasoning with respect to natural rights, and are these differences important for Christian engagement with public policy in this field? Gunton's thesis is that it is 'not simply a matter of natural theology over against a theology of revelation', or of teleology over against eschatology. Rather, he says, we need a theology of the natural world and its revelation to us of both itself and God.[3] It is not simply a matter of positing a Christological and Trinitarian theology of nature over against a natural theology, but of perceiving and giving expression to the role of the Holy Spirit in a theology of nature.

Mediation and the Role of the Holy Spirit

In the essay we are considering, Gunton draws heavily on the Johannine account of God's giving of the Spirit to the church in an attempt to develop an adequate theology of nature and of general revelation. He writes:

> without the revealing action of the Spirit, we shall not know Jesus as the way of God. But because the Spirit is not the Son, and the Son is not the Father, there are differences of function and action, and therefore differences of mediation. The clue to the doctrine of revelation is accordingly to be found in unravelling the different patterns of mediation with which we are concerned.[4]

'Mediation' is an important word in this quotation. A fuller recognition of the distinctive role of the Spirit in revealing the mysteries of God to us will, says Gunton, allow the possibility of mediation through otherness: 'The Father is indeed made known by Jesus, but as one who is greater than he (John 14.28), and so beyond all we can say and think: one revealed by humiliation and cross, but revealed none the less as other.'[5] Knowledge of God is mediated pre-eminently through Christ but also, by virtue of the power of the Holy Spirit, through the 'otherness' of, for example, music and the findings of modern science. If the Holy Spirit is the presence of God in many and diverse human attestations to God's creation, then each of these realities can potentially mediate the presence of God to us. God himself mediates his revelation to us. Our question is whether and/or how such a theology of mediation might be developed with respect to a teleologically derived ethic of natural rights.

The context of Gunton's observations is twentieth-century Protestant theology, framed in response to Kant, which tended to elevate revelation to a first-order doctrine and to repeat 'the Kantian and foundationalist error that epistemology is prior to the practice of a discipline'.[6] Barth, says Gunton, demonstrated effectively that the doctrine of creation is as much a product of revelation as other doctrines of faith but failed to develop an adequate account of the Holy Spirit as mediator of the knowledge of creation: 'Although he [Barth] has a doctrine of creation, there is reason to suppose that he scarcely begins to do justice to the ontological question of the kind of reality that the world is.'[7] Barth, he says, held back from seeking revelation in the structures of the created world, thereby producing a stunted and inadequately biblical theology of revelation. This, says Gunton, leaves Christian people without the means of expressing the logical link between a theology of nature and an account of the human capacity to appropriate general revelation. What is needed is a fuller account of the world's worldliness that allows 'God to be God' and 'the world to be the world'. Indeed, 'a theology of nature is the gift of biblical revelation'.[8]

A similar need was identified by Dietrich Bonhoeffer in the 1940s, and it is interesting to observe what little progress had been made in Protestant ethics in the ensuing fifty years. Bonhoeffer began the section of his *Ethics* entitled 'The Natural' by observing that the concept of the natural has fallen into discredit in Protestant ethics.[9] Like Gunton, Bonhoeffer was aware of the divorce of creation from redemption in Protestant theology and of the grave consequences for a Christian outlook on the world:

> Before the light of grace everything human and natural sank into the night of sin, and now no one dared to consider the relative differences within the human and natural, for fear that by their so doing grace as grace might be diminished. It was its treatment of the concept of the natural that demonstrated most clearly that this Protestant thought was no longer conscious of the true relation of the ultimate to the penultimate.[10]

Bonhoeffer himself defines 'the natural' with reference to God's providential preservation of the fallen created order until his kingdom comes on earth. The word 'natural' implies an element of independence from a being's status as creaturely. 'The natural' is the form of life that embraces the entire human race and may be understood as both an end in itself and the means to an end.[11] As an end in itself, 'the natural' is from God and oriented toward God though not necessarily recognized as 'creaturely'. As the means to an end, that is, within a theological world-view, it is the penultimate directed towards the ultimate, the created oriented towards the end-times when Christ will come again. Any action to undermine 'the natural' denies that it is preserved by God until Christ's coming.[12]

For Bonhoeffer, certain strands of Protestant theology had allowed the natural or penultimate to be diminished in significance for the sake of the ultimate. This one-sidedness was manifest in a 'two spheres' kind of thinking that kept the realm of the natural subordinate to that of grace, the spiritual separate from the secular, and, in its most extreme form, the world apart from Christ: 'The monk and the nineteenth-century Protestant secularist typify these two possibilities.'[13] This world-view opposes the rational and the revelational, the sacred and the profane, the natural and the supernatural, and severs 'the natural' and 'natural right' from the operation of God's grace. It might be difficult to break the spell of this kind of thinking but, says Bonhoeffer, such an outlook is profoundly unbiblical and neglects to affirm the truth of the world as reconciled to God in Christ: 'The New Testament is concerned solely with the manner in which the reality of Christ assumes reality in the present world.'[14]

For Gunton, writing with similar concerns but fifty years later, it was necessary to distinguish between a theology of nature (a theological account of what things are by virtue of their createdness) and a natural theology (a theological account of what things are which is based on the supposition that the world is in some way continuous with God and reveals the truth about human nature independent of revelation in Christ). This distinction is a necessary prerequisite for a theologically adequate investigation of the relation of revelation to reason, free of the foundationalism that grounds reason in human nature and assumes 'that something eternally and universally true can be founded on human rational and scientific effort alone'.[15] With this distinction in place, however, Gunton could ask whether the '"secular" features of the world's being are as relevant for an understanding of the world's capacity to be the vehicle of revelation as those which are apparently religious'.[16] In light of this, our question is the same but with particular reference to the implications for Christian engagement with teleological ethics of natural rights.

Teleology and Natural Rights

The practical focus of our consideration will be the neo-Thomist John Finnis's teleological account of natural rights. Four points about his work must be noted. First, Finnis argues that medieval and modern writers express the same demands of justice, albeit in different contexts and using different terminology. Hence his claim of equivalence (or 'as near as damn it', as he says, when one takes into account the differences of context and idiom) between human natural rights and human rights.[17] This claim probably fails on strictly historical grounds though the debate is only tangential to our argument here.[18] Second, Finnis holds that modern rights-talk amplifies 'undifferentiated reference to "the common good" by providing a usefully detailed listing of the various aspects of human flourishing'.[19] The manner in which he does this is different from that employed by Aquinas but, again, this issue is not central to our purposes.[20]

Third, Finnis believes that all persons are capable of discerning basic human goods because of the universal nature of human experience.[21]

There is no need to ground ethical obligation in God's will because the reasonableness of self-evident human requirements carries its own force. A philosopher of jurisprudence in the Aristotelian tradition of natural law, Finnis treats ethics as practical because it involves 'questioning and reflection *in order to be able to act*'.[22] Ethics, he says, is about practical knowledge or knowledge that seeks the realization in practice of goods attainable by human persons. Basic human goods (bodily life, knowledge and aesthetic experience, harmony between individuals and groups, harmony between the different dimensions within the self, etc.[23]) can be grasped pre-reflectively and immediately by practical reason.

Fourth, like Aquinas, Finnis recognizes an essential directiveness in human reason.[24] This directiveness was recognized, he says, by Plato and Aristotle, and supplies the essential content of reasons for actions.[25] Its pre-moral and trans-cultural status derives from the fact that the basic requirements for flourishing pertain to all human beings; basic human goods are the fundamental requirements of practical reasonableness for all societies. Points three and four are of most interest to us here.

For Finnis, a good explanation can be given of the reasonableness of particular acts without reference to the existence or will of God. Some people, he says, allow belief in God to provide them with an added dimension of reasoning for pursuit of the common good. For them, God functions as the basis of their obligation, and explication of the requirements of practical reasonableness is a direct expression of their religious concern. Others, he says, think that 'God' is a term burdened with widely varying associations. Peculiarly theological investigation of the requirements of practical reason is unnecessary for the moral life. God might be the conclusion to moral reasoning but is not necessarily the premiss. In any case, little is to be gained by positing the existence of God because human goods are grasped pre-reflectively and immediately by practical reason, or by attempting to derive human rights from an objective sense of 'right', because basic human goods provide all the objective knowledge needed for human flourishing.

Our question is whether such a 'Godless' but teleological ethic of natural rights might be deemed to express the mediated reality of God through human reason, or whether the risk of delusion and compromise is too great. Does the reality of God's Spirit make itself known in the midst of processes of identifying and protecting natural rights? What access might we have to the reality of the Spirit here?

Teleology and Eschatology: Dual Focus

Following Gunton, we may not simply reject as inferior a teleological ethic when set against an eschatological ethic. Radical Protestant ethics is often anti-teleological and suspicious of eudaemonistically construed ethical thinking because the latter claims to take human beings on what Socrates called 'the upward progress of the mind into the intelligible region'.[26] Teleological ethics with roots in Plato and Aristotle tends to hold that moral conversion and progression is possible through reason, the identification and acceptance of basic and shared truths, the shunning of ignorance and the striving for knowledge and the fully perfected soul. For radical Protestant ethics, such faith in reason usurps faith in Christ and must be replaced by the evangelical and eschatological hope of new being in Christ. Eschatology eliminates or significantly downgrades teleology.

For Gunton, however, this attitude fails to give an adequate pneumatological account of the kind of reality that the world is within divine providence, even in its fallen state. Merely to reject a teleological ethic that expresses the fundamental human desire to flourish and attain well-being on the basis that such an ethic has not died with Christ hinders a full theological conception of the relation between creation and revelation. A more adequately Trinitarian construal of nature is needed to determine systematically the relation between God and the world: 'distinct beings and yet personally related by personal mediation as creator and creation'.[27] By implication, it is not enough merely to reject teleological notions of natural rights as inadequate because they are not conceived as rooted in and moving towards God. Trinitarian theology offers other possibilities for an understanding of creation informed by revelation: 'The fact that the world is rational at all is a mark of its coming from its creator, but even that is an insight that has been attained only in cultures where the Bible has been a determinative influence, suggesting that it is the fruit of divine revelation.'[28]

Rather than rejecting a teleological ethic merely because it is not a revelation ethic, Gunton's challenge is that we think theologically about the truth and untruth of reason. Rather than simplistically opposing the rational and the revelational, or setting natural theology against a theology of revelation, he wants us to contemplate the mediated reality of God's Spirit in the world. Whatever else it is, says Gunton, revelation in Christian theology is mediated; the truth of the gospel is realized for us, or mediated to us, by the Spirit of truth.[29] For our purposes this means, on the one hand, that a Christian theology of revelation does *not* expect human reason to ground itself or to seek an understanding of human existence, including natural rights, apart from revelation. Finnis, as we have seen, roots natural rights and human rights (which, for him, are equivalent) in universal and teleological truths about human nature and the rationality of human persons. The obvious theological problem is that this nullifies the relation of natural rights to divine providence in a manner that potentially cuts off practical reason from the source of human life and the possibility of renewal. On the other hand, Christian eschatology directs us not only towards the end-times but also to the present responsibilities to work for God's praise and glory. We must seek the Holy Spirit's mediation of God's glory in the things that have been made (Ps. 19.1).

Gunton puts the matter in terms of a ladder between the created and uncreated:

> Revelation—God's personal interaction with the world through his Son and Spirit—suggests ways of seeing parallels between uncreated and created rationality, but we need not be too anxious about finding a ladder between them. God has let that down already in the incarnation of his eternal Son within the structures of worldly being.'[30]

My preferred image is that of a dual-focus lens that allows us to 'see' or to think both eschatologically and teleologically, to see both the wood and the trees, to confess the truth of Christ risen and ascended whilst working in secularist contexts with teleological frameworks of ethics. Dual-focus lenses have two points through which light passes. Their various applications in, for example, laser technology offer processing advantages because either or both focal points may be used at any given time. The 'focal points' for our purpose are eschatological and teleological ways of conceiving of natural rights. Finnis's ethic of human rights has served as our teleological way of thinking, and we shall look shortly at Bonhoeffer's eschatological definition of natural rights on the basis of the gospel. The point here is that we need a dual focus to keep both near and far objects in focus simultaneously, to keep looking towards the eschatological hope while employing teleological rationales.

An Eschatological Focus on Natural Rights

So far, then, we have seen that we must neither leap to condemnation because an ethic is teleological rather than eschatological, nor accept a teleology in which we reach toward God rather than God reaching to us. Neither of these options is adequate. The former is unlikely to be sensitive enough to the work of the Holy Spirit in the world. The latter founds an ethic of natural rights on universal truths about human nature rather than with reference to the triune being of God. Instead, says Gunton, we need a desire to learn from the economic activity of the Spirit of God—which is oriented towards particularity.

A central argument in *The One, the Three and the Many* is that the economic activity of the Holy Spirit brings to completion that for which each person and thing has been created: 'the Spirit's peculiar office is to realize the true being of each created thing by bringing it, through Christ, into saving relation with God the Father'.[31] By extension, the way forward in developing a Christian ethic of natural rights must be based on the operation of the Holy Spirit in bringing to perfection the work of Christ and God's saving purposes. We need a pneumatologically and eschatologically informed conception of human reason so that we may discern God's indwelling of the world and, on the basis of theological confession, explore the implications for Christian moral reasoning and engagement in politics.

Once this is established, Bonhoeffer helps us more than Gunton with maintaining an eschatological focus on natural rights because of his definition of 'the natural' as the form of life preserved by God after the Fall, and directed towards redemption and the coming of Christ. For Bonhoeffer, the definition of 'the natural' yields a related understanding of 'natural rights' as an expression of the respect due to God, the Creator: 'in the rights of natural life it is not to the creature that honour is given, but to the Creator. . . . The rights of natural life are in the midst of the fallen world the reflected splendour of the glory of God's creation.'[32] Of him/herself the individual can claim no rights before God, but rights may and should be recognized in relation to other individuals and in society.

Natural rights are guaranteed not by human law nor by consensus but by God; they are what is required to protect, preserve and enhance natural life until Christ comes again. For Bonhoeffer, it is for the sake of Christ's coming again and because of the work of the Holy Spirit in enabling the world to become itself that natural life must be lived within a framework of rights, and consequently, of duties. Thus, for instance, we may say that bodily life contains within itself the right to its own preservation: 'Since it is God's will that there should be human life on earth only in the form of bodily life . . . it is for the sake of the whole man that the body possesses the right to be preserved.'[33] Barth's treatment of natural rights is comparable and emphasizes the

Christological factor. Human rights, he says, are 'the codified prudence of all others in opposition to me'.[34] I cannot break free of my neighbour because Christ is present for me in him or her. My neighbour's rights are found in Christ and I must submit to them because he or she is the bearer of God's command to me.[35]

Natural Rights and Intercessory Prayer

This strongly Christological and eschatological focus on natural rights is a necessary prerequisite for the dual focus mentioned above. Only if we believe that God's Spirit mediates to us the hope of the gospel and its demands is there any reason to employ the dual focus of the historico-teleological and eschatological ways of looking at natural rights. Only if we believe that natural rights should be respected *for God's sake* is there reason enough to engage in advocating human rights. If we act for God's sake, however, the high-energy density of God's presence promises what Michael Welker calls 'a charged field of experiences'.[36] In this 'field', Gunton's question about how the 'secular features of the world's being' are relevant for an understanding of its capacity to be the vehicle of revelation becomes intensely pertinent.[37]

Gunton's tentative answer, namely that we pray in faith for God's assistance to see 'what is there before our eyes', is answered only as the Spirit enables believers to bring prayers of intercession before God, and as the eschatological hope sends us back in faith to the historical in order to seek God's presence in the everyday work of identifying and protecting natural rights.[38] An ahistorical eschatology would amount to a flight from the created order. As Bonhoeffer wrote: 'Christ died for the world, and it is only in the midst of the world that Christ is Christ'.[39] Only unbelief can wish for something less than Christ or shun involvement in the world. It is only in the world that we may let the reality of the Holy Spirit come to us in ever-new ways, not least as we seek both to support and to learn from practitioners (many of them disciples of Jesus Christ) who work every day to identify and lobby for the protection of human rights.

Our opening question concerned the differences between teleological and eschatological reasoning with respect to natural rights, and whether these differences are important for Christian engagement with public policy in respect to human rights. In response, we have outlined major differences between teleological and eschatological ways of thinking and various ways of construing their relation. Our conclusion is that

God's Spirit can enlist the services of different ways of thinking, including teleologically oriented accounts of practical reasonableness. We have stated uncompromisingly that the intrinsic universality of human existence does *not* supply the only necessary recourse for knowledge of basic human goods, because the origin of all goodness is God; the truth of human existence is revealed in Christ, not decided by consensus or courts of law. Every earthly ethic is disturbed and challenged by the gospel of God.

This does not mean, however, that the only proper Christian witness is opposition to all ways of thinking that do not refer directly to the eschatological hope. Rather, God's Spirit-filled ordering of the cosmos means that spirit and flesh, the ultimate and the penultimate, historical and teleological, need not be distinguished neurotically.[40] God's Spirit mediates God's presence in the natural order. Divine purposes are achieved in diverse and often hidden ways. God is revealed in and by creation (Rom. 1.19–20), and therefore we must take seriously the Spirit's mediation of the presence of God in the historical.[41] This does not relieve Christians working in secularist settings, where teleological rather than eschatological ethics operates, from their calling to proclaim Jesus as Lord in direct fashion. Nor does it mean, however, that their faith is compromised when their work entails teleological modes of thinking (e.g. Finnis's discernment of basic human goods with reference to the universal nature of human experience and local discussion of how to realize the common good).

Working with a dual focus means conceiving natural rights both eschatologically and pneumatologically *and* bringing teleological reasoning to bear within this conceptuality. It is not simply a matter of opposing Christian and non-Christian ways of thinking. Nor is it a matter of finding compatibility between the divine command 'Do not murder' and the human right to life; or regarding the command 'Do not commit adultery' as a possible translation into the human right to marry and found a family, and so on—though this might be argued at some points. Rather, it is a way of thinking that presents us with an agenda of moral reasoning in close connection with intercessory prayer. Much listening and learning from human-rights practitioners and activists remains to be done if this work is to continue. More thinking is also required about how to testify to the Holy Spirit's mediation of God's presence (e.g. by thinking of natural rights as a way of expressing God the Author's mark on his creation—one of many ways in which God's law convinces us of sin—and also as performative claims needed for the building of ethical communities). In the meantime, if Gunton's

A Brief Theology of Revelation helps us both to develop the necessary theological conceptuality and to facilitate its practical working-out in the identification and protection of natural rights, he will have a living memoriam.

Notes

1   Colin E. Gunton, *A Brief Theology of Revelation: The 1993 Warfield Lectures* (Edinburgh: T&T Clark, 1995).
2   Gunton, *A Brief Theology of Revelation*, p. ix.
3   Gunton, *A Brief Theology of Revelation*, p. 41.
4   Gunton, *A Brief Theology of Revelation*, p. 122.
5   Gunton, *A Brief Theology of Revelation*, p. 123.
6   Gunton, *A Brief Theology of Revelation*, p. 59 n. 31.
7   Gunton, *A Brief Theology of Revelation*, p. 41.
8   Gunton, *A Brief Theology of Revelation*, p. 59.
9   Dietrich Bonhoeffer, *Ethics* (London: SCM Press, 1955), p. 101.
10   Bonhoeffer, *Ethics*, p. 101.
11   Bonhoeffer, *Ethics*, p. 101.
12   Bonhoeffer, *Ethics*, pp. 126–7.
13   Bonhoeffer, *Ethics*, p. 63.
14   Bonhoeffer, *Ethics*, p. 64.
15   Gunton, *A Brief Theology of Revelation*, p. 50. For Gunton's more developed thoughts on foundationalism, as the search for a universal and indubitable basis for human knowledge, see *The One, the Three and the Many: God, Creation and the Culture of Modernity*, the 1992 Bampton Lectures (Cambridge: Cambridge University Press, 1993), pp. 129–35.
16   Gunton, *A Brief Theology of Revelation*, p. 62.
17   John Finnis, *Natural Law and Natural Rights* (Oxford: Clarendon Press, 1980), p. 198.
18   For a brief account of the debate about differences between Aquinas's objective sense of 'right' and modern subjective senses, see Brian Tierney, 'Natural Law and Natural Rights: Old Problems and Recent Approaches', *Review of Politics* 64 (2002), p. 390.
19   Finnis, *Natural Law and Natural Rights*, p. 221.
20   This observation is based on Ralph McInerny's argument that this kind of treatment of basic human goods equates to Aquinas's teaching about the good: 'Grisez [and Finnis] thinks that the form of such particular precepts is "X should be done, pursued, protected", where X takes as its value one or the other of the basic goods. . . . For Thomas, the form of a particular precept is "X should be pursued as reason directs the pursuit to one's overall good", where values of X are the ends of natural inclinations.' See Ralph McInerny, 'Grisez and Thomism', in *The Revival of Natural Law: Philosophical, Theological and Ethical Responses to the Finnis–Grisez School*, ed. Nigel Biggar and Rufus Black (Aldershot: Ashgate Publishing, 2000), p. 69.
21   Finnis, *Natural Law and Natural Rights*, pp. 64–90.
22   John Finnis, *Fundamentals of Ethics* (Oxford: Oxford University Press, 1983), p. 1, italics original.

[23] For a full list, see Germain Grisez, Joseph Boyle and John Finnis, 'Practical Principles, Moral Truth, and Ultimate Ends', *American Journal of Jurisprudence* 32 (1987), pp. 107–8.

[24] Finnis, *Natural Law and Natural Rights*, p. 387.

[25] John Finnis, 'Natural Law and the Ethics of Discourse', *Ratio Juris* 12 (1999), p. 354.

[26] Plato, *Republic* 517b, tr. Desmond Lee, 2nd edn (Harmondsworth: Penguin Books, 1987), p. 321.

[27] Gunton, *A Brief Theology of Revelation*, p. 63.

[28] Gunton, *A Brief Theology of Revelation*, pp. 61–2.

[29] Gunton, *A Brief Theology of Revelation*, p. 18.

[30] Gunton, *A Brief Theology of Revelation*, p. 63.

[31] Gunton, *The One, the Three and the Many*, p. 189.

[32] Bonhoeffer, *Ethics*, p. 108.

[33] Bonhoeffer, *Ethics*, p. 108.

[34] Karl Barth, *Ethics*, ed. Dietrich Braun (Edinburgh: T&T Clark, 1981), p. 380.

[35] 'Right as it is now and is in force can open my eyes to the neighbour whom I constantly overlook in the pride of my own impulses and from whom I would rather be free': Barth, *Ethics*, p. 383.

[36] Michael Welker, *God the Spirit*, tr. John F. Hoffmeyer (Minneapolis: Fortress Press, 1994), p. 275. See Mark 16.17; Luke 24.49; Acts 2.38–9; Heb. 2.4; Titus 3.3–7.

[37] Gunton, *A Brief Theology of Revelation*, p. 62.

[38] Gunton, *A Brief Theology of Revelation*, p. 61.

[39] Bonhoeffer, *Ethics*, p. 71.

[40] This last phrase is used by Welker, *God the Spirit*, p. 258.

[41] Gunton, *A Brief Theology of Revelation*, p. 41.

Afterword

Robert W. Jenson

The essays here collected and posthumously dedicated to Colin Gunton reflect his own thinking and intentions quite remarkably. The individual pieces, and the form of their collection, mirror his work both formally and materially, and it is that phenomenon I will for these few pages consider. I have decided not to go through the essays seriatim, perhaps saying that this one makes this point and this other one makes another point. The essays do not, in my judgement, need a guide; and if they did, it should come at the beginning.

Colin Gunton had almost limitless ambitions for the King's College London theological faculty itself, and for making it a centre from which to reinvigorate British systematic theology. Perhaps this manifested itself most directly and visibly in the sheer numbers and variety both of the students he and his colleagues attracted to King's and of the scholarly and churchly associations he maintained through his projects there. When he died, the other faculty were buried under a multitude of research students who were suddenly without a supervisor and had to be otherwise provided for. His former students are spread over Britain and the world; and those colleagues around the world who knew themselves personally and theologically bereaved by his death make a sort of 'Who's Who' of Protestant theology. Moreover, his students and colleagues included—nearly!—all sorts and conditions of scholars.

Thus, the editor could have recruited many times the number of this volume's contributors. And among those in fact recruited we find both an *ordinarius* and recent recipients of their degrees, we find both pastors and academics, we find churchmen identifiable confessionally on a broad spectrum from Baptist to Orthodox.

To be sure, Colin's embrace did have limits. One night at the Guntons' home, after we had drunk comfortably, Blanche Jenson asked him whether for the sake of the unity of Christ's church he could belong to an episcopally governed body. He thought for a while, and

217

finally did not exactly answer. Instead he slapped the table and simply pronounced, 'I am a dissenter!'

Thus the English ecclesial establishment is not conspicuous in this volume. There is a Roman Catholic, but he is a remarkably faithful Barthian. Missing are Lutherans like me, which evokes a theological point I will consider later. On my side of the Atlantic, his associations tended to be at Princeton, Regent College in Vancouver, and Fuller Seminary—and not, let us say, Notre Dame or Harvard. The Orthodox, to be sure, always got a pass despite their hierarchy, partly, I suspect, because in Britain they too are outsiders.

The content of the essays also mirrors his work. They are all 'Trinitarian' explorations. This was the plan of an editor who knows Colin's thinking well; in discussions during Paul Metzger's residence at the Center of Theological Inquiry—where I write these lines—he would sooner or later bring up what Colin Gunton thought or would have thought about the matter. And whatever topic Colin addressed, he indeed sooner or later got around to the Trinity. I suppose I must claim part of the credit or blame for this preoccupation, for I put him onto the project of his dissertation, comparing Barth's and Hartshorne's doctrines of God. Once he saw the great difference between a decisively trinitarian invocation of God and another kind, he never turned back.

In counterpoint to this stringent focus, our volume provides a good many words and a generous sampling of theological *loci*. This too is fitting for a Gunton memorial, for both the rate and the variety of his production were amazing. Essays and books, on a daunting variety of matters, flowed from his desk. When the afflatus was upon him the very process of writing seemed to have a preternatural metabolism; in a scant three-months' residence here at the Center of Theological Inquiry he drafted the entire first volume of his projected three-volume systematic theology.

For all the spread of these essays, they not only have a focus, they have an order: they make a multi-author *loci theologici*, from prolegomena to eschatology. And here the correspondences I have been indicating cease. For the order of the essays is—necessarily of course—traditional; whereas the plan of Colin's systematic theology, of the parts he in fact got to draft and those he did not, was thoroughly untraditional—even anti-traditional. Thus, for example, in this collection prolegomena make an essay of their own and appear in their traditional place, but in the draft of Colin's first volume prolegomena as such disappear completely—they do not even get the mildly independent attention they receive in Barth's *Kirchliche Dogmatik* or in subsequent 'anti-foundationalist' systems. The epistemological topics usually taken up as prolegomena are simply absorbed into material dogmatic sections, titled 'The Economy of the Spirit', 'The Economy of the Father', and 'The Economy of the Son'. And note also the order: Spirit, Father and Son. When his literary executors have put the first volume into shape for publication, you will be able to read and judge for yourselves—in my opinion it is, even as the torso of what was to be a much longer work, a remarkable and creative achievement.

There is a second aspect of Colin's scope that is not strongly reflected in this collection—and of course could hardly have been without making a whole second collection: his penchant for digging out dimly remembered figures of English theological history and discovering great insight in their thought. One of course knew of John Owen as a notable Puritan politician and preacher—but what *exactly* did he preach? And why should we care? Colin would tell you. One was aware of Edward Irving because one knew there had been Irvingites—but just what distinguished Irvingites from other esoteric groups? And is there anything to learn from their initiator? Colin would tell you.

Finally, I earlier mentioned the lack of Lutherans in the volume and said I would comment on that observation. For I did not intend a merely denominational remark. Through most of its history, Christian theology has been divided between—and sometimes by—two Trinitarian-christological tendencies. In the ancient church Antioch and Alexandria argued with each other, whether in fellowship or in schism; the West always remained a bit Antiochene and the East a bit Alexandrian, and at the Reformation the Reformed and the Lutherans renewed the argument, now within the West. How exactly are we to state the eternal Son's personal identity with the man Jesus? What difference, if any, does this hypostatic identity make for the 'natures' so identified? How indeed are eternity and time mediated, generally and in Christ?

Reformed theologians have feared that Lutheran thinking threatens the distinction between Creator and creature; and Lutheran theologians have feared that Reformed Christology is too weak to support practice and shape other doctrine. The doctrine of 'communion of attributes' became the test. Does Christ as man so share in the attributes he has as the Logos that he divinely transcends time and space, also 'according to his humanity'? Or does Christ as the Logos so share in the attributes he has as the man Jesus that he somehow suffers in his own divine person? Antioch and Geneva have said 'No' to both questions;

Alexandria[1] and Wittenberg have said 'Yes'—though after Luther was gone, his followers fudged on the second.

Contrary to what might have been expected after centuries of Reformed–Lutheran cohabitation, the division continues to show itself, though now it rarely occasions that *rabies theologorum* from which Melanchthon was glad to escape into heaven. And from the time we first met, Colin and I regularly and often unexpectedly experienced it.

This never kept us from close cooperation. The last essay he wrote, he and I wrote jointly. And in it we even came to an agreed proposition about the centre of the controversy: '"Jesus is the Logos" is an identity-statement.' But then he continued to be preoccupied with the necessity and nature of mediation between God and creature and I continued to be fearful of the notion. He continued to speak, though with many restrictions, of a Logos who somehow 'was' not yet Jesus, and I went on labouring heavily to avoid such discourse. We planned one day to try together to find a way of finally overcoming the ancient divide, but it was not to be.

But what is the relevance of these last four paragraphs to this volume? The collected essays mirror Colin's concerns also in this: the lines of argument in all or most of them are controlled by a certain reticence about the communion of attributes, and by attention to the problem of mediation between time and eternity. Again, I will not go through them seriatim. Instead, I will leave it to any readers who may find it interesting to play conceptual detective and discover in each where this Reformed—and Guntonesque—habit of mind shows itself. Nor should readers take this paragraph as criticism of the essays, for, after all, I must acknowledge that the Reformed positions may be right.

It is sad that so many honours came Colin Gunton's way only after his death—including this collection. He would have loved to read it.

Notes

[1] One should remember that in Cyril's formula, that the Logos 'suffered in a non-suffering way', the verb attached to the Logos remains 'suffered'.

Index

Lightning Source UK Ltd.
Milton Keynes UK
UKOW06f0614080415

249285UK00012B/337/P